Perseverance

A Memoir

Richard Weisenbach

ISBN 978-1-0980-6994-0 (paperback)
ISBN 978-1-0980-6995-7 (digital)

Christian Faith Publishing, Inc.
832 Park Avenue
Meadville, PA 16335
www.christianfaithpublishing.com

Printed in the United States of America

Without hesitation, I dedicate this effort to
Patricia (O'Brien) Weisenbach my best friend and co-pastor.

Contents

Introduction

Don't ask me why I save things, but I do. Whenever an event occurred or I received an important letter or document, I made a judgment—"Is this worth saving?" I usually saved it, since I could always throw it out later. The earliest piece of paper I have kept is a mimeographed letter that my childhood pastor Rev. Alex B. Morrison sent to me and my brother Bill on the occasion of our decision to "Accept the Lord Jesus Christ as your personal savior on Friday night, February 22, 1952." I was ten years old, and Bill was eight. The letter was folded and kept safe in my Scofield Reference Bible, a gift Mother and Dad gave me at Christmas time in 1954.

Because of my habit of placing important papers aside, I have quite a collection of letters, cards, and college papers. When I decided to go into the parish ministry, my collection grew; letters of inquiry from search committees, minutes from meetings, annual reports, and weekly newsletters were all carefully slipped into file folders awaiting the day when I had the time and inclination to organize and put to paper a somewhat orderly account of my life guided, I believe, by the grace of God.

I suppose my main motivation in preserving all these papers is to share a record of the loving guidance, provision, and correction of God. The more I think about it, the more I realize this little book is an expression of my attempt at grateful stewardship. God has been so good, and I dare not let a single blessing slip away without taking note and breathing my gratitude.

I also want to pass on to my children Pamela, David, and Kimberly and their families some tangible record of all the memories, activities, and struggles of all these years.

A third reason is to pass on to the six congregations that Pat and I have served a small slice of their history, hopefully giving cause to praise the Lord Jesus Christ, the head of the church.

"Remember the wonders he has done, his miracles and judgements he pronounced" (Psalm 105:5).

Heritage

As far as I can tell from the little digging I have done, I'm German, through and through. All four of Dad's grandparents were born in Germany. I don't know when the families came to America, but all their children on both sides were born in the United States. It's the same story on my mother's side. All of her grandparents were born in Germany, and all their children were American-born. I later discovered through Ancestry that I have about 6 percent Swedish blood. Who knew!

Dad's parents, Anton Weisenbach Jr. (September 7, 1888–December 3, 1932) and Anna Weisenbach, née Fanger (September 10, 1892–June 16, 1968), were born and raised in South Philadelphia, Pennsylvania. Dad had an older sister Elisabeth and a younger brother William.

Mother's parents, Louis Karl Strohmetz (February 25, 1874–May 31, 1931) and Catherine Strohmetz, née Bauer (July 25, 1875–February 13, 1948) were also native to South Philadelphia. Mother had an older brother Christian and five older sisters, Clara, the twins Katherine and Margaret, Ida, and Elisabeth (who died in childhood, perhaps due to the Spanish flu).

Mother often spoke of Uncle John, her mother's brother; sadly he was deaf. He lived with the family and had a job till he quit because all the men got a 50¢ raise and he only got 25¢; he never took another job. He did contribute to the family by cutting everyone's hair and repairing their shoes. She also related about a dollhouse he made that was very detailed and must have been a source of great fun.

As a child, Mother would tell others about her sister Elisabeth who died the same day that the Titanic sank. "As that ship sank down into the water," she would recount in a very dramatic whisper, "my sister 'dawied.'" Mother's acting career started early.

Mother and Dad met at Peace Presbyterian Church in Philadelphia. Mother's dad was the Sunday school superintendent, and her mother was the organist. Their congregation was organized to meet the needs of the German-speaking population of South Philadelphia.

As I wrote this, I began to wonder. World War I was declared by Pres. Woodrow Wilson on April 6, 1917, and Mother was born two months later in June 8, and Dad followed in September 14 of that same year. That year was a tumultuous one—recruiting, training, equipping, and transporting an army of a million or more across an ocean. At the time, our military numbered 250,000. The social upheavals were just as daunting, especially if you were German.

I have no knowledge of how Anton Weisenbach Jr., age twenty-nine at the time, or Louis Strohmetz, age forty-three, dealt with the shifts of opinion surrounding them. Was their pastor forced to stop preaching in German? Did the families buy war bonds? Where they shunned by neighbors? Of course Mother and Dad were too young to notice this upheaval, but I wonder what their parents may have been forced to endure. At the time, one-third of the country were foreign-born or children of parents who were born outside of the United States. It all raises questions I wish I had raised when Mother and Dad were with us. Even without their remembrances, it is probably safe to say that those years were challenging to say the least.

Mother often reminisced about her childhood spent on the streets of South Philly. "We played all day, 'Red Light,' skates, and dolls." "Just be home when the lamplighter comes," her mother would say.

Mother and Dad

First Date, Proposal, John Wanamaker's Department Store, Wedding, First Apartment, First Jobs, 741 Street Road, Renovations, Conversion of mother, Conversion of Dad, Dad's retirement, Fiftieth Wedding Anniversary, Family Reunions, Dad's Heart Attack, Dad's Passing, Mother's Passing

First Date

Mother and Dad's first date was a youth group hayride. The young people paired off and Al Weisenbach made sure he would be with Ruth Strohmetz. I guess, as the evening progressed, they held hands and then Dad made a move to steal a kiss.

Mother said, "I never kiss a boy on the first date."

Dad replied, "Everyone else does."

"Well, not me," was her quick response.

Not to be shut down, Dad said, "You don't know it, but you are going to marry me."

Incredulous, Mother snapped back, "Not if I have anything to do with it."

Years passed, and Dad was looking for a relationship and Mother was playing the field. Finally Dad put it to her, "Ruth, I will not be coming around anymore."

"Suit yourself," Mother replied.

Dad continued his tale of woe explaining, "Every time we are together, you wish you were with someone else."

"Well, you have half of me," she explained.

Then Dad uttered one of his most poignant lines, "Not the half with the heart in it."

Mother told us that story many times, and obviously she was touched; nevertheless Dad backed off, and they didn't see each other for six weeks.

Then, it happened. Mother and her sister Ida were in the balcony at church getting ready to sing a duet. Just before the service began, Dad came in with his mother, sister, and brother. He turned around and caught Mother's eye. She looked at him, and as she told the story, "The heat started in my feet and ankles and just kept coming, higher and higher." At this point in her account, Mother's hands were above her head and all ten fingers were wiggling, a big smile growing on her face.

After the church service, Dad asked, "Is anyone taking you home?" After that, they started dating each other exclusively.

After an activity together, they would go back to Mother's house at 1724 Snyder Avenue. To find any privacy, they were forced to sit on chairs in the dining room or kitchen. Her sister Ida and her special friend John had exclusive claim to the sofa in the living room. Mother recalled, "After Ida married, we got the sofa!"

Proposal

On April 15, 1938, Dad got down on one knee and popped the question. One year later, they were married at Peace Presbyterian Church at seven o'clock in the evening. Their ceremony was the same day as her parents' thirty-six years earlier.

I must add just a paragraph or two about Mother's experience at the John Wanamaker's Department Store.

Mother's father died in 1931. He was fifty-six, and Mother was fourteen. She was forced to leave school and go to work to help with the family finances. Three of Mom's older sisters had worked at Wanamaker's in Center City, and now it was Mother's turn. She was in the tenth grade, probably fifteen or sixteen years old. She was assigned a job in the infant's wear department. There she was guided by a wonderful supervisor named Brownie Russell. Mother was very grateful for her love and support at such a critical time in her life.

Mr. Wanamaker realized that there were many families, during those depression years, who were forced to ask their children to go to work without finishing high school. So he graciously offered classes on the ninth floor of his store.

Mom graduated as class president with a degree and a class ring, and they even had a prom. She also learned to play the clarinet and joined the John Wanamaker Commercial Institute Band. The band would enjoy a two-week vacation every year in Island Heights, New Jersey. All the young employees would have a crowded day of activities, and the band would accompany every evening parade and drills. Cadets from West Point Military Academy would assist in the instruction. Mother's mother would often thank God for John Wanamaker. "He was our answer in our time of need."

Wedding, Apartment, First Jobs

Mother and Dad's wedding was small with a sit-down reception in the church's back room. Dad's mother and sister did most of the preparations and cleanup. Mother said that she and her sisters were in charge of hospitality.

Mother shared a brief conversation she and Dad had as they left Mom's childhood home. As Dad pulled away, Mom's mother waved goodbye to her youngest child, and Mother waved back and began to cry. Dad noticed of course and said, "I'll take you back if you want." Mom wiped away her tears and motioned to move on.

They had received or saved about $200.00 by this time and decided to buy furniture for their apartment; the honeymoon could wait. They did go to Echo Lake Farms in the Pocono Mountains during the summer and took a two-day trip to the 1939 World's Fair in Flushing Meadows, New York.

Their apartment was at Twenty-Ninth and Girard, and it cost $20.00 a month. They lived there for two years. Mother continued to work at Wanamaker's earning $13.00 a week.

Sadly, Dad's teenage years were very similar to Mother's. His father died in 1935 at the age of forty-two, and Dad was sixteen and forced to leave school. His first job was a doggy for Western Union. He delivered telegrams for 32¢ each.

One of his customers, Russell Baum, was the owner of a paper-folding company. Dad remembers, "He was a good tipper." Mr. Baum would often give Dad $1.00 and say the sweet words, "Keep the change, Al." Dad ultimately landed a job with Mr. Baum's company. On his first day, Mr. Baum said, "Any married man working for me should be making $20.00 a week," and that was a $3.00 a week raise. Dad stayed with the company for four or five years.

Mother and Dad remained at their Girard apartment until my birth in October 1941 forced a change. They were able to purchase their first home just south of Roosevelt Boulevard, 4827 A Street. Dad's mother loaned them $500.00 for a down payment.

741 Street Road, Renovations

Everything changed, however, after the December 7 bombing of Pearl Harbor. Dad got a job as a sheet-metal worker at the Johnsville Naval Air Station. He would drive through the town of Southampton on his way to work. He took a liking to the little town in the northern suburbs of the city, and it was there that he saw a house for sale and took Mother to see it. They agreed to engage a realtor, but just as they were about to sign some papers, they learned that the house, the former home and office of a doctor, had been sold to someone else—they were heartbroken. Mother recalls crying as she hung the clothes in the backyard. Then they got word that the buyer was having second thoughts and was willing to consider selling. He had paid $5,000.00 and offered to sell it to Mother and Dad for $5,250.00. Sold!

The house needed a lot of work, probably the reason the first buyer changed his mind. Mother and Dad stripped all the wallpaper by pulling the garden hose right into the house. They removed twenty doors, installed three steel beams, and torn down two walls.

One sign of Dad's cleverness was how he took the legs off Mom's ironing board and attached a hinge to one end and arranged it to drop out of a spot he built against the wall in the kitchen, just like a Murphy bed. I always admired that contraption.

When they finished, they were the proud owners of 741 Street Road, Southampton, Pennsylvania. Their labor resulted in a home with a living room including a large fireplace, dining room, wraparound porch, kitchen and breakfast nook, three bedrooms, two full bathrooms, guest room, and a detached two-car garage. There was a sizable backyard with four apple trees, a plum tree, and a space for Dad's vegetable garden. There was also a basement that held a coal bin, Mother's washing machine, and Dad's workbench. They lived there for twenty-one years. By then the town had exploded from three thousand in the 1940s to 12,000 in the 1960s. As a result, their house had been rezoned commercial. They sold it for $26,000.00.

Conversion of Mother

There was no Presbyterian Church in town, so the family went to a Baptist church up the street. Mother and Dad had been raised in the church, but I suspect that they had not seriously considered their relationship with God in any personal way. I say this because Mother shared how she first heard the gospel from a neighbor.

Dad, so the story goes, had left Johnsville Naval Air Station after the war and began selling cemetery property at Sunset Memorial Park. He called it his layaway plan. He visited a home in the neighborhood and presented his sales pitch, but the family wasn't interested. Then the woman of the house said, "You have visited our house. Can I visit yours?" Dad agreed. The woman was in a wheelchair; nevertheless she came to our house and spoke to Mother and Dad about God's love and forgiveness through Jesus Christ. Mother responded positively to the woman's presentation and received Christ as her Savior. She was thirty-three. That decision became a critical cornerstone in the life of our entire family

In 1934, Esther Swigart, a teacher at Girard College in Philadelphia, bought a property in Southampton, "for the purpose of establishing a haven for those who appreciated weekends of relaxation, restoration and Christian fellowship in the countryside." Esther had dedicated the property to her mother and called it Bethanna, which means House of Grace.

In 1950, Miss Swigart met Marion Kinsler, a retired missionary to Korea. These two servants of God decided to provide a home for needy children. Over the years, Bethanna Home for Boys and Girls grew to provide for thousands of children living in eastern Pennsylvania.

Mother heard about this place at church and decided to visit one afternoon. She began by helping Miss Swigart with the cleaning. Over the months, her involvement deepened, first by organizing the children into a choir that presented a musical program, increasing the visibility of the home. This was followed by forming a women's auxiliary. Finally she was asked to join the board of directors and later became chairperson.

In March 1990, she was honored at the annual fellowship banquet with the establishment of the Ruth E. Weisenbach Volunteer of the Year Award, she being the first recipient. All four of her sons were able to attend the occasion. She was surprised and grateful to see all of us. Bethanna would go on to name a new dormitory after Mother. The Ruth House remains a substantial reminder of Mother's contribution to this very worthy ministry.

Conversion of Dad

Of course, Mom got Dad involved at Bethanna doing repairs and other various projects. After a while, Esther Swigart shared the love of Jesus with Dad, and he responded to the gospel message on April 4, 1951. He was thirty-four. Although fully trusting his Savior, he was never comfortable bearing witness to others about his faith. And he didn't feel the need to be baptized as a believer. "I shouldn't have to prove my Christian faith to others," this was his long-held understanding; but while attending Faith Community Church in Roslyn, Pennsylvania, he came under the preaching of Rev. George Slavin. A sermon from Acts 8 convinced him to change his mind.

"Ruth," he announced one Sunday evening, "I have to go to church early tonight. I'm getting baptized" (October 16, 1960). Mother burst into tears. Dad was forty-three and claimed Joshua 24:15 as his life verse, "As for me and my house we will serve the Lord."

Dad was always aware that he had never completed his high school education. So, in the spring of 1997 at the age of eighty, he set about to achieve his goal. His final requirement was to write an essay, and he chose to write about Mother, but he couldn't complete the task in the time allowed. He didn't graduate. I'm sure he was crushed and embarrassed, but Dad was a "plugger" and he moved on despite this major disappointment.

I must mention here that Dad had a great sense of humor. He loved to tell jokes and often saw the funny side of things. I suspect this trait of his personality helped him get past many a challenge.

Here is an example of Dad's quick wit. I guess it was a time when Mother and Dad were visiting us in Wakefield. We were finishing dinner and Dad was telling a story about his earlier years, featuring a South Philadelphia neighbor whom Dad referred to as "this black fellow." Before he could continue with his tale, our daughter Pam interrupted him with a question. "Hey, Gramps. Does it really matter that your neighbor was black?" Becoming aware of his racist comment, he acknowledged that his story really didn't require us to know such a detail. He continued with his story and finally ended it.

None of us can remember how it ended, but what we do remember is what happened twenty minutes later. He had another story. He began with, "That reminds me of a fellow I knew from work. I don't remember what color he was…" This caused a complete breakdown of our table manners. None of us could stop laughing and have enjoyed telling and retelling the story. I'll never know if Dad had another story to tell or maybe he was biding his time at the table for his chance to spring his surprise. Either way, we will never forget the experience as one of Dad's finest hours.

Dad had many memorable sayings. Our daughter Kim even assembled a booklet that matched each saying with an appropriate picture. Here's a sample:

"A pixture no artist could paint.

"My compliments to the chef."

"It couldn't have happened to a nicer guy."

"I'm not a well man."

"There we're six men in the boat and the oars leaked."

"I need to see a man about a horse." (When he had to go to the bathroom)

"Mention my name and you will get a better seat." (When you had to go)

"Would you believe, I never took a lesson?"

"I never hit the children except in self-defense."

"I'd rather stand in the cold shower and rip up $20 bills."

How often a situation will arise and I can hear Dad inserting one of his well-worn sayings.

Of course Mother could match Dad in the humor department. She had her monologues, and she called them funnies. We all had our favorites.

She said she started telling her stories when she was a teenager, but when she grew older and more serious about her Christian faith, she questioned the appropriateness of telling some of them. Then she realized she could use her gift of entertaining for God's glory, not just for fun. As time went on, her repertoire expanded to include stories that encouraged Christian faith, sacrifice, and service to others. For years, especially during the spring and holiday season, she would be engaged as the entertainment at scores of women's clubs, church groups, and annual banquets. Dad drove her to her venue, enjoyed dinner, and sat listening to her speak, sing, and accompany herself on her autoharp. She wrote to me on December 20, 1982, "Very busy this week doing *the Herdmans*. Out every night!"

I said we all had our favorites, *the Dutch Lady at the Opera, the Cat and the Pitcher, the Bee, the Best Christmas Pageant Ever*, and others. And we can never forget her favorite two-word exclamation, "Oh birds."

I asked Mother to share one of her monologues while we served at First Parish Congregational Church. The worship service had a mission theme, and Mom told the story of "Sophie" who washed floors in order to contribute to the needs of a missionary she knew. Her story and presentation were very compelling. After the service, several people, not knowing who Mother was, told me to, "Get that woman who spoke this morning onto our Outreach Committee. She was great!"

Mother and Dad sold 741 Street Road in 1966 and moved to a split-level home in Holland, Pennsylvania. They remained there for twenty-three years. Then in 1989, they moved for the last time to 514 Dock Drive, Dock Acres, a retirement community in Lansdale, Pennsylvania, managed by the Mennonite Church.

Dad wrote to me on October 1, 1981, remembering my birthday, "Oh me, my little boy forty years old! Truly the years fly by." His last sentence read, "I have about five months and I will be free, free, free. No more work! Oh happy day!"

Dad's Retirement

We were all aware of his upcoming retirement and we're planning a party. Mother arranged with Joe and Eleanor Biebl to go out for dinner with a stop at Bethanna to drop off something. Dad had to carry a box into one of the buildings. As he opened the door, he was surprised to find many friends and all four sons greeting him. My brother Bill put together a slideshow and scrapbook, and the four of us boys sang three barbershop tunes including "My Wild German Dad." It was a great night! "It couldn't have happened to a nicer guy," was Dad's closing comment.

Like many retired people, Dad sought activities to fill his days. Of course Bethanna and repairs at their Holland home along with the garden took much of his time, but he also spent a few hours a week at a step-down Sears store nearby; it carried tools mostly. Another activity was teaching the AARP Drive Safety Program. I don't recall how long Dad taught that course, but I know he enjoyed it and even got written up in the local newspaper.

Pam and Dave lived together in Pennsylvania for a time. Dave worked with his uncle Ron Markloff, Pat's brother-in-law. Pam worked at TGI Friday's, and once a week, they would drive to Gram and Gramp's for a real meal; pork chops, sauerkraut, mashed potatoes, and gravy were a favorite. Then at 9:00 p.m., Dad would serve the nectar of the gods, butter pecan ice cream (pronounced butter peeecan). Mother and Dad provided a touch of home for several years. Around 1992, Sharon Reynolds began to visit with Dave and Pam, and she of course married Dave on October 9, 1993. More about that special event later.

Fiftieth Wedding Anniversary

Another great memory occurred in April 1989, April 15 to be exact. The occasion was their fiftieth wedding anniversary. It was a great event. My three brothers and I had been planning for about a year. You can see the fiftieth coming a long way off, so it was hardly a surprise. Just being together was a special treat for all of us, but the highlight for me occurred on that Saturday morning right after breakfast.

We had decided that an open house from 11:00 a.m. to 3:00 p.m. would be best. We had arranged for a professional photographer to come at 10:00 a.m., but just before that, I asked if everyone would gather in front of the TV to watch a video.

I had worked on this project for about three months. The idea was to transfer 180 color slides and prints into a video and match it with appropriate music. I asked Mother for some favorite pictures, and she gave me some real beauties—Mom and Dad on a date in 1936, their wedding day, their first apartment, us four boys as children, the first grandchild, family reunions, celebrations, and graduations. As I sorted through the photos and the slides, memories filled my mind and tears of gratitude filled my eyes. As you can imagine, it was hard to limit myself to 180.

I matched the pictures with music, Tommy Dorsey, Barbra Streisand, Paul Anka, Kenny Rogers, and of course some of our favorite hymns done by Ken Medema, Ralph Carmichael, and even my brother Bill, who made a few records while a music major a Nyack College. I was pleased with the result, and I couldn't wait to share it with the family. Everyone brought their coffee cup or juice glass into the family room, and I started the tape. It was a real celebration of God's faithfulness to our family and a clear demonstration of the priceless gift two parents gave their children when they decide to keep their wedding vows, no matter what! We were all so happy to give that gift to them. Their gift to us was a yearly family reunion that we enjoyed during the next nineteen years.

Family Reunions

Five months earlier, December 8, 1988, Mother sent us this letter of announcement.

> Dear Sons,
> The enclosed brochure describes the resort we have reserved for our family get together after our anniversary bash next year. We are scheduled to arrive at Willow Valley in Lancaster, Pennsylvania. Our rooms are in the main building called the Atrium, a very classy place. There is an indoor pool, lighted tennis courts, sauna, Jacuzzi, and the fitness room. A nine-hole golf course and a free bus tour of the area if you're interested. There are three restaurants in the building. One is a smorgasbord! Two dinners and two breakfasts are included in the package. We are looking forward to a great time.
> Love Dad and Mom
> PS Great area for shopping too!

We had a great time, eating, swimming, shopping, and talking. Just for the record, 1989–1993 was at Willow Valley, Stroudsburg, Pennsylvania. In 1994–1995, we gathered at the O'Brien's hideaway in Tannersville, Pennsylvania. From 1996 to 2005, we traveled to Ladore, a Salvation Army camp in the Poconos.

Each year, we appointed a tour director to be responsible for the theme and to distribute various responsibilities involved in food preparation. We had a scavenger hunt, played Family Feud, carved pumpkins, wrote poems and songs, had a puppet show, marked the millennium, dressed as pilgrims, celebrated our German heritage along with Mother and Dad's eightieth birthdays, and reenacted our version of *the Sound of Music*. Great times were had by all!

During one of our last gatherings, Bill's family conducted an oral history of Mother and Dad. Interesting details emerged—Mother's name was to be Elsie Ruth, but it got changed. Thank goodness! She hoped to be a minister's wife, but Fred Rhody married somebody else. Thank goodness again! Dad had to leave school early but spent many hours in the library. He said, "I got through school by the skin of my teeth. I wasn't very smart." To this, we all disagreed strongly.

Then Bill asked, "What was a sad memory?"

Dad replied, "The year I had to repeat a grade."

Mother sighed deeply and said, "Losing two grandchildren, Brie [May 28, 2002, age twenty-three] and Matthew [February 4, 2004, age eighteen])."

Bill ended the interview with, "And what was a happy moment?"

Dad quickly said, "Marrying Ruth."

Mom spread out her arms and said, "This...our annual reunion."

Dad's Heart Attack

On Saturday night, May 23, 1998, I got a call from Mother. "Dad has had a heart attack. He is in Grandview Hospital's Intensive Care Unit. He is not conscious." We four boys met with Dr. Greenspan who gave Dad a 50-50 chance of recovery. We requested bypass surgery. He was transferred to Lehigh Valley Medical Center.

Dr. Lynn Morris said, "Your Dad is very sick. I see four problems: poor blood supply to the heart, malfunctioning heart value, his kidney has shut down, and he is over eighty years old."

On Thursday, May 28, he underwent an eight-hour operation to perform four heart bypasses and the replacement of his mitral valve. About a week later, in June 2, he regained consciousness and began talking, trying to explain about the moss bark tree. "Indians use this in their courting rituals." We all looked at one another and began laughing. "Well, at least he is trying to have a conversation."

By June 3, all wires and tubes were disconnected. Dr. Phillips reported, "He's in the pink. I think your Dad has experienced a miracle!"

On April 17, 2001, the family gathered at 514 Dock Acres to mark Mother and Dad's sixty-second wedding anniversary. My brother Dave had built a wooden cross for the sanctuary of the Dock Acres Chapel. All four sons and their families were there to present the cross, dedicated to our parents. There is a plaque outside the doorframe of the sanctuary to mark the occasion. The following day, Dad sent this note.

> Dear Richard.
>
> No doubt about it, you fellows are the greatest. Our name will live in infamy because of your generosity. Dock Acres needed a cross and you were there to fill that need. We cannot put into words our thanks. Truly, "Our cup runneth over." Much love to you all.
>
> Love and love,
> Mother and Dad

The procedure that Dad survived usually adds about six to seven years to one's life. That was Dad's experience. On Tuesday, December 17, 2002, I listened to a message on my phone; it was from Mother. "Dad is at Grandview Hospital. They need to transfer him back to Lehigh Valley. He is very sick. Please come." I think I set a record of four hours and forty-five minutes (3:30 to 8:15 a.m.). Our son Dave joined Mother and me for a visit. Emily, brother Bill's daughter came the next day.

We were all so grateful for the amazing recovery he made that day. He was transferred back to Grandview in December 19 after an electric shock to restore his heart's natural rhythm. Mother was too weak to visit in December 19 due to a diabetes flare-up, but Dad came back home on Sunday, December 21.

Mother began writing down some instructions about funerals, not funeral, but funerals. She specified the funeral home, Huff and Lakjer, where important papers were kept—cemetery information, suggestions for the service, hymns and scriptures, a solo by Janet Gross, and the song she should sing, "Finally Home." "The music is in a book in the organ bench." It became pretty obvious that Mother was thinking ahead.

Fortunately, in anticipation of his future, Dad wrote his thoughts and requests concerning his funeral.

> I don't know why God has decided to call me home, but this is one of the oldest benefits of being under His wing. Who can say what lies ahead for me? Please include these scriptures in the service, Romans 5:1–11 and 8:28 and John 4:7–12 and 20–1.
>
> God must've had me in mind when this part of the gospel was written. It has to be faith that does it all. I was not that smart, rich, or good-looking, nothing that would set me apart. Yet when I was led to the Lord by Esther Swigart, all good things happened. I shouldn't say all good things necessarily, but I always had that gut feeling that while I had my problems, I somehow knew that all things would work out okay.
>
> Looking back, if I have any regrets or failures, I think these passages from scripture explain it all. Somehow I could not reach out to those people I did not like. Ruth always kept saying to me, "Be nice, Albert." How fortunate to be forgiven our shortcomings.
>
> Love,
> Dad

All the above scripture verses were included in his funeral service.

Following this second heart episode, he lost some of his memory but was with the family at Ladore in 2004.

Dad's Passing

After many challenging experiences, Mother finally realized she needed to admit Dad to the Terrace, a special care unit on the Dock Acres campus. While there, he fell and broke his arm, which made using his walker just about impossible. He was ultimately transferred to the Cottage, the Alzheimer's unit.

Pat and I were visiting and planned to leave for home, but the unit called to say that Dad was entering the end. I decided to stay with Mom, while Pat drove back to Massachusetts alone. Mother and I arrived at the unit just moments after Dad died. It was just one month after leaving home. He died on March 14, 2005.

The service was held in April 1 at First Baptist Church, Lansdale, Pennsylvania, and all four boys spoke. I reminded everyone of Dad's favorite sayings by speaking just a few words and then challenging everyone to complete the phase. They completed every one.

The Strohmetz and Weisenbach families gathered after the service, and our son Dave provided a baton for everyone. We put on some rousing band music, "Seventy-Six Trombones" I think, so we all could conduct just like Dad would have done. We then returned to their home and tried on some of Dad's clothes and hats.

My brother Bill wrote the following tribute to Dad that was included in the order of worship:

> Albert Rudolph Weisenbach, husband, father, and friend to many, died on Monday, March 14, at the age of eighty-seven following a brief illness. He is survived by his wife of sixth-five years, Ruth Strohmetz Weisenbach, their four sons, Rev. Richard and Patricia of Wakefield

(MA), Rev. William and Cynthia Stuen of Katonah (NY), Mr. Paul and Christy of Rochester
Hills (MI), and Mr. David of Morison (FL) and
by their grandchildren Pam, David, Kim, Ona,
Emily, Peter, and Max and eight great-grandchildren. Grandchildren Brie Weisenbach and Matthew Stuen preceded him in death.

Dad spent most of his working years in sales
and had the ability to strike up a conversation
with anyone, anywhere. He believed in what he
sold from cemetery property to fuel oil. He completed his full-time working career at Sears selling sewing machines that he first learned how to
use. At Sears he would often talk young couples
out of buying machines with features they would
never use and became the department's top sales-
person as a result of his knowledge and integrity.

Dad was an occasionally impatient, but
active churchman and served as a trustee for many
years at Davisville Baptist Church in Southampton, Pennsylvania. His deep faith, shared by our
mother, meant that the first 10% of everything
that came in went to God. In their eyes this guar-
anteed that there would always be enough for
everything else necessary… There always was!

Dad was a clever handyman and could make almost anything
he could imagine. For example, unable to afford a riding mower,
he made one out of an old tricycle front end and the walk-behind
mower he already owned. He was also a true believer in function over
form and most of his inventions reflected it. Reputedly, he could fix
anything with a hammer and/or duct tape. This trait of Dad's was
genetically inherited by his sons.

Too busy, or perhaps unable to develop a deeply
personal relationship with his sons when they

were children, he worked hard to do so when they became adults. Each of us celebrate our own very special relationship with him that continues to influence and shape our lives, the lives of our children and the lives of our children's children.

On Father's Day 1999, I wrote the following about Dad for our church's newsletter:

Dear Dad,

As I see it, God used you to shape me into who I am today. Of course, there were other influences, other people and circumstances. But, Dad, you were the key player.

I, like your three other sons, watched you, took mental notes, and followed where you walked. You certainly made mistakes, but let me embarrass you—just a little—by reminding you of what I think you did right.

- You never lied to me.
- You never used foul language.
- You continue to love Mother, as you would usually write on your greeting cards, "Always and Always."
- You determined to give 10% of your hard-earned salary to others, usually through your church.
- You worshipped your Savior Jesus Christ every week.
- You speak your mind and have the courage to make yourself understood even if you are in the minority.
- You take pride in your sons and often shed a tear of appreciation.

- You are basically a humble man who never dreamed he would get as far as he did.
- You are predictable, dependable, and trust-worthy.
- You are admired by your friends and family.
- You have a refreshing and wholesome sense of humor and are quick to laugh at yourself.

That's enough for now, Dad. I don't want to give you a swelled head.

Thanks, Dad.

Mother wrote a card to Dad on his eighty-fourth birthday.

September 14, 2001
To Albert on his eighty-fourth birthday
"How do I love thee, let me count the ways."
1. Your thoughtfulness in getting me things that you know I like.
2. For helping in the kitchen and doing the mundane things like cutting the onions and cucumbers, apples, and peaches.
3. For putting programs on TV that please me.
4. For bringing me goodies to the TV room.
5. For loving me even when I am cranky.
6. Most of all for the sixty-two years we've shared together—good times and bad, happy times and sad ones too, but the happiest times of my life! May God spare us more years in the future.

Your Ruth, now and always

I honestly can't remember if we gathered for our reunion in 2005. I can't imagine that we would assemble without Dad. In 2006, we all set out for Bedford, New York, for the wedding of Bill and Cynthia's daughter Emily to Mike Burke. In 2007, we met in June at Bill and Cynthia's to celebrate Mother's ninetieth birthday. For her ninetieth, some of us took Mother out to lunch at the Olive Garden in Lansdale.

On January 18–20, 2009, we went through the difficult task of moving Mother out of her unit that had been her home for almost twenty years. We had to squeeze her furniture and possessions into one room at Dock Meadows. I remember taking countless items to her and asking, "Do you want to keep this?" How sad to be the one to force her to give up such treasures and pass them on to others. Pat reminded me that we did fill two pickup trucks with Mother's furniture, eventually distributing them to her grandchildren. My brothers and cousin Karen Miller received some items as well.

Mother's Passing

Mother remained at the Meadows for just eight months. She died on September 13, 2009.

I remember those last hours that Friday and Saturday when I said my final goodbye. We prayed together and repeated the Lord's Prayer and Psalm 23. Then she said, "I've had a good life, Rich. You go home now. Tell everyone I love them. Journey mercies, son."

"Journey mercies, Mom," I whispered.

My brother Bill wrote this account to his church family at First Presbyterian Church of Katonah, New York, a beautiful description of her last five days.

> Last Wednesday evening, my mother, Ruth Weisenbach, was taken from her assisted living home in Pennsylvania to the local hospital with very high blood pressure. By 11:00 p.m., her CO_2 level was above one hundred and I, as her POA, had to choose between letting her die and putting her on a vent. I chose the latter because

it appeared the underlying problem, fluid in the lungs, could be resolved the next morning returning her to health. I drove to Pennsylvania early Thursday only to be told that the only viable procedure was the insertion of permanent chest tubes with the remainder of her life in a nursing home.

Following her written instructions, I ordered the vent removed. When she regained consciousness, I told her what had happened, and she agreed on hospice. Over the next several hours, all of her sons, daughters-in-law, and grandchildren spoke their tearful goodbyes over the phone.

I sat with her the remainder of the day and all day Friday. My brother Richard drove down from Boston late Friday to spend the night, and I returned home. Rich, also a pastor, had to go back to Boston on Saturday. Grandson Peter and niece Karen made visits that evening and Sunday morning as well. After church on Sunday, I returned to Pennsylvania, by which time she had slipped into coma. She died peacefully and painlessly at 7:18 p.m. as I held her hand. I can barely describe the privilege I felt being present when she moved from this life to the next.

Mom was a woman of incredible faith who embraced her death with the eagerness of a child in a toy store. My three brothers and I are planning a memorial service at her Baptist Church in Lansdale for this Saturday, September 19, 2009. Mom's entire family are so grateful for her life of ninety-two years and all feel abundantly blessed by her love and example.

I wrote this in May 1999, a tribute on Mother's Day.

Her name is Ruth Elsie Weisenbach. She will be eighty-two years old in June 8. She lives in Pennsylvania with her husband Albert of sixty years. When she reads this, she'll probably weep warm tears of joy and gratitude to God (like I am doing as I write this).

Mother, I trust in God's grace that you will live for many more years, but we have both put that into our Lord's hands. So while I am able to write and you are able to read, I thought I should get this on paper. I love you, Mother, and I thank God for you.

As I think of you, which I do almost every day, two qualities come to mind, faithfulness and humor.

First of all, your faithfulness to God. You have always worshipped your Savior every day as you take time to read and study the Bible and as you and Dad gather at church every week. You and Dad have always given 10 percent of your income to others. I know that has impressed your sons. You have always said yes to service opportunities that came your way—choir, solos, children's choir director, and Board of Directors at the local children's home, just for starters.

Then, there is your faithfulness to Dad. You respond to his needs, adjust to his desires, speak, write, and display your love for him and have found a balance between submitting to him and speaking up for yourself. Good for you, Mom!

Then, there is your faithfulness to me. Helping me learn to read music and play the clarinet, taking a big loan to send me to college, and supporting me when I changed college majors and girlfriends! Your faithful prayers, every day, no doubt, have sustained me and my family through fifty-eight years and four churches.

And then there is your humor. Everyone who knows you knows about your monologues. You have entertained social groups with your "funnies" for decades. I know most of them by heart, but I'm also thinking of your humor off stage—your humor in real life. One of many fun memories you have given me is your broad smiling face and laughter so enthusiastic that tears run down your cheeks. You know how to enjoy life, Mom. Your joy is infectious and such a gift to me and Pat and our children and grandchildren. We all enjoy and have come to depend upon this quality. Faithfulness, loyalty, dependability, humor, joy, and happiness!

Thanks, Mother.
Your firstborn son

She responded with this note.

Dear Rich,

What can I say about your RAW material? Of course it filled me with pride, but I was humbled as well. However, it's good to hear while I am still on this earth than to wait until my memorial service for others to hear. I appreciate so much your love and concern through these years. I too hope I will be around for a while.

With deep and lasting love,
Your Mother

Most all the family were able to journey to First Baptist Church, Lansdale, Pennsylvania. Pastor Kent was very helpful and arranged every detail for us. All four of our boys were able to speak along with some of the grandkids.

Brother Dave's words will long be remembered. "Mother loved her boys, the ministers, Rich and Bill, and the other two." Dave inherited Dad's wit and expressed a great deal of self-assurance with his remarks. All went very well, and fortunately both funerals for our parents were recorded on CDs.

A second abbreviated service of remembrance was conducted for Mom at the Meadows in September 21 for the residents who knew and loved her. (We arrived about twenty minutes late, because a young driver hit us while we were driving on County Line.)

About a week later, I wrote that part of my sadness over Mother's passing is that it feels like my number one fan isn't there anymore, but then I'm reminded of Hebrews 12:1 and that "great cloud of witnesses," a full grandstand cheering us on. Praise the *Lord!*

A portion of Mother and Dad's ashes were interred in the Memorial Garden of First Parish Congregational Church, Wakefield, Massachusetts. The remainder were laid under the weeping cherry tree on the corner property of Bill and Cynthia's summer home in Bayside, Maine. All four of us along with our spouses and Mike and Emily gathered along with our son David in August 2011. We suggested that memorial gifts for both Mother and Dad be directed to the Bethanna Home.

As I hope you can tell, my parents provided a very significant influence in my life and that of my three brothers. There's much more that could be written, but I trust that what I have shared communicates the high degree of love and gratitude I hold for Ruth Elsie Weisenbach, née Strohmetz, and Albert Rudolph Weisenbach. I will remain forever grateful to God for the blessings these two people have bestowed upon my life

"The boundary lines have fallen unto me in pleasant places; surely I have a delightful inheritance" (Psalm 16:6). Praise God!

Childhood Memories

Elementary School, William Tennent High School,
Southampton Hardware, Patricia O'Brien, Spiritual Goals.

I was surprised to discover that just as Mother and Dad were born in 1917, the year America entered the Great War, I was born the year World War II was declared.

Pearl Harbor on the Hawaiian island of Oahu came under attack on Sunday morning, December 7, 1941. The attack came in two waves, 7:56 a.m. and 8:54 a.m., from 360 cruiser-based Japanese planes led by Mitsuo Fuchida. The Japanese lost only twenty-nine planes, but the attack crippled our Pacific Fleet; nineteen ships were sunk or run aground including the battleships USS Arizona, Oklahoma, California, Nevada, and West Virginia and damaging three others. Also the attack inflicted major damage on three cruisers and three destroyers and 328 US planes. This surprise attack killed 2,403 men and wounding 1,143 others.

"December 7, a date that will live in infamy," declares President Roosevelt in an address to Congress the next day. The Senate voted 82-0 for a declaration of war, while the House of Representatives voted 388-1, Congresswoman Jeanette Rankin (R-MT) voting against as she did in 1917.

Two months earlier, October 24, I arrived, the first of four boys born to my parents (eight pounds and eight ounces). Years later, Mother suffered a miscarriage of a fifth boy. Mother has reminded me that I tried to console her by reminding her that a pie was always cut into six neat pieces. I guess I saw seven pieces as problematic.

The only memories I have of our home on A Street were captured by early photographs. One was of me being held by my dad's grandfather Anton. (He gave me my middle name.) The other is one of me sitting on a horse fashioned by Dad, I was in a "baby parade" and took the prize for most original. I was awarded $7.50 in defense stamps. I can actually remember that I was scared of falling off my mount.

I do remember some of the remodeling of our Southampton home in 1945, the garden hose in the living room to help remove the wallpaper and being very worried that one of the three steel beams Dad had to add would slip from its position bringing the whole house down.

The following are a few scattered memories:

- Our house caught on fire in the late 1940s, so we all stayed with our neighbors, Uncle Dick and Aunt Edna Yerkes.
- In April 1958, it snowed for sixteen hours and cut power to our town. Our house became a welcoming spot for food and heat since we had a big fireplace.
- Mother's mother lived with us for a few years. She died in 1948 at the age of seventy-three. Mother was thirty-one. The funeral director carried her body out of the house in the wicker basket while mother wept.
- Mother tried to get me to practice the piano, but I was strongly reluctant to do so. I did take up the clarinet when I entered fourth grade. As I think about it now, that was the instrument she played.
- Our town had a parade every Fourth of July. Dad entered us boys two or three times wearing costumes he made himself. I remember one year we portrayed the three revolutionary soldiers, one with a flag, one with a fife, and one with a drum. We might have won a prize.
- I would play Monopoly on the side porch with my brothers. The game usually ended early in a strong disagreement, anger, and tears. Paul added, "Yes, but it was always fun."

- Dad had a big garden, and a farmer Mr. Harrington would come each year to plow it before planting. Dad, being a very generous man, would usually offer free vegetables to whoever happened by. "Rich, Bill, go pick some beans and tomatoes for our friends."
- Dad made root beer. Not having enough strong glass bottles, the natural yeast would burst a few bottles overnight.
- Dad had a workbench in the cellar. One afternoon, I straightened it up for him. Dad spoke up, "Thanks, Rich, but don't ever do that again. I can't find a thing!"
- At Christmas time, Dad would purchase a very cheap tree on Christmas Eve, probably not more than $5.00. He would then cut off the branches from one side, sharpen the ends of those branches, drill holes in the trunk of the opposite side of the trunk, and fill out the tree with the new branches. Then he pushed the tree against a wall. Merry Christmas! Paul adds, "Of course we four boys were forced to wait at the top of the stairs."

  My brother Dave remembers the Lionel trains. Uncle Bill, who married Mom's sister Margaret, gave us his set when he switched to HO. It came with a huge platform and two complete trains, freight, and passenger. I bought several Plasticville buildings to fill out the layout.

- Dad had a temper, especially when us boys would not settle down and go to sleep. Brother Bill and I shared the same bed till we got bunk beds, so we were constantly fighting about who was on whose side. He had hung the cord of the toaster on a hook behind the cellar door. When we heard the cellar door open, we got real quiet. Bill added that "we fought each other with our elbows." Paul wrote, "Can't remember. Dave and I were perfect."
- Mother organized a junior choir at church. I guess we sounded pretty good because on one Sunday, Pastor Morrison enjoyed our piece so much that he asked us to sing it again. By the way, Pat O'Brien was in that choir, and she

recalls saying, "Mrs. Weisenbach is our director. What a strange name."

- One Sunday night, us four boys sang in church. Our song was, "I've Got a Mansion just over the Hilltop." I remember that we didn't get a good start, and Dad had us stop and begin again.

- Another time we were rehearsing but my brother Dave was sick, so Dad had to fill in the melody. Halfway though, the melody grew silent, and Dad was weeping.

- Probably once a month, the whole family would ride down to 314 Fitzgerald Street in South Philadelphia to visit Nanny, Dad's mother, and Aunt Betty and Uncle Fred. Dad smoked cigars back then. The smoke got really bad, but the trip was worth it because Uncle Fred had a TV! Some nights, we would stay long enough to see the *Ed Sullivan Show.* On the way home, we would ask Mother and Dad to sing their one duet, "Let the Rest of the World Go By." It was always such a comfort to hear them singing together. We were able to take long car rides thanks to the ever present wee-wee jar.

- Speaking of the TV, we didn't have one until one day, while we were across the street watching *Frontier Playhouse* (Bill remembers *the Lone Ranger*) at the Tomlinsons', Dad called and told us to come home. The show wasn't over, and we always got to stay till it was over. We came home, and much to our surprise, we watched the rest of the show on our own TV. It was a gift from Nanny.

- Another memory of 314 Fitzgerald Street was the Mummers Parade. This event is unique to Philadelphia and had its official beginning in 1901. It contains five divisions—Comic, Wench Brigades, Fancies, String Bands, and Fancy Brigades. It is presented every New Year's Day with each division providing music, elaborate costumes, and moveable scenery.

    It is rooted in South Philadelphia. Both parents were raised in the area and Dad, growing up with the tradition, really enjoyed going every year. It was always cold, so we stood for a couple of hours, went back to Nanny's for hot soup, and then go back out again. Dad always took a ladder to get us a better view.

- We never did discover who put the cat down the hole in the back of the fireplace, since that hole was for ashes, nor who put the rubber band on our dog Cinder's back leg. I think it was Bill. He later confessed to letting the screen door slam on Cinder's hind quarters.

- Once a week, we would travel to Bristol to get eggs from the Brigal farm. We would take Buck Road, and it had a long hilly stretch, so we would beg Dad, "Go faster!" We would often fly off our seats and enjoyed the tingling feeling it provided.

- We would later deliver a dozen eggs to family and friends. Each year, we would return to the farm to buy five hundred ears of corn at a penny an ear. Guess who husked that corn? Then, rather than having corn on the cob, Mother cut the kernels off the cob and canned most of it. Paul remembered that Mother and Dad invited friends over for corn and watermelon.

- When we first arrived at 741 Street Road, the backyard had four apple trees. Dad removed the front two and erected a tetherball for us and a clothesline for Mom. I don't recall ever getting much fruit from those apple trees, but my brother Bill remembered the time Dad would throw a rope over a branch and tug for all he was worth, shaking apples to the ground. It was our job to rake them into piles and take them to Mom who would make batches of applesauce. We did have a tree fort in the back tree and plenty of ammunition for apple fights.

- Paul recalled an event that I had forgotten. It wasn't my experience, but it impacted the family. Paul and his friend from across the back fence thought that it would be exciting to see who could break the most windows in Uncle Dick's three-story chicken coop. He and Dave Swan broke every one! I believe that Uncle Dick knew who had done the deed and told Dad. Mother and Dad were confused and very angry. I think that brother Dave and Dave Swan had to repay as much as they could.

- I remember Dad soaking a rag in used crank case oil, sticking it to the end of a long pole, lighting it, and burning out tent caterpillars. Crispy caterpillar bodies would rain from the sky. Paul wrote, "We all watched him do that. A real thrill."

- Dad made a tire swing in one of the remaining trees. To do this, he stood on a chair and reached up to nail a piece of wood in place. Unfortunately he slid off the chair and fell to the ground landing hard on his left shoulder. I remember him holding his shoulder with his right hand rolling on the ground and moaning loudly. I was scared to death. He had dislocated that shoulder two other times. Bill recalled this fall was his third and required a trip to the hospital. The surgeon operated, shortening some tendons. Paul recounted, "Once while driving, Dad's shoulder 'went out' and he stopped the car and banged it back into place."

For the rest of his life, probably fifty to fifty-five years, he was unable to fully extend his left arm. I don't ever remember him referring to that accident or his handicap.

One of Dad's first jobs was as a bread man, and his route was in Trenton, New Jersey. He got up at 2:00 a.m. to drive to the bakery, load his truck, and begin his route. He had to carry a large tray of the morning's goods from his truck to every customer. This part of the job might have taxed that shoulder.

A final memory is of Mother ringing a noisy cowbell that Dad had hung by the back door. Mother would ring that bell to call us boys home. All the neighborhood knew it was dinner time at the Weisenbachs.

Elementary School

I started school in 1947. I would walk from our home on Street Road to the three-room stone building up the street. I suspect it was the first school building in Southampton. There were "Safeties," fifth- and sixth-graders who wore cool white belts with silver badges and who helped us cross the street.

Mother told me that I had to be "registered" on the first day of school. The only register I knew about was the hot one in the hall behind our fireplace. I didn't like the sound of her announcement. (My brother Bill had walked across that register one morning, and the design of the grate was burned into his bare feet.)

I made it through those first three grades but not after cutting my little finger when I dropped the class fishbowl on the way up from the basement after changing the water.

Later I remember being sent out of the classroom because I mimicked my teacher. She would clap her hands together to have the class come to attention. From my back row chair, I clapped right after she did, and she didn't appreciate it. She sent me out of the classroom to stand alone in the hall. On my way, the steam register spit at me. I guess I finally did get "registered."

Many of my elementary school memories involved recess. We played some great games, such as hi-low water, jump the brook, dodgeball, kickball, and, when we got older, softball. We would pick two captains, and ours were usually Henry Kohler and Ken Fessler. They were the tallest kids in the class. Henry usually picked me to be on his team. We had a midmorning twenty-minute recess and a full hour at noon.

Another activity besides Sunday school and church was Cub Scouts and later Boy Scouts. I remember my best friends were Bob Severn (who died in 2018) and George Stockberger III (Butch for short). Butch's dad sold Chevrolets, while Bob's father sold Fords. We would often try to start up a debate between the two of them. The three of us were together from first grade to our senior year. We still exchange Christmas cards and go to reunions every five years. We missed Bob at our sixtieth in September 2019.

We were in the Cub Scouts together, and Mrs. Francois, George's mom, was our den mother. Later we three joined the Boy Scouts with Mr. Templeton, and we called him Mr. T. He was a wonderful leader. I learned camp cooking and fire building, some astronomy, knot tying, basic first aid, Morse code, the Scout Law and pledge, respect for my elders, and working with others to achieve a common goal. Sadly I never got more than a few merit badges past first class.

When I was eleven, I got a paper route delivering the *Philadelphia Evening Bulletin.* I think I had about fifty papers serving customers on Cherry Lane, Cybus Way, Redwood Drive, and Pinewood Road. Mr. T was one of my customers, and our house was the last on my route. Thursdays were the worst. All the advertising made the papers very thick, and Saturdays were the easiest.

I would walk up Second Street Pike to the front yard of Bethanna where the papers would be dropped off. During the summer, I'd usually stop along the way at the Wagon House for an ice cream cone, 15¢ for a single dip and 25¢ for a double. I continued till ninth grade when my after-school hours were filled with other activities, usually music or sports.

I don't want to skip over eighth grade too quickly. All the eighth-graders from Southampton and Warminster were sent to Craven Hall. The building was later preserved by the community as a historic landmark. We were there for a year because the new high school building wasn't finished yet. It would be named in honor of William Tennent (1673–1746).

Reverend Tennent was born in Ireland and came to America settling in Neshaminy, Pennsylvania, in 1718. Shortly after his arrival, he left his membership in the Anglican Church of Ireland and petitioned the Presbyterian Church in America for membership. His request was granted, and he soon established the Log College (1735) in order to teach his sons William, John, and Charles as well as other boys who were interested in an academic Christian education. All three of his sons became ministers and went on to become leaders in the Great Awakening. His school would later become Princeton University. The origin of sixty-three colleges and universities can be traced to the influence or work of the men whom Tennent trained. In 1926, a stone monument was erected and dedicated to this very special Christian pastor/educator.

William Tennent High School

Our new school would accommodate all the students in grades nine to twelve gathered from Southampton, Warminster, and Lacey Park. We Southampton kids considered the Warminster kids as different and the Lacey Park kids as, well, really different. Mr. Exum was our homeroom teacher, and he later became vice principal. He was my football coach and eventually invited me to speak at my brother Paul's baccalaureate service in 1965.

With four boys in the house, there were chores to be done, from setting the table, washing and drying the dishes, putting out the trash, to mowing the lawn. I earned a quarter every week. My younger brothers took over once I was in senior high school.

Southampton Hardware

I was fifteen when I started to work at Southampton Hardware on Saturdays. I was the stock boy, keeping myself in the back room for several months and then picking up added tasks as my knowledge increased. This was a very good experience, for not only did I earn some money and learned a bit about the kind of stock hardware stores sold, but also I became good friends with the owner's daughter.

Patricia O'Brien

Her name was Pat, and she was a grade ahead of me but only seven months older. When I started at the store, the O'Brien family lived in the back of the same building. By 1956, Mr. O'Brien had completed construction of a large beautiful home next to the store. I remember having spinach soup for lunch—never my favorite—while I worked at the store or helped with some simple construction tasks at the new house.

I enjoyed the construction trade and would later go on to work with local builders during breaks from college. I found employment with three different companies, Dick Eitner Homes, Harry Epp and

Son, and Al Bartram and Son. I enjoyed myself, learned a few things, and was able to help with my college expenses.

Occasionally my father worked at the hardware store, and our two families would get together at times. There were four O'Brien kids and four Weisenbach kids. The big difference was that the O'Briens had a girl and three boys, while there were four of us Weisenbach boys. My brothers paired off—Pat's brother Dave and my brother Bill, Pat's brother Jack and my brother Paul, and Pat's brother Tom and my brother Dave.

As I remember, Pat and I didn't make many personal connections, but we saw a lot of each other. Besides there were many activities that brought us together, such as youth group at church along with the orchestra and band and chorus at school. I enjoyed our times together, but I was going steady with another girl during those years. Her name was Barbara Stevenson. Of course Pat had several boys she liked.

Barbara and I were as serious as fifteen-year-old kids can be, but I always felt that what Barbara and I experienced as teenagers was a good preparation for my future. I never thought of marriage when I was with Barb. We were just happy companions. She later went off to nurse's training in Philadelphia, and I went to Muhlenberg College in Allentown. I remember, at age seventeen, a conversation we had agreeing to go our separate ways. She later met a seminary student named Frank Robinson whom she married. The last I heard, they have retired from parish ministry and are living in Florida.

When I learned to drive at the age of sixteen, the family car was a 1956 Plymouth Belvedere, aqua with a black top. I had two accidents with that car. I remember signaling for a left turn and turning right instead. The car behind me passed on my right and got as far as my right rear door. I can still see Dad's face as he got out, looked at the damage, and slammed the door.

The second accident was along County Line Road, in front of Sunset Memorial Park. My girlfriend Barb was next to me in the front seat, and Ed Erkert and Janet Maddox were in the back. I foolishly turned to kiss her and consequently grazed a telephone pole, damaging the same right rear door. I remember getting out of the car and finding a piece of chrome trim lying on the ground. I picked it up and with tears streaming down my face looked to heaven and prayed for God's help. I drove home and told Mother and Dad what had happened. I lied and told them that a truck forced me off the road. With those tears still staining my cheeks, I tossed the keys on the kitchen table and said, "I don't deserve to drive."

I will never forget Dad's reply. "Well, son, I knew this would happen. I didn't think it would happen this soon, but we will get it fixed." Then he offered the keys back into my grateful hand. This loving action of my father, expressed on that Sunday afternoon, helped form a reliable foundation upon which to build a future. Thanks, Dad!

Senior high school provided many opportunities to learn and grow, not only physically but also academically, socially, emotionally, and spiritually. Being in different grades, Pat and I were never in the same classes, but we both played clarinet in the band and orchestra and sang in the chorus. We were also regulars at Bible Club with Harold Schmidt as our leader as well as early prayer meetings before classes. Through church and Youth for Christ meetings, we were exposed to challenging pastors, teachers, evangelists, and missionaries.

Our pastor's wife Ruth Morrison taught a Sunday school class, and it was she who gave me my first devotional book with a page for every day. It was entitled *My Continual Burnt Offering* by Harry Ironside. That book helped me develop the habit of reading something every day, a good habit to pick up.

When I heard a quote I thought was worth remembering, I would write it in the front or back pages of my Bible.

Here is a small sample indicating my goals at the time.

> If this world was worthy of my Lord's life, it surely is worthy of mine. (Marshall Case, February 7, 1959)
>
> Who I am is more important than what I do. (Harold Schmidt, April 13, 1959)
>
> Faith and unbelief are both progressive. (Ken Grey, August 4, 1961)

Good can often times be the enemy of best.
(Pastor Cressman, October 28, 1961)
Am I called to Patty or to God's service?
(Ken Grey, January 20, 1962)
God doesn't pull, he directs. (Pastor Burrell
Fraser, June 30, 1963)
The most important thing about prayer is
to pray. (Dr. Paul Smith, July 11, 1963)
Be careful how you handle God's money.
(Pastor Alex Morrison, December 29, 1969)

I must add the critical part music played in those early days, starting with Mother's willingness to lead a children's choir at church. As we grew older, she always expressed great joy at hearing her family sing whenever we all got together. Music was very present in high school too, both vocal and instrumental. And of course, music was everywhere at church, especially in our youth group.

Our church had a bus and our leaders used it to get us to various meetings and activities, and singing together was part of the ride. One of our favorites was a song written by Thomas Chisholm and music by Harold Lowden. It was called "Living for Jesus" based on Romans 12:1–2. As I reflect back, this song expressed my teenage desire to serve the Lord someday. The words of commitment are quite clear and I meant every word.

By the way, Harold Lowden taught music at the Bible Institute of Pennsylvania (now Cairn University). Thomas Chisholm wrote the words to "Great Is Thy Faithfulness," among many others.

Living for Jesus
Living for Jesus a life that is true,
striving to please Him in all that I do.
Yielding allegiance, glad-hearted and free,
this is the pathway for blessing for me.
Chorus:
O Jesus, Lord and Savior, I give myself to Thee,
For Thou in Thine atonement didn't give Thyself for me.

45

I own no other Master—my heart shall be Thy throne:
My life I give, henceforth to live,
O Christ, for Thee alone.

I recently discovered that Pat confessed Christ as her personal Savior on the same day I did, February 22, 1952. Our church must have organized some sort of program for us kids. She wrote the following in the front of her Scofield Reference Bible.

My Covenant

Lord, I give up all my own plans and purposes, all my desires and hopes and accept Thy will for my life. I give myself, my life, my all, utterly to Thee to be Thine forever. Fill me with Thy Holy Spirit. Use me as Thou wilt, send me where that wilt, work out Thy whole will in my life at any cost, now and forever.

I believe that God took Pat at her word and has, through the years, used her as His instrument. She is reluctant to speak of her critical role in initiating a spiritual search on the part of her parents, but her father often referred to it as the event that changed the direction and character of the O'Brien family. And I believe that her decision to be faithful to her Lord and Savior has been the rock-solid basis for our marriage and ministry.

Our partnership was clearly displayed when the leadership of First Parish Congregational Church, seeking to hang a picture of the minister in the Fireside Room along with that of several previous pastors, chose to have the picture include Pat by my side.

I wanted to be a serious, faithful Christian, and as I look back, God supplied special people to pray for me and with me all along the way. Among the many were Pastor Morrison, Pastor Burrell Fraser, Charlie Vogel, Ed O'Brien, Dick and Jean Cook, Mae Erb, Bill Freeland, Ken Grey, Mr. James Exum, Coach Dick Acker, Dr.

David Bremer (chaplain), Muhlenberg College, local Allentown pastors, Cressman and Kenyon, the Bartholomew family, Dr. Arthur Glasser, Dr. Glenn Barker, Dr. Earl Jackson, John Carter, Dick and Beth Cairns, Eleanor Walker, Dexter Wheeler, Dick Sanderson, Ed Chapman, Ron Kent, George and Kathi Ensworth, Vernon Von, Dr. Takeshi Yoshihara, Randy Hongo, Tom Masaki, Larry McCracken, Peter Galateria, Horace Hylan, Robert Woodyard, Jan Martin, Roy Evans, Ruth Ross, Dr. Glenn Jamison, Rev. Peter Brown, Rev. John French, Rev. John Stoekle, Rev. Ralph Peterson, Rev. Dean Pedersen, Rev. Ed Whitman, Dr. Lee Maynard, and of course my parents and Pat's parents, our adult children, and my precious partner Pat.

I cannot overemphasize the spiritual boost I and others received through the life and ministry of Dick and Jean Cook. They were our volunteer youth group leaders who were used by God to pour themselves out to a group of about twenty of us teenagers. They were Christian people who loved God and loved us. Dick was a machinist, and Jean a mother of three.

Every Saturday night, they planned an activity for us followed by devotions and food back at their house. We went to Youth for Christ meetings, bowling, swimming, waterskiing, winter and summer camp, and tent meetings. The Cooks eventually left us to become missionaries in Western Canada and then house parents for Overseas Missionary Fellowship (OMF) children. I believe that next to our parents, the "Cookies" influenced me the most during my high school years. I will be forever grateful to God for his provision of these godly servants.

The Cooks afforded us opportunities to serve the gospel. We would travel to Christ Home, a Christian facility for the elderly, or a rescue mission in Philadelphia. Once a month, a group of us would arrive on a Sunday afternoon to conduct a worship service. Someone would lead in group singing, scripture reading, prayer, and testimony. There would often be a special duet or quartet. I usually went with the group to share an encouraging word.

At one of those services at Christ Home, I announced that I would soon be going to Muhlenberg College in Allentown, Pennsylvania. One of the ladies, Mae Erb, lit up and announced, "I'm from

Allentown!" Our relationship grew, and my generous parents would include Aunt Mae in many of our family gatherings. She became a fixture at our house until she passed away.

Extracurricular activities were a major part of my high school experience, band, orchestra and chorus, football, and track. I had been playing the clarinet and singing at school and church for years, so with the coming of Mario and Mary Trezza, I was able to participate fully. The Trezzas were tireless teachers, offering private lessons and leading us in groups. Mr. Trezza led band and orchestra, while Mrs. Trezza led the vocal groups. Every year, they combined their efforts to present spring concerts, which usually included several selections from well-known musicals. Great fun!

During football season, I had to drop out of the band. I played on the team for all three years of senior high. My first position was a defensive guard and then a linebacker. I later played end and then halfback, but I always had trouble catching the ball. I guess I was good enough to get a partial tuition scholarship at Muhlenberg College, but more about that later.

Just as Mother was a sprinter during her teen years at John Wanamaker's, I was recruited by the track coach Dick Acker to run the 100 and 220 (yards not meters). Later I developed enough endurance to advance to the quarter mile and finally become a member of the mile relay team. Coach Acker was truly dedicated to our success, exposing us to many opportunities to compete, even during the winter. As a result of his leadership, we never lost a league meet during my high school career.

One memorable moment of my running career came at the Penn Relays held at Franklin Field, University of Pennsylvania. Coach Acker allowed me to run anchor leg at that very special event. I got the baton after the first three runners completed their quarter mile. When I received the baton, we were ahead by about ten yards. When the runner behind me got his baton, he sprinted to catch up and overtook me. I picked up my pace and hung on his outside shoulder. At about the three-hundred-yard point, we both began our kick. He had used too much of his energy at the outset, and I overtook him to regain the lead. I still can picture the final fifty yards! Coach Acker used a newspaper photo of that finish to announce the opening of track season for many years after my graduation.

Our team went on to set a high school record for the mile relay at the state meet that year, 3:25.6! Coach later wrote in my yearbook, "Hope in some small way I have been helpful to you in your future. Your athletic deeds of courage will long be remembered. Few coaches have the pleasure of working with a track man such as you. Coach Acker." One final note, Coach Acker was the one who suggested that I investigate Muhlenberg College, his alma mater.

I honestly can't remember how I was able to buy my first car, a 1929 Ford Model A. I do however remember getting it to run. I actually drove it to college once or twice, brother Dave remembers one harrowing drive home in a snowstorm when he and Dad kept me from driving off the road. I sold that car for $200.00 to a missionary kid who drove it all the way to Atlantic City, New Jersey.

Critical Decisions

Muhlenberg College, Interest in Foreign Missions, Gordon
Divinity School, Dr. Glenn W. Barker, Our wedding

In 1959, at the tender age of seventeen, Mother and Dad drove me
the 120 miles north to the campus of Muhlenberg College. I went
a month early because the football team began practicing in August.
Mother and Dad drove back home that night, and I went to my
dorm room, 368 Martin Luther Hall.

Our dorm was a three-story brick building with the hallway
running from one end to the other. Number 368 was in the middle
of the hallway, and unlike other rooms, it had space for three students, not two.

I'll never forget my first night in that room. There was another
football player down the hall, and I could hear the echo of his radio,
but I wasn't about to knock on his door. I was too scared! In fact,
I cried that first night. The thought of four years stretching out in
front of me and Mother and Dad taking out a $1,400.00 loan to pay
for it and fear that I might flunk out or not make the team filled my
seventeen-year-old mind. If anyone had told me that I would eventually go on to seminary for three more years and then graduate school,
well, I'm not sure what I would've done.

Football practices lasted all day long for about a month before
our first game. As I reflect back, we didn't have a very keen coaching
staff. The college was deemphasizing athletics at the time. To make
things even more challenging, we were in the mid-Atlantic conference matched with teams like Delaware, Bucknell, Temple Univer-

sity, and Lehigh. Our records for those four years were nothing to boast about. My senior year, we were 2-7!

I remember two salt tablets after practice to make up for all the sweating, steak dinners before a game, the grumpy man who washed our practice uniforms, and the few times I felt I played a good game.

I was surprised to find a newspaper clipping in Aunt Betty's journal. Betty was Dad's sister. In October 15, we bombed Lebanon Valley College 27-12. "Houseknecht's first touchdown pass, to end Richard Weisenbach, was the result of a muffed field goal attempt. On the attempt, the center pass went awry and Houseknecht picked up the ball and threw a fourteen yard pass to Weisenbach in the end zone." How about that!

My tuition scholarship was a great blessing, and my membership on the Dormitory Council provided a free room during my sophomore, junior, and senior years.

In my senior year, I was given a special opportunity to work in the commons, where we ate our meals. The Conrad Seegers Student Union was the new building on campus and named for our seventh president. When Allentown was named an All-America City, the newly elected governor of Pennsylvania, William W. Scranton (1963–1967), was the guest of honor at a citywide banquet held at the college. I had the privilege of serving him, dressed in my black slacks, black bowtie, white shirt, and red cutaway jacket. Hot stuff! This position provided me with free food during my last semester. Actually, I might have come out ahead financially that last year.

During the first week of classes, all the freshmen were ushered into the school theater to hear a welcoming speech designed to tell us the basics of college life. The only thing I remember was the speaker inviting us to look to our right and then to our left. Then he told us, "Those two students will probably not graduate with you. Chances are they will transfer or drop out!" As it turned out, I was the only student from 368 Martin Luther Hall that graduated four years later. Bernie Semell transferred, and Dick Weathereau left after one year.

Unlike Pat, who had received a full scholarship and earned straight As in nursing school, I struggled academically and ended my first year with a 1.8 cumulative average. I had great difficulty with

German—believe it or not—and chemistry and physics. I decided I had to get out of my intended track toward civil engineering and choose something else. English/psychology came to the rescue.

Dad was disappointed with my change; after all he was paying for it! But I just couldn't hack it. The change however afforded me the opportunity to take extra courses in British literature and public speaking. I also took two electives, art and architecture and music appreciation, which opened up interesting avenues.

Muhlenberg was founded in 1848 by Henry Melchior Muhlenberg, patriarch of the Lutheran Church in America. It began as a seminary, I referred to it as "a small Christian college for small Christians." We did have compulsory chapel, and they did take attendance.

There were a few students who were more serious than most about their personal beliefs and behaviors. We were the Muhlenberg Christian Association (MCA). As the yearbook stated, "The Muhlenberg Christian Association is interdenominational, yet bound together by a mutual love of Jesus Christ. Its sole purpose and sole reason for being is to glorify Jesus and to make Him known throughout the campus." I remember very little about our bimonthly meetings, but we did, in March 1962, have a spiritual retreat at Kirkridge Retreat Center in Bangor, Pennsylvania. All I remember was that Pat was with me.

My participation in MCA allowed me an opportunity to meet the school chaplain. His name was Rev. Dr. David Bremer, a wonderful man who tolerated my superconservative opinions and patiently nurtured my faith. He even gave me an opportunity to preach in the daily chapel service. A quote printed on the bottom of one of our daily chapel bulletins captured my attention and helped smooth my rough edges.

> What makes a man a Christian is neither his intellectual acceptance of certain ideas, nor his conformity to a certain rules, but his possession of a certain spirit, and his participation in a certain life. (John Baillie)

I know this quote pushed me along a more accepting and less judgmental path for sure. There will be Lutherans in heaven!

The college newspaper *the Muhlenberg Weekly* had a feature called "In the Spotlight" by Bill Burton. I was featured during the latter part of my junior year. Here is a part of that article.

> Here at Muhlenberg, Rich is a member of the football and track teams, M club, and MCA. When participating in intramural sports, wrestling and softball, he represents the 200 Club. He is also a member of the class of 1963 Executive Council, treasurer of the men's dormitory council, and was chairman of the recent World University Drive held on campus.
>
> He was injured in a good part of the recent football season but he did start the first three games of the year. He'll be running the two twenty- and the four forty-yard sprints for the track team this spring.
>
> Rich is a psychology major who has some very interesting aspirations. He is a pre-theological student who hopes, upon graduation, to attend Columbia Bible College in Columbia, South Carolina.
>
> After this, he has till further plans; he is looking forward to working in the foreign missions field, probably in the Far East under the direction of the China Inland Mission, a non-denominational group. Still further, Rich has been dating a student nurse from Germantown Hospital who has similar plans and they are preparing to carry out their plans together.

When I began college in the fall of 1959, I was a young seventeen-year-old. One of my required courses was freshman English.

Our first assignment was to write a one-page theme to be entitled "Who Am I?" Here is my first effort for Ms. Stang.

"Who am I?"

September 24, 1959

God, in his immeasurable creation, made man and placed him on this earth to glorify Himself. I am but one of those creations. When God creates a man He gives him a special personality. Every man is different, he doesn't follow a blueprint. If a person was appointed to find me he would be looking for a teenage boy with a very methodical and organized outlook of life. For example, I try to keep my room as neat as possible, I do my homework far in advance, and I write a little note to myself to be sure to carry out my plans. I believe in planning my work, then working my plan. In addition I feel that being dogmatic about something, if I'm sure I'm right, is an asset rather than a liability. I don't want to think as the crowd thinks, the crowd maybe wrong. Moreover I am not overly extravagant. Buying secondhand books is a wise investment. Finally, I am proud of a good, well-executed job, done not for recognition, but for the sole purpose of self-satisfaction.

This first theme is a bit embarrassing! Ms. Stang gave me a D.

As I look back from the perspective of fifty-five years, I realize now how critical and formative my college years were. I became much more open to different ideas, especially about my Christian faith. My relationship with Pat was deepening, and our desire to prepare ourselves for a future in God's service was uppermost in our prayers and planning.

By God's grace, I graduated on June 9, 1963, with a 2.8 C+ average. That was enough to gain admittance into Gordon Divinity School (GDS), Wenham, Massachusetts.

I must mention one critical conversation Pat had with our high school friend Frank Severn. When Barbara Stevenson and I decided to go our separate ways around Christmas time in 1959, I began to develop a closer friendship with Pat O'Brien. However there was one major problem—she was in a growing relationship with a classmate named Don.

During the summer of 1961, she became quite conflicted concerning which young man she might seek a partnership with. Looking for counsel, she posed the question to Frank who knew Don, me, and Pat. "Whom do you think I should choose?" By God's grace, Frank suggested me.

Pat took a long walk with Don and explained her decision. I'm sure it took gentle love and courage for Pat to speak with Don, and of course he must have called upon God for His peace. During the next twelve months, our relationship deepened. To the best of my memory, we kissed each other for the first time on the Fourth of July 1961. Yes, we saw fireworks!

By the spring of 1962, Pat and I had decided to marry, probably after she finished her nursing training. She graduated on September 8, 1964. Eleanor Whalen, assistant director of Nursing Education, wrote the following: "Patricia has maintained high theoretical and clinical grades. A quiet, mature girl, Patricia adjusts well to most situations. As her time in nursing increases she is developing into a knowledgeable, feeling nurse." Pat had scored in the nineties in every subject and enjoyed a full scholarship.

We formalized our decision to marry in the visiting room of the nursing school affiliated with the Germantown Dispensary and Hospital. The decision was not a surprise to either of us. It was clear that this was the right decision, and I had previously asked her father for his permission and blessing. I guess all those years of sweeping the stockroom floor at Southampton Hardware finally paid off.

During those years, the most important issue for us was how we might minister together. Having been raised in a Christian home and church, we were taught that the question of how we might serve God should always be front and center. We were challenged by our pastor and visiting missionaries to be open to an overseas call.

Interest in Foreign Missions

One of the stronger influences was brought into our lives by Uncle Ken Grey. He and his wife Maybeth had been missionaries with the China Inland Mission/OMF. After serving overseas, they were asked to be house parents to the children of missionaries who took advantage of the mission policy of affording their children the opportunity to gain their education in the United States.

God provided the mission with a spacious home for this purpose in Ivyland, Pennsylvania, just a few miles from our home and church in Southampton. Uncle Ken brought his kids to our church and youth group. He saw the ministry afforded by Dick and Jean Cook and sought to have his charges benefit. It was God's blessing to all of us.

The mission home was a large farmhouse complete with a long driveway, barn, and pond. Our youth group made frequent visits to discuss the Bible, swim, ice-skate, and eat together. We were introduced to the ordinary life of two very experienced, loving, and prayerful Christian adults at a level we could understand. And of course, they prayed for the future of each of us.

While at Philadelphia College of Bible (1958–1961), Pat's interest gravitated toward ministry opportunities in Asia. My roommate in seminary was a student from Japan, Takeo Miyamura, just another of God's push in that same direction. In addition, we had the chance to sponsor a Chinese orphan through Evangelize China Fellowship. Her name was Née Née Liu. We began our support at $10.00 a month on May 4, 1964. Our support continued to June 6, 1969, when Nee Née moved back with her parents. The mission assigned a second orphan, Yushu Chen, asking us to continue our support. The question of overseas service would remain a matter of prayer, discussion, and observation for the next several years.

The plan to serve in Asia had been growing throughout the last two years of college. In October 1961, I attended a mission conference held at the Evangel Fellowship Church just down the street from the college. J. Morris Rockness, associate home director of the China Inland Mission/OMF, was one of the invited speakers. I wrote to him on February 28, 1962, requesting some information about their missions work. Here's a few lines from his response.

> March 2, 1962
> Dear Dick,
>
> It is gratifying to know that the Lord is guiding you in your thoughts concerning his will for your life. As you have committed your life to the Lord for his service you can press forward with confidence that he will give you a confirmed leading for each step that lies ahead.
>
> I am enclosing herewith a copy of our handbook which should give you an outline of our history, its present scope of ministry, and our doctrinal position, principles, and practices and, from pages eighteen to twenty four, the qualifications and requirements which we look for in prospective candidates. As a mission we do not dare to put pressure on young people to join us, as we feel that they should do so only as they are constrained by the Holy Spirit. May I say that we would rejoice if this should be the Lord's will for you.
>
> Yours sincerely in Christ,
> J. Morris Rockness

Pat and I have always been grateful for the soft-sell approach of this mission organization. We received answers and guidance when requested but never pressure. So from high school/youth group days to seminary, God planted seeds that grew in my heart; Pat's life goals, praying parents and friends, and a seminary roommate all served to move me toward full-time Christian ministry of some type somewhere.

I met Dr. Arthur Glaser, home director, at a mission conference in late 1962. I wrote to him inquiring as to his suggestions about further education.

> January 8, 1963
> Dear Richard,
>
> I am glad that you felt free to write and inquire further into the matter of your formal preparation for the Lord's work. With regard to Bible training prior to seminary, you are in the best place to judge as to this need. If you feel you do not have a sufficient grasp of the scriptures, then I would urge you to make securing this a high priority.
>
> I have recently been in rather close contact with the board of PCB and have come to appreciate in a new way the manner in which our Lord is using it to prepare young people for his service. My only question as to the suitability of the school for you is that its total program is undergraduate. To be candid, I think that if you were to take studies in the scriptures, you ought to be made to work hard, on a graduate basis. It would be preferable if you could work toward some academic goal bearing on your undergraduate work at Muhlenberg.
>
> From my impression of your intellectual stance, I do not think that Westminster or Fuller Theological Seminary are the schools for you. You are more of an activist rather than philosophical in your outlook. Have you contacted Gordon Divinity School at Beverly Farms, Massachusetts?

This school is highly regarded in certain quarters and essentially Baptist in its orientation.

This comes with cordial greetings in Christ. Please feel free to reply should this letter not quite answer your problem.

Yours warmly in Christ,
Arthur Glasser

Gordon Divinity School (1963-1966)

Within the month, I wrote to Dr. David Kerr, dean of GDS. He replied by sending a catalog and sharing a bit about the school.

> January 16, 1963
> Dear Richard,
>
> Since we cannot speak with you personally, perhaps you will permit us to say something about Gordon and its program. We have a faculty whose qualifications are of a high order since each member has studied at outstanding schools in the United States and abroad. What is more important is that each is wholly committed to Jesus Christ as Lord and Savior. Each also believes that the Bible is God's written word and that its teachings, inspired and illuminated by the Holy Spirit, provide the only satisfying answers to the multiple problems of our crisis times.
>
> Sincerely yours in Christ,
> David W. Kerr
> Dean

I responded back to Dean Kerr with a statement of my Christian faith and call to Christian service. On February 25, 1963, I received tentative admission with the class of September 1963. My transcript from Muhlenberg was all that remained to complete the process.

In April 16, I wrote to Dr. Glasser again letting him know of my/our plans. He responded,

> April 22, 1963
> Dear Rich,
>
> With regard to your plans, I think that you are wise in putting the matter of the time of your marriage completely in the Lord's hands. If you were to marry in the summer of 1964, we feel that that might quite possibly be the Lord's will. Long engagements are not good.
>
> Should the Lord continue to lead you toward the CIM, you would file application soon after your marriage.
>
> While at Taylor University this past weekend, I met some fine fellows who will be going to GDS this fall. The seminary certainly draws a good quality of students. And if God is leading you to take your theological training in Gordon, we know that you will get a good exposure not only to Christian truth but also to all of the contemporary thought of our day.
>
> Of course, you recognize that seminaries are not strong in giving one a deep and comprehensive grasp of the Scriptures. You will have to continue to work on this on your own. We at the mission believe that the strongest contribution to one's current effectiveness is their daily walk with God, their daily Bible study. So you will need to struggle and make sure that you maintain your quiet time, etc. This comes with cordial greetings in Christ.
>
> Yours sincerely in Him,
> Arthur Glasser

I began at GDS in September 1963. In October, I wrote a letter home. Mother kept that letter and I was able to retrieve it after she died.

> October 9, 1963
> Dear Family,
>   The Lord is continually blessing my stay here and making each experience a joy. I have my second Greek test tomorrow and feel pretty confident about it. The Lord has really given a motivation to learn. I find myself studying on an average of three hours a night and enjoy it because of the satisfaction it gives me when I finish. These blessings and joy are God given and a direct result of your prayers and those of Patty, Aunt Mae, Uncle Ken, and others, so please continue.
>   I am leading a youth group in a Baptist church in Somerville. Another student works in the same church and we go every weekend.
>   Thank you so much, love to all.
>
> Rich

School required two years of fieldwork, supervised ministry, in a local church. The closest Baptist church was in Somerville, about forty-five minutes toward Boston. I would travel with another student from school who was serving at the same church. Pastor Don Crosby offered me a bed and breakfast each weekend. I would assist in the worship service and then lead a small group of youth in the afternoon. I was paid $20.00 a week. I remember my experience was a bit of a chore. The congregation was struggling, and Pastor Don was getting frustrated with the slow pace of progress.

I did develop some good relationships at the church and kept in contact for several years after leaving them. I was quite surprised, while serving in Wakefield, to run into one of the Somerville youth while visiting a church member in an assisted living facility in Reading. She was the receptionist who recognized my name as I signed in.

Of course the bulk of my time and energy was spent on my studies. As Dr. Glasser had observed, "You are more of an activist rather than philosophical in your outlook." He was so kind in describing my less than stellar academic record.

My first year included courses in Basic Greek, Historical Theology, Man and His Relationships, Preaching, Protestant Theology, Intermediate Greek, and two units of fieldwork. I finished my first year with a 2.3 GPA. I have always considered myself a plugger, not outstanding in any particular way, but just a man who sees what ought to be done and goes about doing it. Sometimes, by God's grace, the results are very special. The next year, 1964, proved to be a special year indeed!

During that first year at GDS, I along with about ten other unmarried "divies" lived in Frost Hall. This huge stone building is tucked away in a corner of the Gordon College campus and, at that time, housed the entire seminary—library, classrooms, professors' offices, and even the cafeteria—so we only left the building to go to chapel.

It was built by Fredrick H. Prince (1859–1935), an American stockbroker, investment banker, and financier. He was friend to both Joseph P. Kennedy and Pres. Franklin D. Roosevelt. In the 1890s, he purchased 994 acres in Wenham, Massachusetts, and he called it Princemere. In 1911, he built Frost Hall and then went about constructing riding trails and carriage paths throughout the property. Twenty years after his death, Gordon College was able to move their campus to Wenham from their original home at the Clarendon Street Baptist Church in Boston.

In June, I had to make an important decision about our future. Because of our upcoming wedding, I would be moving out of my third-floor room in Frost Hall. Pat and I would need a place to live, and I needed a new fieldwork location. There were two possibilities. One was to work with Rev. Chris Lyons, senior pastor of West Congregational Church in West Peabody. One of his seminary assistants, Mike Easterling, had graduated in May and Chris was looking for a student to replace him. It was an exciting possibility.

West Church was a vital place, ministering to the community and attracting several college and seminary students and even a few professors. They also ran a bus to Gordon College, which provided transportation from campus to the church. Along with regular worship and several groups for students of all ages, several church members provided a student or two with Sunday dinner and fellowship.

I would assist Pastor Lyons in the pulpit with funerals and weddings, preach periodically, do some visitation, and oversee their entire youth program. The position would pay $55.00 a week and required thirty-five hours per week.

Our housing would be provided for us if we were willing to be house parents at one of Gordon College's dormitories. The college had four roadhouses on Grapevine Road, housing about a dozen students each. Hopefully, Pat and I could become dormitory monitors. Pat had gotten a job at Beverly Hospital about five miles down the road. I would be able to walk to class. It seemed doable. "Lord, is this for us?"

The other opportunity was to travel about twelve miles up Route 128 to the Union Congregational Church in Magnolia. Dr. Glenn Barker, professor of New Testament at the seminary, was the interim pastor at the church and was looking for an assistant. We would not be paid but would be provided with a spacious nine-room apartment located above the church's vestry. This placement would fulfill my fieldwork requirement because I would assist Dr. Barker along with developing a fledgling youth ministry.

Dr. Glenn W. Barker

Glenn Wesley Barker was born on June 10, 1920. In 1945, he married Margaret Robinson of Portland, Oregon. Sadly he died in 1984 at the age of only sixty-four. The order of worship at his funeral contained the following information:

> He was a scholar, theologian, teacher, pastor, and administrator. He was educated at Wheaton College and Harvard University from whence

he graduated as a Doctor of Theology. He was professor of New Testament at Gordon-Conwell Theological Seminary till 1972 when he became the dean of the School of Theology and professor of Christian Origins at Fuller Theological Seminary. He then took up responsibilities as provost in 1977. He made significant contributions to important works such as the Expositor's Bible Commentary, the Encyclopedia of Christianity, and the International Standard Bible Encyclopedia. He served on committees of the Association of Theological Schools and the Western Association of Schools and Colleges. To the last, he was a lover of nature and sports enthusiast.

I would add that he loved his students. Pat and I have often reflected back upon the choice we made. It was one with momentous implications for our future. Little did we realize how critical this decision would be. Obviously we chose to join Dr. Barker at Union Church. This began a relationship that developed into something very special. Over the next twenty years, Pat and I would find ourselves being blessed by the prayers, lessons, opportunities, and example of a magnificent Christian family.

I didn't know it at the time, but Dr. Barker had slipped a look at my admissions file to discover that I played football in college, was married to a nurse, and would graduate in 1966. He used this information to get to know me a little better by inviting me to be part of his intramural touch football team. He also knew that I would be graduating the same year as his planned sabbatical to Heidelberg, Germany. He was hoping and praying that I might be able to develop sufficiently over the coming two years to take over pastoral responsibilities when he and his family left for Europe. By God's grace, that is exactly what happened! Our decision in the summer of 1964 would prove to be a major cornerstone in our lives. I believe that God's Holy Spirit nudged us and then confirmed to us the rightness of that choice. Praise be to God!

Our Wedding

Of course, a second major event occurred on August 8, 1964. Patricia Ann O'Brien became my wife! Oh, happy day. The service was held at Davisville Baptist Church (DVBC) and conducted by our pastor Alex Morrison. I paid him $15.00, which he returned. Would you believe that I sang the song "Because" as Pat walked down the aisle? Everyone in the congregation was invited, and we had a reception of punch and sandwiches followed by a wedding cake. Pat's mom did most of the work, including the sewing of Pat's dress. Frank Severn was my best man, and others who stood with me were my brothers Bill and Paul and Lenny Ochs, a friend from college. Pat's maid of honor was Iris Strauss, a friend from nursing training. She was joined by Liz Hoagland, Jane Severn, and Nancy Board. Here is a copy of the vows we pledged to each other.

> I, Rich, take you, Pat, to be my wedded wife. With deepest joy, I receive you into my life, that together we may be one. As is Christ to His body, the church, so I will be to you, a faithful, sacrificial husband. Always will I perform my headship over you even as Christ does over me, knowing that His lordship is one of godly love and holiest desires for my life. I promise with my deepest love, my unselfish devotion, and my tenderest care. I promise to you that I will live first unto the Lord, rather than for others or even you. I promise to direct our lives always into a life of faith and hope in Christ Jesus, ever honoring God's guidance by His Spirit through the Word.
>
> I, Pat, take you, Rich, to be my wedded husband. With the deepest joy, I come into my new life together with you. As you have pledged to me your life and love, so I too happily give you my life and in confidence submit myself to your headship as to the Lord. As is the church in her

relationship to Christ, so will I be to you. I will live for you, loving you, obeying you, learning from you, and ever seeking to please you. God has prepared me for you, and so I would ever strengthen, help, comfort, and encourage you. Therefore, Rich, throughout life, no matter what may lie ahead for us, I pledge to you my life as a loving, obedient, and faithful wife. "And whither thou goest I will go; where thou lodgest, I will lodge. Thy people shall be my people and thy God my God" (Ruth 1:16).

We took a few pictures in the backyard of the church, opened a few gifts, and then headed back to 875 Rozel Avenue to change clothes and drive our 1957 Chevrolet station wagon, a gift from Pat's parents, to our honeymoon cabin along the shores of Moosehead Lake, Beaver Cove, Maine.

We drove up US Route 1 as far as Exit 9 on the New Jersey Turnpike, New Brunswick. We spent our first night together at the Howard Johnson's Motor Lodge. We had a room right next to the pool, and it cost $20.00! We had a very fulfilling night.

After breakfast at HoJo's restaurant and before heading up north, we found a Baptist church and attended the morning service. We made it to the church in Magnolia by nightfall and slept in a pretty empty nine-room apartment. We left the window open and were kept awake by a puzzling sound. In the morning, we discovered that it was the waves of the ocean.

I had gotten a copy of *Maine Camps and Cottages* and chose a cabin based solely on the price, $8.00 a night, fully furnished with electricity from a generator. I had no idea where Beaver Cove was or Moosehead Lake for that matter. It turned out to be about an eight-hour drive without I-95 or GPS. We turned into the narrow dirt driveway in the late afternoon, and the owner Vernon Davis was waiting for us.

We spent a week or ten days enjoying each other and the beautiful lake, the largest in Maine. Pat's attempt at our first meal was memorable. She was used to cooking for her big family of ten. We had a lot of leftover spaghetti that night. Walks, swimming, shopping, and berry picking filled our days. Then it was back to Pennsylvania to collect our furniture, pack it into a U-Haul trailer, and head back up to Massachusetts.

On August 11, 1964, Pat wrote to her parents from our honeymoon cottage.

> Dear Mother and Dad and kids,
> Hi! We are here safe, sound, and very happy! We arrived here at our cabin on Moosehead Lake at about four thirty yesterday afternoon after shopping in the nearest town, eight miles away! We stayed overnight in our apartment in Magnolia Sunday night. Then we left early yesterday, ate breakfast, and headed for Maine. We're almost at the top of the state.
> It is really beautiful and restful here. We are 150 feet from the lake, which is quite a bit larger than Schroon Lake. We have a nice little cabin, with porch, front room with a table and chairs, kerosene lamp, and Franklin stove, which we fire every morning and evening. There is a small bathroom in back of the bedroom. We have only cold water, so we heat water for everything. Really fun! I'm really enjoying cooking and keeping house. We have electricity from sundown to 11:00 p.m. from a generator. Today we slept in and then went raspberry picking after breakfast and came home with half a pail full. We got our bathing suits on and took lunch down the lake a ways for a cookout. Then we sunbathed for the rest of the afternoon.

We are really enjoying each other and the rest. It's great to be Mrs. Richard Weisenbach!

We are thinking of you all, praying for you, and perhaps now, more than ever, thanking the Lord for you, my wonderful parents and family. Thank you too for making our joyous wedding possible. We certainly enjoyed it and I think everyone else did too. Well, bye for now.

With deep love,
Pat and Rich

Pat's brother David and his wife Ellen Spangler were married just a month before us, which meant that we had the early opportunity to choose some furniture that had been collecting in a barn in Bustleton, Pennsylvania. Along with a few pieces made by Pat's great-grandfather, we received gifts of a rocking chair and end table from Aunt Mae and a cash gift to purchase a dining room set from Larry and June Bartram. We picked up a desk from Mrs. Ritter, a church member. Other pieces gradually made their way into the apartment to meet our needs.

Union Congregational Church, Magnolia, Massachusetts (1966–1971)

Brief History of Union Church, Ordination Plans at DVBC-
Rejection! Seminary Graduation, Installation, Pamela Lynne,
Thoughts about Funerals, Land Purchase, Tithe Sunday,
UCC Ordination, Installation, David Barker, Kimberly Joy,
Foreign Missions? Play School, Youth Club, New Parsonage

M oving far from home was a challenge for us and especially our
parents; back in 1964, it was a seven- to eight-hour ride. I
guess we were so busy at the school, the hospital, and the church that
we didn't have much opportunity to think of our parents. I'm sure it
was a difficult adjustment for them. We did travel back to Pennsylvania for Pat's graduation from nursing school in September 8 and
then again for Thanksgiving and Christmas. Visits at Christmas have
become a tradition to this present day.

Just for the record, here is a very brief history of the beginnings
of Union Congregational Church of Magnolia.

Brief History of Union Church

The first church in Magnolia was a non-denom-
inational "Union Church" for the summer residents. Those who lived year round in Magnolia wished to have a building of their own, and
a "Congregational Society" of twenty members

69

was formed in 1887. In June 1892, Mrs. D. W. Fuller offered a lot of land on Norman Avenue for the building of a "Winter Chapel." Building was started in the fall of 1893 and the first service was held on Children's Sunday in June of 1894. The building cost $4,650.00 to build, formal dedication of the sanctuary was delayed until all debts were paid. This was done on November 8, 1903.

The funds for maintaining the church were largely gifts of the "summer people" of Magnolia plus whatever funds could be raised by Summer Fairs held by the Ladies Aid Society.

In the early 1940s more land was purchased from the Fuller estate and a vestry, with an apartment for the pastor, was built as an addition to the original building. This vestry became the meeting place for community groups as well as a facility for a fairly active Sunday school program.

In 1966 more adjacent land was purchased from Michael and Ruth Wood and in 1970 a five room parsonage as built on a third piece of property contiguous to the church campus.

Dr. Barker began his interim ministry at the Magnolia church in the fall of 1963. He was paid $50.00 a week. Pat and I joined him in August 1964. We moved into the parsonage and took up whatever tasks Dr. Barker suggested. I assisted in the pulpit and began a ministry to the youth and taught a Sunday school class and a Tuesday night class for adults. I also visited as often as possible with members of the church and community. Pat taught a Sunday school class and visited with me when she could. We both joined the choir. We also performed a few chores, such as putting out the trash, cutting the grass, raking the leaves, and shoveling the snow.

Earl Jackson wrote the stewardship letter that November, mentioning some of the accomplishments of the year.

> The end of November 1964 brings the close of our church year. Much has been accomplished this past year. As a result of Dr. Barker's confirmation class, our membership has increased. Two sides of our church building have been painted. The basement rooms have been partially finished and can now be used. One classroom has been repainted and re-furnished by the Harris family, and another room is on its way to being redone. Outside lights now illumine the front of the church at night. A fence has been put up as a boundary on one side of the church property. Yes, many things were undertaken and completed, but many more things have remain unfinished.

He then went on to challenge the congregation to finish what had been started.

The budget for that year (1964–1965) was $7,980.00, and we spent $7,138.57 including $253.84 for missions. During July and August of that year, the Barker family drove to Colorado Springs, Colorado, where Dr. Barker taught a course in New Testament for staff members of Young Life, they returned in September. I was by myself for those nine weeks. Sadly I have no record of what I preached those two months, and you can be sure that I was grateful to welcome the Barkers back home.

While away, Marge Barker wrote the following note to the congregation:

> July 1965
> Dear friends at Magnolia,
>   You surely surprised us in a most pleasant way by the send-off you planned for the Sunday before we left. We are so grateful to you for this

expression of your warm friendship. The nice additions you gave us to our camping equipment have come in very handy, and we are most appreciative of them. There is really a very special place in our hearts for the Magnolia church and for all of you there. We miss you, but are glad that you will be having a blessed summer together under Mr. Weisenbach.

Greetings and gratitude to all
The Barkers

In July 1965, I received this note from the church.

Dear Mr. Weisenbach,

At the church meeting held on May 31, 1965, it was unanimously voted that an invitation be extended to you to continue as our resident assistant minister until next summer, under the same conditions as the past year.

Since Dr. Barker is on vacation until September, we would like to have you assume his duties as our full-time minister at a salary of $50.00 per week until he returns. Even though you will be attending school for the rest of July and will not be free to give full time to the duties of the church, we want you to accept full salary of $50.00 as a small token of our deep appreciation for all that you and Mrs. Weisenbach have done for us.

Yours truly,
Union Congregational Church
Miriam Karcher
Clerk

Those months during the summer of 1965 provided the opportunities to discover what the pastor of a local church is actually required to do. One thing I learned immediately was that ministry required personal discipline. I had to schedule my time quite carefully. If anything was to get done, I had to get to it. Personal study, program planning, visitation, and sermon preparation called for a routine that I had to establish. There was no other person making suggestions or giving guidance. No one was keeping a close watch over my stewardship of my time.

Another thing I discovered was that I was enjoying myself! Studies and sermon preparation were challenging, but I felt very fulfilled with the results. I enjoyed visiting people as well, even those in the hospital. It was intimidating at first, but I realized the person was so grateful to see me and the visit need not be too long; twenty minutes was more than enough time. I would always offer to pray at the conclusion of the visit, and this was almost always appreciated. I didn't please everyone that's for sure, but the vast majority of the congregation, the community of Magnolia, and local clergy affirmed my activities and my manner.

As much as I enjoyed my new role as a young local minister, Pat and I were still thinking that ministry overseas was the goal. In March 1965, I wrote to Rev. Arthur Matthews, candidate secretary of the OMF, asking his advice about the steps that should be taken after graduation from seminary. He spoke of language school and encouraged me to get as much experience in a local church as possible. He continued, "Mr. Lee, our overseas director has gone on record as saying that our applicants should have an adequate period of successful experience in full-time Christian work, preferably in a local church."

Ordination Plans at DVBC-Rejection!

At the time, our plan was to graduate, go to language school, and become ordained at our home church. Ordination in the United Church of Christ (UCC), the denominational affiliation of Union Congregational Church of Magnolia, was not something I had ever seriously thought about. So I wrote to Pastor Morrison.

November 26, 1965
Dear Pastor Morrison,

I have about two weeks remaining in this trimester and then I'll start my last, Lord willing, in January 1966. I should complete my formal studies in April and graduate in the latter part of May. The church here in Magnolia has asked Patty and me to remain as their full-time pastor. I presented this possibility to Mr. Arthur Matthews, candidate secretary of the OMF, and he advised us to stay here for one year gaining invaluable pastoral experience, enlisting in the University of Toronto in June 1967, and making application to the mission after completing their one-month course in linguistics.

I would therefore like to be ordained after graduation. We plan to be home before Christmas, possibly December 16–19. Can I see you then?

In His care,
Rich Weisenbach

He wrote back on December 7, 1965.

Dear Rich,

With regard to your question concerning your possible ordination after graduation in May 1966, I would say that I see no reason why you could not be ordained without official completion of your courses or the receiving of your degree. I agree with Brother Matthews that your experience as pastor will be invaluable in the future.

Rich, our local ordination council endeavors under the leading of the Lord to view and examine each candidate with regard to his particular ministry and the leading of the Lord concerning his future. I am enclosing in this letter page 18 from our church manual, which states our requirements concerning ordination and the procedure that you should follow. If you desire help concerning the preparation of your statement of doctrine or any of the other matters, I should be pleased to counsel with you when we see you, Lord willing, in a few weeks.

Until that time, if our Lord tarries and we are spared, may God's richest blessings rest upon you both as you serve our wonderful Lord now and prepare to reach the unreached in the years that lie ahead.

Devotedly yours in our Savior's love,
Alex B. Morrison
Pastor

After my meeting with Pastor Morrison during our Christmas visit to Pennsylvania, I wrote to him again on January 12, 1966.

Dear Pastor Morrison,

Time is quickly passing, and my plans for ordination are beginning to become finalized. I would like to be ordained at Davisville Baptist Church before my formal completion of studies since my time after graduation will be taken with church activity here in Massachusetts. I have composed a service of ordination, which follows the standard form, and I am including a brief resume of this service. Dr. Glenn Barker has seen this and feels it to be quite adequate. None of the personnel have been contacted, awaiting the approval and recommendation of yourself. I honestly feel that nothing would be objectionable. I would very much desire to substitute this service for the regular evening service on April 24, 1966, using formal vestments without hoods.

Could you please let me know if this meets with your approval and schedule and also advise me as to the extent to which the church will assume financial responsibilities?

The only people you may not know are

Rev. David H. Bremer, Chaplin, Muhlenberg College
Rev. Dr. Glenn W. Barker, chairman, New Testament department, Gordon Divinity School
Takeo Miyamura, classmate
Yukinobu Sato, classmate
Call to worship: A. B. Morrison
Invocation: D. H. Bremer
Statement of ordaining council of DVBC: A. B. Morrison or church clerk
Scripture: T. Miyamura
Vocal solo: Y. Sato
Sermon: G. W. Barker
Charge to candidate: K. T. Grey
Charge to the church: B. Frazier
Vows of ordination. A. B. Morrison
Prayer of ordination: G. Slavin

Welcome to the Christian ministry and presentation of ordination certificate: A. B. Morrison
Benediction: R. A. Weisenbach

We would also plan a reception in the lower auditorium after the service. I would appreciate your ideas on the service, possible meeting dates of the ordination council, and when my statement of faith must be submitted.

In His care,
Rich

The pastor responded,

> Greetings in the precious name of our wonderful Lord!
>
> Thank you for your letter of January 12, which I have at hand. I will present your request for the possibility of substituting your ordination service for a regular Lord's Day service. I will also present your request with regard to the inviting of the various men you have noted in your communication to me.
>
> While you have mentioned the possible date of your ordination, you have not mentioned when you would be available for examination by the board of pastors in this area. Since you are seeking ordination in April, it is essential that you immediately make preparation to meet with this board that will be called to convene upon vote of the Davisville Baptist Church.
>
> Your next steps should be these: 1. submit to me for my reviewing and that of the deacons your statement of faith as outlined in our church manual. 2. We will then by order of the church call the council to examine you. 3. Following the meeting and, Lord willing, positive recommendation of the council, you will establish a date for your ordination (no ordination council will convene if they are aware that an ordination date has been established, for this makes them merely a puppet board).
>
> I shall be awaiting word from you as soon as possible concerning your availability to meet with the council and also shall await the receiving of your statement of faith per our church manual. We greet you in our Savior's name and send the love of the brethren from the faithful saints

here in Southampton to you all in Magnolia, Massachusetts.

Devotedly yours in the Savior's love,

Alex B. Morrison
Pastor

I wrote back on February 5, 1966.

Dear Pastor Morrison,

Enclosed are three copies of my statement of doctrine as required by the church manual. I would like to meet the council during the week of April 18. Any day 12–16 would be suitable. Which would be best for them?

Honestly I do not feel that the council would be a "puppet." They are under no obligation whatsoever to approve me. If they do not, I will simply postpone the service. Confirming the date is important to me so that I can begin to ask the participants to reserve that Sunday evening.

Although our church has perhaps never experienced a service of this kind, with all parts directed toward ordination, I feel that since this is the most important act any local church can do, it should direct full attention to it. This time can be extremely enriching not only to the participants but also to the church as a whole. Please let me know the church's decision at your earliest convenience.

In Christian sincerity,
Rich Weisenbach

Things were moving along and I was extremely busy planning, studying, and corresponding with Pastor Morrison as well as the five others I had asked to participate in the service. In addition, we were expecting the birth of our first child in June. Pastor Morrison wrote again on February 28, 1966.

My dear Rich,

Thank you for your letter, which I presented to the board of deacons at a special meeting I called last evening for their vote of your planed ordination examination. At a special meeting of the church this coming Wednesday, your request will be presented, and following their vote, I will be authorized to call an examining council. I shall call the council to meet at DVBC in April 14 at 10:30 a.m. According to your letter of February 5, this should be satisfactory.

Now, the board of deacons discussed several suggestions you made and have asked me to reply to you these thoughts and decisions. You mentioned a reception following your ordination. We have not had such receptions at church on the Lord's Day and do not feel it wise or expedient to begin now. Also we do not feel that formal vestments are in keeping with the witness and ministry of DVBC and have rejected such use in the past and are doing so now. You mentioned what financial responsibility the church would assume. Again we have not previously had any such request. To my knowledge, it is customary that it be the responsibility of the candidate. Our church will provide you with an engraved ordination document.

The deacons voted to make the 7:15 p.m. service available to you for April 24 at your request. However, they asked me to suggest that you might possibly consider having a Lord's Day afternoon service instead. This would not necessitate pastors Fraser and Slavin getting supplies for their pulpits and also permit others, who might feel it necessary to be in their own churches during the evening hours, to be present at your ordination.

I will have the secretary send out letters with enclosed cards to the council for your examination of April 14 at 10:30 a.m. unless I hear from you.

May the Lord continue to bless you and Patty and your ministry for His honor and glory in Massachusetts. Please feel free to contact me with any questions and rest assured that we will do all we can to help as the Lord directs.

Sincerely in the love of our glorious Savior,
Alex B Morrison
Pastor

I'm sure the reader will get a hint as to the "witness and ministry of DVBC" from Pastor Morrison's response. It is easy to see from the requests I was making that I had changed a bit since leaving my home church in August 1959.

I wrote to Tom Stevenson, chairman of the board of deacons, about his suggestion to conduct the service in the afternoon rather than the evening. He responded saying that the evening would be fine. (I was very grateful, but upon reflection, I think the afternoon would have been better.)

After gaining permission from Davisville Baptist, I wrote to Uncle Ken, Pastor Fraser, Dr. David Brenner, and Rev. George Slavin. Three of these four were able to participate, but Reverend Slavin could not. With a bit of wise foreknowledge, he chided me concerning my assumption of a favorable outcome in April 14. I have often wondered what he might have anticipated.

Dear Rich,
I expect to be at your ordination council, but find it impossible to be with you Sunday evening.

Now, because you will be entering the ministry, may I with fatherly gesture gently rebuke you. Your letter above should have read on line two, "has consented to ordain me on Sunday evening… Provided I am so recommended by the examining council." You will be giving counsel to young men someday and they must not count their chickens before they are hatched.

May the Lord bless you.

By His grace,

George H. Slavin

Well, I had written my doctrinal statement and drove to Pennsylvania for the examining council.

Let me make clear that because DVBC is an independent church free of denominational ties, such an examining council would simply be a grouping of local, like-minded ministers approving a candidate of their choosing. The credibility of such a council of the vicinage does not extend beyond that particular vicinity. A council conducted by a denomination would give the candidate credibility throughout the nation. This is important especially when a pastor chooses to move to another church.

I really don't remember much of the process or who was there except that pastors Rev. George Slavin and Rev. Burrell Frazier said they would attend. I remember sitting in the sanctuary in a chair to the right of the communion table. I read my paper and awaited questions for the sake of clarification. I suppose some of my answers were acceptable, but the fact that I referred to "sacraments of the church" instead of "ordinances of the church" may have sent a negative signal.

A greater problem was my understanding of eschatology, "a branch of theology concerned with the final events of the world and mankind, including the second coming of Jesus Christ, the resurrection of the dead, and the Last Judgment."

As one might imagine, there is a difference of opinion among Christian scholars concerning these events. Each understanding is put forward with scriptural support, but I didn't think that espousing one point of view, exclusive of others, was something I would choose to do. This became a serious problem to some members of the council.

Every Christian church/denomination has a list of beliefs—beliefs that they consider nonnegotiable. The Apostles' Creed is a very common theological statement summarizing Christian basics. Some Christian groups will include one particular eschatological viewpoint, among the many, to their list of basic beliefs. DVBC is among them. Because I did not align myself to their singular perspective, I was stepping outside the boundaries of acceptability. I honestly didn't think that such a difference of opinion would be a problem. I was wrong!

The council decided that I needed to make my beliefs "clearer" in regard to my eschatology. I remember going back to Pastor Morrison's home, spreading my statement out on his sofa, and hearing his suggestions. But in the end, I would not change my beliefs to satisfy the council. I failed their examination.

I had to alert Dr. Barker and the others who had consented to participate in the service that I had failed to receive the council's approval. The service of Christian ordination set for April 24, 1966, at DVBC was canceled. Dr. Bremer sent his kind response.

> Dear Rich,
> Thank you for writing me about the change in plans for the ordination service previously scheduled for Sunday, April 24. Having served on the examining committee for ordination for our own church, I understand how these plans are subject to change. I know your day of ordination will be a very high point in your life, and if I am free to share it with you, I will be delighted to do so.
>
> Sincerely,
> David H. Bremer
> Chaplin

I was confused and embarrassed. My father said, "Write your paper and stuff it down their throats!" I must tell you that Dad had left Davisville years before. He and Pastor Morrison had serious differences. He began attending Faith Community Church, served by Pastor George Slavin.

My dear mother had to call her family members to say, "Rich failed his examination for ordination" It must have been one of her saddest chores!

I had gone to Pennsylvania by myself, and driving back to share the news was very sad and difficult. I cannot remember if the Magnolia congregation even knew about my plan for ordination, but I cannot recall any negative reaction. In God's timing, this sad development grew in its influence upon our future.

If I'm not ordained, can I apply to the mission? Can I continue to serve Union Church? Should I begin praying about ordination in the UCC?

I was still in seminary with graduation a month away. The Magnolia church wanted me to continue and the Barkers were headed to Germany.

Seminary Graduation-Installation, Pamela Lynne

I graduated on Saturday, May 21, 1966, and was installed as full-time pastor the next day. Dr. Barker had timed it perfectly! He wrote and conducted an informal service of installation for Sunday, May 22.

> Order of Installation
> Scripture: Dr. Glenn Barker
> Charge to the pastor: Deacon Earl Jackson
> Charge to the church: Deacon Wilbur Johnson
> Leader: You, as a church, have expressed your conviction of God's leading in the calling of this man to be your pastor. Do you therefore now, before God, pledge to him

your prayers, your understanding, and your faithful support?

People: We do.

Leader: Do you promise to hear with open heart the preaching of the Word to participate reverently and faithfully in the service of worship and by every means to seek the strengthening of your individual spiritual lives in the life of this church?

People: We do.

Leader: Having called this man to be your pastor, do you promise to follow his leadership as he follows Christ, seeking, with him, the salvation of the lost, the comfort of the needy, the nurture of the saved, and in all things seek to make this the church God would have it be, according to the teaching of His Word?

People: We do.

Leader: Do you promise to support this church by your prayers, your talents, and your substance and to so share the responsibilities involved in its ministry that your pastor may be able to give himself effectively to the ministry of the Word to which God has called him?

People: We do.

Leader: To the fulfillment of these promises, before God, I charge you. May the blessing of God be upon you and upon the one whom God has chosen to be your pastor.

Prayer of dedication: Dr. Glenn Barker

Everyone was invited to remain for an informal reception, which was held in the vestry following the service.

The next Sunday, May 29, I preached my first sermon as pastor. I chose Luke 8:4–18, the parable of the sower. I emphasized verse 18, "Therefore consider carefully how you listen. Whoever has will be given more; whoever does not have, even what he thinks he has will be taken from him."

I chose this, reminding the congregation that with Dr. Barker as their pastor for two and a half years, they had received much. We must strive to build on that firm foundation as we go forward.

During the first week of June, the church had a farewell supper for the Barker family. Marge Barker sent the following note that I read the next Sunday:

> June 2, 1966
>
> Dear friends at Magnolia,
>
> Please accept our warmest thanks for your great kindness to us on our last night with you. How happy we were to be present with you for the lovely fellowship supper with a real German flavor throughout. We are sure we will feel more at home when we get to Germany because of this send-off.
>
> We were truly surprised and overwhelmed with your lovely gift of pewter by Guy Parker. What a splendid choice in every way, and how delighted we are to have this choice set of bowl and candlesticks gracing our dining room table. We deeply appreciate your thoughtfulness.
>
> Magnolia has a special place in our hearts, and we look forward to hearing of many accomplishments there in the days ahead. With so many dear people and a consecrated young minister all working together, we know you will really move ahead.
>
> With prayers for God's rich blessings on you all and with grateful hearts,
>
> Love, from all the Barkers.

In June 18, we welcomed our first child, Pamela Lynne, and the next day was Father's Day. I preached from Ephesians 5:18 and titled the sermon "the Cure for Delinquency." I've been a father for twenty-four hours and a pastor for twenty-one days, and already I have all the answers. I had a lot to learn, and by God's grace and Pat's partnership, I picked up a few parenting and preaching skills along the way.

After the arrival of Pamela, Pat left her position at Beverly Hospital to become a full-time mother. We have a picture of me holding Pam in my arms the day she came home from the hospital. All that filled my mind was the awesome responsibility that was upon my shoulders. This little child was totally dependent upon Pat and me. All we could do was pray to the Father, "Oh, Lord, help us to be the support she needs."

We lived in the apartment above the church's vestry, a large room used for community and congregational gatherings. Pam found it to be a perfect indoor playground.

Those first few months became a real challenge, especially the preaching every week. Planning and composing a sermon along with the committee meetings and visitations required courage, discipline, and a great measure of God's grace.

I developed a routine for Sunday mornings. I would get up early, probably five o'clock. I could get to the sanctuary without going outside since our apartment, the vestry, and sanctuary were all one building. I would put on my bathrobe, go into the pulpit, and rehearse the sermon to an empty sanctuary. Then I would go upstairs to the bathroom, open the medicine cabinet, and take some Pepto-Bismol to calm my stomach. I don't recall how long I had to do this, but my guess is that I stopped taking the medicine after about a month or two. I did continue rehearsing in the sanctuary for quite a while.

More recently I review the sermon at the office or at home on Saturday night and again on Sunday morning. Eventually preaching became a privilege and a real joy, probably because of the happy combination of Mother's acting skills and Dad's salesmanship.

Beginning in October 1964 to June 1966, I assisted Dr. Barker in four funerals. On July 13, 1966, I conducted my first funeral alone. It was held at the Pike Funeral Home in Gloucester for Elizabeth Cruickshank. She was eighty-eight years old. I have no remembrance of the service, but it was the beginning of many funerals to follow. After the service for Mrs. Cruickshank, I conducted fourteen more during the next seven years while pastor at Union Church.

Thoughts about Funerals

Over the years, I have conducted 848 services so far. Since retirement in 2013, supply preaching and funerals have been my main ministry opportunities. I have come to regard the funeral service as a very special time to meet some very critical needs.

At first, like visiting in the hospital, meeting a grieving family was difficult. What can I say? How can I meet their needs? I soon came to realize that my main task was to visit the family and ask some obvious questions and then listen carefully. I soon found out that allowing the family to rehearse their loved one's last days and hours can be very beneficial. After a while, the family begins to remember all the many memories that have been shared over the years. These family gatherings usually take about an hour and a half. Along with these expressions of sadness mixed with joy and gratitude, I help plan the funeral service and invite their ideas, suggestions, and participation if anyone chooses to say something. It is a great privilege to share the Christian hope with others, even those who have little interest. Just sowing seeds is a special God-given privilege. The family is always grateful, and I have received scores of cards and notes expressing appreciation. People do not forget these occasions.

I also keep in contact with the family for a full year by sending four booklets written by Dr. Kenneth Hauck, founder of Stephen Ministries. He wrote these booklets during the year following the death of his wife, Joan. I send one of these booklets every three months along with a brief note and two scripture references. Dr. Hauck shares his feelings and faith as he faces his new reality. I truly believe that the families I have met and the funeral services I have been privileged to conduct have become a major part of my ministry through the years.

It was one of my greatest gifts from the Lord to be able to labor alongside Dr. Barker for almost two years. I have remembered many of our conversations and have tried to follow his instructions. One example of his leadership was when he urged me to "visit every home in Magnolia." Union Congregational Church is the only church in town, so I saw the whole community as my responsibility. I needed to become aware of the people and the issues of those souls in my care. The majority of the town is Roman Catholic, served by St. Joseph's Chapel, but there is no resident priest. St. Ann's would send someone to conduct mass each week, but there was no other ministry provided. (Sadly the chapel property has been sold and the building razed.) This presented an opportunity for our church to develop a weekly program for the children, we called it Youth Club, but more about that program a little later.

During those beginning months, I began to visit. My records show 220 visits from 1964 to 1966. I visited for several reasons—I used the time to get to know church members more completely and to explore their gifts for ministry. Seeing shut-ins and hospital patients and welcoming newborns as well as those who were grieving, I found it all quite fulfilling. Then there were inactive church members who had their story to tell and new attenders who had their questions about the church and her beliefs and activities.

Land Purchase

Another suggestion Dr. Barker made was to always investigate any possibility of purchasing property that was contiguous to our own. We were given that opportunity when our neighbors Michael and Ruth Wood offered to sell the back portion of their yard. We took advantage of the offer and on July 22, 1966, paid them $2,500.00. We didn't realize it then, but this decision proved invaluable four years later when we were given the chance to purchase another piece of land connecting our piece from the Woods to a piece on the corner of Fuller Lane and Field Road. We would eventually build a modular home on this second property to serve as the church parsonage. The following announcement was included in the order of worship for Sunday, August 28, 1966.

> Concerning our recent land purchase, those who desire to give special gifts toward the quick liquidation of the debt may do so in one of two ways. Members and friends may desire to give the cost of one or several square feet of the new property, a square foot costing 44 cents, or some may prefer to give a member's share of $28.00. All gifts will be gratefully received and publicly acknowledged unless otherwise specified by the donor. [From these facts, one can easily calculate that the property was 5,682 square feet, and at that time, we had eighty-nine members.]

That same Sunday, the order of worship indicated that seven individuals became members.

> It is our joy to welcome into our fellowship seven who have been recommended by the Advisory Board. All have made a thrilling confession of faith and now desire to unite with us here at Magnolia as full members. They are Richard and Beth Cairns, Richard and Bonnie Coté, Mrs. Lynne Khambaty, and Pastor and Mrs. Richard Weisenbach. Be sure to greet each heartily.

During a special part of the service, I asked each candidate the following questions:

- Do you believe in God as your heavenly Father?
- Do you accept Jesus as you Savior and Master?
- Do you believe in the Holy Spirit as your Comforter and Guide?

- Will you continue striving to know and do the will of God as taught in the scriptures?
- Will you be loyal to the church of Christ wherever you are and uphold it by your prayers, presence, gifts, and service?

Then each knelt as I prayed for each one.

I do not know whether or not Union Congregational Church conducted a Vacation Bible School before I arrived, but I had my first experience in August 8–19 of my first year. For two weeks, we led the children in songs, Bible lessons, activities, snacks, and recreation. It is always a nice surprise when I meet some person in town who remembers those days.

I cannot remember the year we discontinued the every-member canvas, but it probably was not in 1966, although it might have been. *The Gloucester Times* article took notice of the change. The paper reported,

> This is a revolutionary decision since the Union Congregational Church is one of only three or four churches on Cape Ann that has been completely supported by free will offerings and pledges.

The change came about after speaking to the Stewardship Committee. The members felt uncomfortable visiting church members and friends asking for money. Many times the canvas was the only time some folks ever received any contact from the church. I felt this was very unfortunate and needed to stop. My home church never had an every-member canvas, so I hoped this congregation could do the same.

Tithe Sunday

In most churches, November is stewardship month. Union Congregational was accustomed to this schedule, but in October 30,

90

I gave them a challenge. I urged each individual or family to calculate what a tithe would be. "If you gave ten percent of your weekly income to our church, what would it amount to?" You can imagine that this idea got people thinking!

I labeled the first Sunday of November "Tithe Sunday." Our total for that first Sunday was $254.95. In 1967, it was $401.67, and in 1968, it climbed to $502.33. We did have a tithe Sunday in 1969 and 1970, but for some reason, I didn't record the amount. It was a blessing to see the congregation respond to the challenge, and perhaps some realized they could budget more for God's purpose. Just to share the financial facts, the income in 1964 was $7,470.58. In 1970, it had climbed to $20,199.57. My beginning salary was $3,320.00 in 1970, and in my last full year, it was $7,326.00. Missions giving grew from $254.84 to $1,998.61 with a commitment to raise the percentage to 12 percent in 1971 with further increases to be made in the future. At present the church budget provides 20% for missions.

On December 7, 1966, the church received the following note from the Barker family:

> Christmas greetings to you all from the Barkers in Heidelberg. Our thoughts turn fondly to Magnolia often, and we are glad for frequent news from there. We miss you all and are so happy to hear of your faithfulness to the Lord's work there. We have met fine German and American Christian people here and have felt a oneness with them. We shall especially miss being with you as you carol Christmas Eve and return for communion. To us, that was really what made Christmas.
>
> Our best wishes to you all.
>
> Love,
> The Barkers

I began my Christmas letter that year with this greeting.

> To the members and friends of Union Church,
>   It is with a real sense of joy that I sit here at my desk and write a Christmas greeting to you all. Spending our first Christmas with our first church represents quite a milestone for us. How thankful to God we are for each of you. The warmth of our reception and the progress of God's church in Magnolia are the direct result of your help, prayers, sacrifices, and encouragement.

I continued with a reminder of all the holiday activities scheduled and concluded with the following:

> Patty and I wish you all God's choicest blessings during this season and for the coming year.
>   Your pastor in Christ's love,
>   Richard Weisenbach

Pat and I wanted to dedicate our daughter Pam to God's purposes, but since I was not ordained, I felt I should not officiate. Besides, as one of the parents, I would find it awkward to ask questions of myself. So in May 1967, I invited Dr. Roger Nicole, theology professor at Gordon Divinity School, to our pulpit to preach and dedicate five children of the congregation. They included Leslie and Darron Burke, Geoffrey Cairns, Julia Calder, and our daughter Pamela Lynne. We invited the Nicoles to stay for Sunday dinner making that day very special.

UCC Ordination-Installation, David Barker, Kimberly Joy

On September 11, 1967, the following invitation was sent by the scribe of the Essex South Association of Congregational

Christian Churches and Ministers to all the ministers of that association:

Greetings!

At the request of the Union Congregational Church of Magnolia, Massachusetts, the association is hereby called to meet as an Ecclesiastical Council to examine Mr. Richard Weisenbach as to his fitness to be ordained to the Christian ministry.

Since the church has called the candidate as its pastor, the records of the church in this regard will also be reviewed by the council.

Ministerial members of the association and churches represented by pastor and delegate are urged to be present at 2:30 p.m. on Sunday, September 24, 1967, at the Union Congregational Church of Magnolia.

If the examination of the candidate is sustained and his ordination and installation approved, the council will recess until 7:30 p.m., Sunday, October 8, at the Union Congregational Church of Magnolia for a service of ordination and installation.

Proper representation of eleven churches will constitute a quorum.

Wishing you grace, mercy, and peace.

Rev. Edward W. Nutting
Scribe

Sounds pretty official, doesn't it? Being ordained into the UCC was not something I was preparing for, but three factors led to my change of direction.

First was my failure to move forward with the requirements of the council of the vicinage held at my home church in Pennsylvania back in April 1966. They required me to take a stand regarding a singular interpretation of the end times and final judgment. I would not do that because serious scholars disagree on the subject. Believing and teaching others that there is only one accurate interpretation of biblical texts is unfair and unwise. Nevertheless I knew I needed to be ordained if I were to function as a minister through foreign mission or a local church.

Second was the enthusiastic invitation of Union Church to become their pastor. (The tricky part was the fact that Union Congregational Church was a part of the UCC.)

The third factor was the fact that despite obvious theological differences between me and the UCC, I was welcomed by the local UCC ministers and found that my participation was stimulating. My presence and interaction at the monthly association meetings was always respected.

In addition to these monthly meetings of the UCC clergy of the association, Pat and I would attend the Annual Meeting of the Massachusetts Conference of the UCC held in June, along with both the fall and spring meetings of the local Essex South Association. We were often challenged and frustrated at the same time. But we continued to attend, looking for opportune occasions to share our opinions. Unfortunately, as time passed, those opinions were usually put aside by my ministerial colleagues.

I must say that the UCC has changed dramatically since 1967, so much so that I would not seek ordination in the UCC today. The differences are too many and too great. But I must add that given the same circumstances, I would do the same thing I did over fifty years ago.

The Ecclesiastical Council held in September 24 became a challenge for two reasons. The ministers and delegates knew that I had graduated from Gordon Divinity School. The school had a conservative reputation, and the majority opinion of the association leaned more to the liberal side of the theological spectrum.

When I had finished the examination, everyone but the ministers and delegates were dismissed to the church's vestry, while an open discussion was held in the sanctuary. This, of course, brought back memories of the last time I was examined. We waited for a full forty-five minutes while the delegates debated. It came as a great relief to be invited back to the sanctuary to receive a positive result. I am very grateful to those who not only spoke up in favor of theological diversity within the denomination but also actually voted for it.

A second issue was then discussed. The council decided in favor of my ordination, but the records of Union Church came under discussion because the church was asking the association to install me as their pastor. The association tries to protect the minister from agreements that do not seem fair, and issues like expectations and salary are looked at carefully.

As detailed earlier, my salary was $3,320.00, an amount below the standard. The denomination's policy forbids requiring salary levels—each congregation is autonomous and allowed to make her own decisions—but I remember Dr. Earl Jackson, a highly regarded church member, explaining that the church knew that the figure was low but is committed to raising it. His explanation was accepted reluctantly and sounded pretty good to me!

By God's grace, a service of ordination and installation was held on October 8, 1967. Dr. Barker preached, along with six local clergy taking a part. This was followed by a reception in the vestry prepared by the congregation. My parents and grandmother and brothers were able to attend, making the day very special. The church even arranged to have napkins printed, "Reverend Richard A. Weisenbach. October 8, 1967." Nice touch!

I received many cards of congratulations, but one from Earl and Marge Jackson was very touching. Marge signed it, "Always remember your first flock." We have endeavored to do just that.

In June 2017, Pat and I traveled to Hartford, Connecticut, to attend the Annual Meeting of the UCC. I and six other ministers were honored on the fiftieth anniversary of our ordinations. It was very special. (I must confess that my participation in denominational affairs decreased substantially during my years at First Parish.)

Here are a few congratulatory notes and letters I received after my service of ordination and installation.

Aunt Mae wrote, "May God bless you richly." (She enclosed $50.00, which I know was a great sacrifice.)

Earl and Marge Jackson wrote, "It gives us such pleasure to write your new title! How fine that we're permitted to share in this happy, holy ceremony. Very best blessings from all of us."

Pastor George Slavin wrote,

> Allow me to express my congratulations to you on your ordination into the gospel ministry. It is a joyous and solemn occasion to think that the Spirit of the Lord has set you apart to minister His Word and to shepherd His flock... The ministry is wonderful. To speak for the Lord—there is no substitute.
>
> I'm sure your dad and mom are pleased and thrilled. So am I. May the Lord continue to bless you and use you.
>
> By His grace,
> George H. Slavin

I was surprised to hear from Chaplain Bremer.

> I was so delighted to get a copy of the Ordination Service and to know that you folks are now installed in Union Congregational Church of Magnolia. I wish so much that I might have been present on this happy occasion and to share its joys and promise with you... May God bless you richly in your ministry in Magnolia and may you both find the work there full of challenge and promise.
>
> Cordially,
> David H. Bremer
> Chaplain

I guess my favorite note was from Dr. Barker. I had sent him a thank-you note and a check for $15.00.

Dear Rich,

Thank you for your note and for the check, which you sent for the ordination ministry. I want to return the check to you as a start for Pam's education.

It was a real joy to participate in this particular service, which in some sense serves as the end of the beginning. Our confidence in you as a servant of Christ is boundless, and we have nothing but genuine hope that in the days ahead, God will realize through you and Patti His own matchless will. We will continue to pray for your ministry at Magnolia. I believe that it in time will serve as an earnest of what God can do through your lives.

Our very best to you.
Cordially,
Glenn W. Barker

Let me say again that the God-given opportunity to learn from and minister with Dr. Glenn W. Barker was an extreme privilege. After my ordination and installation, the Barkers began attending West Congregational Church in West Peabody. Pat and I remained in close contact with them during the next eighteen years.

We shared the leadership of their daughter Ann's wedding to Gary Lausch on July 21, 1972. That same year, they moved to Pasadena, California, where Dr. Barker became provost at Fuller Theological School. He encouraged me to apply for the doctor of ministry (DMin) program at the school. I was accepted—probably with a big push from the good doctor—and stayed with them during several two-week classes. By this time, Pat and I were pastoring at Kalihi Union Church (KUC) in Honolulu, Hawaii. We saw them every time we passed through on our way to Pennsylvania. Sadly Marge died from cancer in 1982 and Glenn died in 1984 from a heart attack while on the tennis court. She was sixty-two, and he was sixty-four.

I was very disappointed that he did not witness my graduation in 1987.

When our son David was born on January 17, 1969, we named him David Barker Weisenbach in an effort to state just how much we loved and admired this special family. By God's grace, we anticipate a joyous reunion in heaven.

Congregational polity limits the authority of the pastor. I agree with this tradition because Jesus himself called us to be servants, not bosses. As pastor, I have complete freedom in the pulpit as well as the authority to invite whomever I might choose; but the congregation holds the final say regarding my tenure, the budget, who joins the congregation, and who might be asked to leave. The power rests in the various boards and committees appointed and elected by the congregation. Therefore my leadership is best exercised at the committee level. In March 1968, after meeting with the diaconate, I wrote myself a little note.

> I learned something last night. I certainly hope that I'll put into practice. It is for me to counsel with the chairperson of each committee *before* the meeting and then allow them to run the show. Talk little, pray, and guide much. This way I show my trust in their ability, thus increasing it, causing it to grow, and really demonstrating what I say about the church not being mine but theirs. This is a hard lesson. I like to talk and lead. Pat was key in teaching this to me. I find it difficult receiving criticism.

Over the years, I have tried to implement this tactic. I think it is the wisest way to lead. The premeetings with the chair enabled the two of us to settle on an agenda and gave the chair knowledge about where I stand regarding a particular item. The last thing I wanted to do was to surprise or differ with him/her at the meeting. The chair leads knowing where I stand and can bank on my support.

Although ordained to a ministry in the local church, foreign missions remained a major goal for Pat and me. So in 1968, we organized a two-day missions conference, Saturday and Sunday (April 20–21). We were able to contact Park Street Church in Boston and Gordon Divinity School to gain the participation of several missionaries. We planned sessions on Saturday evening followed by a dinner with Arsenia Banaga as guest speaker. Sunday included Rev. Ben Draper of the OMF in morning worship, a time with youth in the afternoon, and a closing panel Sunday evening. I believe this first conference followed by others sparked interest within the congregation, an interest that has grown and continues to today.

In addition to this local missions emphasis, I wrote a letter in May to the OMF requesting the Candidate Secretary Arthur Matthews to send preliminary application papers. He responded by sending an application questionnaire.

Foreign Missions?

Because I was now an ordained minister in the UCC, I thought I might contact the United Church Board for World Ministries (UCBWM) inquiring as to their procedures and opportunities for foreign service. I wrote them in June and again in July only to be told that they had lost my correspondence. In September, I was told, "There were no current openings that commend itself to your situation. I think it would be best if we deferred further correspondence until Mid-November."

In the meantime, Arthur Matthews wrote us in November saying that he had received our preliminary questionnaire and would send formal application forms. He also outlined a possible schedule for Candidate School and a course in linguistics conducted in Toronto, Canada.

I did not hear from the UCBWM until January 1969 when on the thirty-first of January, I was informed, "We no longer have any openings that would fill your situation... Our work in Micronesia is being phased out to such a rapid extent that we are sending no new people this year."

During that year, the UCBWM transferred all their records to the newly formed Overseas Personnel Recruitment Office in New York City. This new office was charged with the placement of personnel from eight different denominations. In May, they wrote,

> Unfortunately, at this time of year, most of the 1969 requests have been filled. I regret that there is no position open, which seems to correspond to your abilities, training, and interests. Requests for placement in 1970 will be coming into our office during the next few months, and we shall certainly contact you in the event that there is an opening, which seems to correspond to your situation.

I never heard from them again. That seemed to us to be a closed door!

We had a second missions conference in 1969 with Arthur Matthews as our preacher at the Sunday service. Pat and I entertained him and Mrs. Matthews for Sunday dinner. We received a thank-you note from Wilda Matthews with this word of encouragement,

> The missionary conference was well planned and much good seed was sown. We pray with you that there will be a new and increased vision of missions and giving. You are surely leading them in the right direction.

On April 5, 1970, we engaged Rev. John Kyle of Wycliffe Bible Translators. It seemed to me that a yearly exposure to missions and missionary speakers was a necessary factor in church growth.

We took the month of June to drive across our nation using Pat's father's red GMC Pickup Camper. The three of us, with two-year-old Pam, visited New Orleans, Louisiana, and Dallas, Texas, to visit the Satos, fellow students at Gordon Divinity School and Pueblo Bonito, to see Lois Wilson, a friend from DVBC. We remember that we all got sick from the water that was highly alkaline. Then we went on the San Francisco, California, and Cheyenne, Wyoming, and then the Kellogg factory in Grand Rapids, Michigan. Our only problem was the need to replace the fuel pump and two tires.

In July, Dr. Arthur Glasser wrote telling us that he and his wife Alice and daughter Carol would be visiting our area and asked if we could get together. I don't remember much from the visit, but we did go fishing in our little cove using the small aluminum rowboat that Pat's father had loaned us.

Dr. Glasser also included a lengthy letter of resignation from his position as home director of the OMF after serving for fourteen years.

Fortunately we reconnected with the Glassers at Fuller Theological Seminary during my DMin course. He had become part of Fuller's School of World Mission along with Dr. Donald McGavern, Dr. Pete Wagner, and Dr. Ralph Winter.

In October, we started the Magnolia Play School under the direction of Beth Cairns, Lynne Khambaty, and Maureen Taillon. The enrollment was thirty-one including four on scholarship. Of those thirty-one children, twenty-four had no other connection with Union Church. There was a waiting list. I am sure that this program spoke clearly to the community as to our desire to serve. This outreach was self-sustaining and even contributed a small balance at the end of the year.

On Christmas Eve, we received a letter from Rev. Herman Dietsch, home director of the Liebenzell Mission of the USA, Schooley's Mountain, New Jersey. It was a thank-you note to the church for the offer of a complete set of the Encyclopedia Britannica. "It seems providential," Herman wrote, "that you could make this offer as we had just received a letter from our mission members in Palau expressing just such a need." (Pat and I had bought the set thinking that our daughter Pam would become a genius by reading and researching.)

> Hi! I'm three years old now and Mommy and Daddy said that I can tell you some of the things that happened to me this year. First of all, I'm a

sister. Mama went to the hospital in January and brought home my brother. His name is David Barker. He was almost a whole month early, but he is fat now. He pulls my hair too.

Next, I got a puppy. Her name is Missie. Sometimes Daddy calls her Messie. We lost our dog Patches in the woods of Pennsylvania this summer, so we got a nice new puppy. I still think about Patches sometimes.

Another thing that I really like is Playschool. Our church started it in October, and all my friends come every morning. I have learned to color inside the lines, build towers with the blocks, do puzzles, cut paper with my scissors, and lots of other things. I have had more fun this year than I have had in my whole life!

I'll have to say hi for my brother David because he is too little to talk. But when he gets big next year, he will talk a lot.

Merry Christmas everybody!

Pamela Lynne

Pat wrote,

Thought I'd try to share some of the things that have made this year fun and challenging—David's and Pam's development; summer guests who keep our fishing lines wet; additions to our larger family, my brother Jack's Julie, Rich's brother Paul's Susan, and my brother Dave and Ellen's Danny; a refreshing camping trip to Moosehead Lake for two weeks; varied worship services and involved people; awareness of my need to work for social justice; nursing; sewing class; daily eye-opening times together with E. Stanley Jones.

My prayer for myself and each of you is that the coming year will be one of living in the freedom of His care.

I added,

As I sit at my desk, it is hard to imagine that this will be our fifth Christmas here in Magnolia. It is even more overwhelming to realize that this is my third Christmas season as the pastor of the church in Magnolia.

1969 has been a year filled with lessons. I haven't learned them all, but one I shall not forget is the utter faithfulness and constant dependability of God. He has consistently supplied every need. And this year was a year of many needs.

It's been a year of blessing as well. I'm thinking of David's safe and healthy arrival especially.

It's also been a year of broadening opportunities. I've recently become the chaplain to the Juvenile Court here in Gloucester. (I wear a clerical collar too!)

May I close by thanking each one of you for your thoughts, prayers, and remembrances throughout the past twelve months.

Pastor Rich for all the Weisenbachs

I began my pastor's report for our annual meeting (1969–1970) with this verse,

"I thank my God for you all every time I think of you, and every time I pray for you. I pray with joy, because of the way in which you have helped me in the work of the Gospel, from the very first day till now" (Philippians 1:3–5).

"The way you have helped me"—it is this phrase from one of the apostles' letters that describes my feelings and attitudes. I have found this past year to be the most fulfilling year of my ministry. There has been years of sowing and watering and cultivating. This year the harvest began.

Growth in many dimensions has been quite evident. The sense of God's Spirit expressed in genuine love and concern thrills me: the need on a Sunday morning when the ushers have to run for more chairs or the deaconess board has to prepare more glasses for communion, your constantly increasing level of financial involvement, the deepening participation on the part of many committee members, and the success of a number of recent projects. All of this and more has been of real encouragement to Pat and me.

The decision to "take the next step" and build a parsonage was very significant. And God has certainty placed His seal of approval upon that decision. We will probably be moving in by the end of the year. The project will be complete within seven months after we voted and already it is one-third paid for.

Another giant step forward was the introduction of Youth Club. I personally believe that this program could be the most significant step that we have ever taken in the field of Christian education. Through Youth Club we are reaching more young people and involving more parents that ever before.

Another encouraging sign is the increasing number of young adults who worship with us. I was even happier when fifteen of these young adults came to our recent membership class.

I, as your pastor, have been privileged, refreshed, and challenged as the year has passed by. May God grant to us all His grace, mercy, and peace through Jesus Christ our Lord.

Richard A. Weisenbach
Pastor

The Christian Education Board had a wonderful report that year. In it, they described the Youth Club as an activity to which I have already made reference.

Youth Club Program, Inc.

Our biggest project for the year has been the formation and start of the Youth Club Program. This is a community program for grades five through eight, which has been endorsed by St. Joseph's Lay Council and Monsignor Sullivan, pastor at St. Ann's, Gloucester. Parent participation is a part of this program. We have thirty-six students, of which eighteen (50%) are Roman Catholic, twelve (33%) are Union Church members, and eight (17%) do not have any church affiliation. The program is held on Wednesday afternoon from 4:00 to 7.00 p.m.

The program consists of one hour of Bible study and one hour of arts, crafts, or physical education and one hour for dinner, which includes a guest speaker, film, or singing. Most of the parent participation takes place at dinner time, with parents preparing the meals, setting up tables, and cleaning the dining room and kitchen.

This is a self-supporting program with a budget of $600.00. Each student pays $19.50 per year, which includes study materials and meals for the twenty-seven sessions.

New Parsonage

In May 1970, I wrote a letter to Dick Coté, chair of the board of trustees, requesting that the church consider seriously the building of a parsonage. The board responded immediately and called for a special meeting of the congregation for June 16. A committee was formed and at a second meeting in September 8 approved a plan to purchase a sectional home from Continental Homes of New England. The site was prepared and a foundation poured to receive the house that arrived in December 10. It came with wall-to-wall carpeting, storm windows, electric heat, garbage disposal, and water heater. It was painted and papered throughout according to choices made by Pat (and Rich). The home arrived on two huge truck beds, twelve feet wide and forty-four feet long.

By God's grace, we received a $10,000.00 loan from the First National Bank of Ipswich that enabled the congregation to pay for the house upon its arrival. The house cost $11,798.10. Costs for excavation, septic system, foundation, completion of the basement, and hookups brought the complete cost to about $18,000.00–$19,000.00.

> Dear members and friends of Union Church,
>
> We look back over the years, this is our seventh Christmas in Magnolia. So much has happened between Christmases
>
> In December 10, the parsonage arrived. This marked the completion of many months of planning and marked the beginning of a new style of life here at Union Church. We are active and growing and the new parsonage will is a giant step into our future.
>
> And, of course, in December 3, we celebrated another arrival, Kimberly Joy. She is growing well and is receiving the best care we can provide. All of us take the opportunity to express our

sincerest wishes to you for a blessed Christmas and fruitful New Year ahead.

From all the Weisenbachs: Rich, Pat, Pam, David, and Kim, Missie, and Boots

West Congregational Church, Peabody, Massachusetts (1971-1977)

Brief History of West Congregational, Denominational
Affiliation, Land in Maine, Ron and Betty Kent, Razing the
Old Building, Sumer Adventure, School of Christian Living,
Worship Committee, Thoughts About Church Finances,
Emphasis on Mission and Community Outreach, Hawaii?

A guest book was given to the church by the Vacation Bible School back in 1966. As I took a glance through it, I saw some familiar names of family and friends. Then there were others I did not recognize.

On June 14, 1970, Dick Sanderson and Herb Stark signed. In September 20, Mr. and Mrs. Ralph Blake and Mrs. Sarah Wheeler visited and signed. I came to discover that these five were from Peabody, Massachusetts, and members of the Pulpit Committee of West Congregational Church. Their pastor Rev. Chris Lyons had resigned after fourteen years (February 1956–March 1970) to take up ministry responsibilities at Wheaton Bible Church, Wheaton, Illinois. These members were visiting Union Church to check me out!

On June 15, 1970, I received this letter from the chair of the Pulpit Committee, Dexter Wheeler.

> Dear Mr. Weisenbach,
>   Those members of our committee who visited your church yesterday are very excited about

your candidacy. We feel that you may very well be that man that God is calling to the pastorate of West Church... I am enclosing additional material about West Church to further aid you in becoming better acquainted with us and our programs... I hope that you are becoming as excited about the possibility of being called here as we are!

In December 15, the chair wrote again. Here is a small part of this handwritten note.

Dear Rich,

Here is some material for your perusal. The Pulpit Committee has prepared an offer to you. I am meeting with the trustees tomorrow night... We're just brimful of joy and excitement I really can't express it in a letter! Looking forward to a meeting with both of you (if Patti is up to it) on Saturday, December 19.

In December 16, I received the news of my election by unanimous vote of the Pulpit Committee of West Congregational Church for the position of senior pastor. "It is my hope that you will be able to preach your candidating sermon early in January."

In January 6, the chair wrote to inform me of a meeting to be held in January 12. "Here is a list of those who have been invited to the meeting. The committee thought it would be helpful for the leadership to meet you and Patti."

There were twenty-two people at that meeting. It went very well—another step in the process. I did candidate in January 24. This was followed by a reception.

I had written the committee confessing that I thought I was too young and inexperienced to take on such a huge responsibility. The chair wrote back, "You have expressed some concern because of your young age. Age is not particularly important, so long as a man has ability and potential and knows that his strengths and talents come from God."

He concluded with these words from the Seminary Placement Office,

> The committee feels that you should not over-look him, either because of his close proximity or because of his youth. He is highly thought of, obviously has a good future, and is highly regarded by a great number of Divinity School students who attend his church. The faculty feels that he has great potential and would do excellent work at West Church.

Dr. Barker reflected years later, "When you went to Peabody, you skipped a church," indicating that I was young for such a large responsibility.

It seems ironic that the church I refused as a supervised ministry opportunity back in 1964 was calling me to be pastor. Another interesting note is the fact the Dr. Glenn Barker was their interim. When I ultimately moved to West Peabody, Dr. Barker became interim at Union Church Magnolia again.

On Sunday, January 31, 1971, I read the following letter to the congregation in Magnolia:

> It is with this letter that I submit my resignation as the pastor of the Union Congregational Church of Magnolia to become the pastor of the West Congregational Church in Peabody, Massachusetts. This resignation shall be effective three months from today, on Saturday, May 1, 1971.
>
> Pat and I came to Magnolia following our honeymoon in August 1964. We leave as the parents of three growing children.

Our ministry began in Magnolia. It was here that we learned, grew, and developed. Wherever we go from here, we shall forever be the product of this local church. Here we witnessed God working among His people, loving them, correcting them, challenging them, and blessing them. The past six and one-half years have been fruitful and rewarding, but not without its imperfections.

It would be presumptuous of us to think that no offenses were incurred, no mistakes made, for these, Patty and I ask your forgiveness.

We leave by faith in the will of God, a way that is not always easy but ever rewarding. Now, may we commend you to God the perfect keeper and to His word, which shall continue to lead you in all truth.

Yours in Christ,
Richard A. Weisenbach

Following the reading of this letter, I prayed, "Father, help us this morning to hear your voice. Remove all that would distract and enable us to focus our attention on you and your promises. Bless us for Jesus's sake. Amen." Then I preached briefly from 1 Corinthians 1:1–10.

When I finished preaching, I stepped out of the pulpit and asked if there were any questions. I realize now that I was trying to force the congregation to agree with my decision. I was prepared to answer any of their questions, and I wanted them to love me even though I was leaving them. "I'm leaving because God is leading me. This is a good thing for all of us!" This was not a healthy way to leave this congregation. They were surprised, hurt, fearful, and angry. I skipped over their feelings, not letting them be expressed. I'm sad and embarrassed to think back upon the way I handled this situation.

I was happy and proud that West Church chose me to be their pastor. I actually expected Union Church to be happy with me. In my selfishness, I totally neglected to consider their needs. I am grieved when I think about it.

When the time came to leave West Church, or KUC, or First Parish in Wakefield, or First Congregational Church of Woburn, I believe I handled things much better.

Leaving a congregation is always a major event in the life of a church, and it is never easy. But it is a necessary part of being a pastor. A new ministry opportunity presents itself, and one is called to discern how one should respond. Any decision to leave can be second-guessed. "I wonder what it would be like if we had stayed." This is only natural, but one must believe that God is leading and leave the what-ifs to Him.

> As I sit at my desk, I fully realize that this is the last pastoral letter I'll ever write to you. We'll be packing in a few weeks and after three or four days of rest will begin ministering in West Peabody. It will not be easy to leave. Our professional contacts with you have developed into deep friendships. When we go, we will leave a large piece of ourselves here, but let me quickly add that we'll be leaving fuller, richer, more complete than when we came among you. Christian ministry is giving and receiving, and we have received much from you.
>
> I've been told that if I would come back after a year, I wouldn't recognize the church. The programs, plans, projects, and organization would be completely different. The only feature with any durability is what the Holy Spirit sustains.
>
> In my ministry therefore, I have endeavored to emphasize the Lord Jesus, knowing that all else will fade away. That ministry will only be effective as you learn this lesson too. The church is the body of *Christ*. He is the head and demands preeminence. Love, honor, and obey Him and

Magnolia will feel the impact of God's Spirit. Put Christ aside, elevate other things, and you're on your own.

I leave commending you to a risen Lord. And I trust that you will come to rest upon His power and direction as the years pass.

In His Ministry,
Richard A. Weisenbach

I believe it is a gift of God that Pat and I were able to settle back in Magnolia after retiring from First Parish, Wakefield. We own a condo just a short distance from the church we once served. The pastor is Abram Kielsmeier-Jones who had served as youth minister at First Parish during our last years there. We rejoined Union Church in 2013 and have worshipped regularly. As I sit in the pew and observe the congregation, listen to their singing, hear Abram's sermon, and participate in the weekly time of prayer and personal sharing, I am filled with praise and thanksgiving to God. Truly God has sustained this congregation.

It has been forty-four years since we left Union Church and moved to West Peabody. During those years, Union Congregational has faced severe challenges, but by God's grace, the congregation is in a healthy place today. It is so encouraging to me to see how God's spirit is displayed among the people. *Praise God!*

The church has been very generous to me since I returned. Abram is especially kind and attentive to anything I might request or suggest. He made sure I was given a key to both the building and his office and have full use of an office of my own in what was the kitchen when we occupied the apartment years ago. The apartment was converted into Sunday school rooms once the new parsonage was useable. The kitchen is too small for a class, but just fine for me.

Brief History of West Congregational

West Church was established in the sprawling farm community of West Peabody in 1883. It existed as a small community church ministering to only a handful of parishioners until a building boom began in the 1950s. The population grew from 23,000 in 1950 to 32,000 in 1960 and hit 46,000 by 1970. In 1956, West Church called a young energetic seminary student to be pastor. In his fourteen years as pastor, Chris Lyons had seen his typical Sunday congregation grow from twenty-five to about five hundred! He had guided the church through two building programs—the first in 1960–1961 when crowded triple morning worship services necessitated the construction of a new sanctuary. In 1967–1968, a growing congregation required further expansion of the sanctuary. An education wing was also added at that time to provide needed classrooms, offices, kitchen, and a second fellowship hall. Long-term plans call for eventual construction of another education wing to provide much-needed classrooms.

The committee also listed as congregational strengths clear preaching of the gospel, strong budget support, excellent physical facilities, and large Sunday congregation, many from Gordon College and Gordon-Conwell Theological Seminary, both students and faculty, and active Sunday school and youth programming and about a dozen small-group Bible studies, which are held weekly in parishioner's living rooms.

They also confessed some weaknesses, such as low mission interest and giving, poor local evangelistic outreach, few youth activities outside of Sundays, and the need to provide lay training for adults.

Priscilla Watson, church clerk, wrote, in January 28, informing me of a congregational vote taken that evening at their annual meeting (110-0, no blanks). It did strike me as surprising that only 110 attended and cast votes at such an important meeting. Their profile indicated five hundred "active" members, so this concerned me. I responded to the clerk's letter on February 6, 1971.

> To the clerk,
> It is with a great sense of God's peace that I accept the call of the West Congregational Church to become pastor. I understand that the terms are those outlined in a letter to me dated

December 16, 1970, and that my responsibilities are to begin in May 1971.

I come as one Christian minister among Christian ministers. Because of the size and urgency of the task set before us, I shall call and depend upon your support, encouragement, and correction. I could humbly ask that the next three months be spent in prayer for us. We will be depending upon your help at every turn.

Yours in Jesus Christ,
Richard A. Weisenbach and family

On May 2, 1971, I was installed as pastor. The service was led by Dick Sanderson, chair of the deacons. There were greetings from the city of Peabody, the Peabody Clergy Association, Gordon College and Gordon-Conwell Theological Seminary, and the UCC. Dr. James King gave the charge to the minister, Dr. George Ensworth preached, and Dr. Glenn Barker gave the prayer of installation. It was a very blessed service. Thank you, *Lord*.

It came as a surprise to me that this service was on my very first Sunday. It shows clearly that the leadership was able to plan and execute a program fit for the occasion. I had very little responsibility for the service save answering some very important questions and pronouncing the benediction.

Pat and I along with seven others joined West Church on June 6, 1971. This encouraging note came from Marge Barker in October.

I hope you know how glad we are that you came to West Church, but just in case you don't, this will tell you! I believe you are just the people we needed and that God can and will use you to make this people into a solid spiritual body. We are so thrilled to see the fruits of your years at Magnolia and enjoy the fine spirit that is there. Some friends from Grace Chapel who come up occasionally have said how refreshing it is to be in

Magnolia—in that place with those people and in an atmosphere that seems to them genuine and with every part of the service meaningful. I thought you should hear this as it is what God created through you. Be assured of our prayers of support in your new work.

Affectionately,
Marge Barker

The idea of writing my memoirs did not enter my mind until I was in the last few years of ministry at First Parish Congregational Church in Wakefield. By God's grace, a very significant change took place throughout the congregation during the thirty years we were there. My first thought was that it might be helpful if I could write about that transition. I would try to describe the issues, decisions, struggles, and mistakes that filled those years. The more I thought about writing, the more I realized that the other four congregations might appreciate some reminder of our years together, so I decided to include all six congregations in this project.

I had kept some material pertaining to our first years in Magnolia, but had little information about our years in Peabody and Honolulu for that matter; fortunately West Congregational Church archives are complete concerning the six years we were there. So my thanks to Kelli Sawyer, secretary, for helping me fill in the gaps.

The position of senior pastor at West Church was quite demanding. There were two worship services on Sunday morning, nine thirty and eleven o'clock, and a third on Sunday evening. Sunday school classes were conducted during both services. Three youth groups met Sunday evening before the seven o'clock worship service. This was a busy place.

I soon discovered that West Church had a very positive reputation throughout the north shore due to the ministry of Pastor Chris Lyons and his ministry team. Being the pastor of this well-known and influential congregation led to some very interesting and humbling opportunities.

I was invited by the associate pastor of Park Street Church, Boston, to be one of the preachers at their annual Lenten forum. In 1975, I was asked to consider the possibility of joining the Gordon-Conwell faculty as dean of Students. I responded with gratitude at being one of many being considered but shared my firm commitment to remain in the local church. A similar offer came from Dick Gross, president of Gordon College. He was seeking to discover my interest in becoming dean of Christian Life. Again I wrote to tell him how humbled I was at the possibility, but I believed my calling was to the local church. That same year, Ken Swetland, director of Alumni Affairs and Placement, wrote to congratulate me upon my election as president of the seminary's Alumni Association. Then there was an invitation from Alton Bay Camp Meeting Association to be the preacher during one of the weekends in August 1975. All of these became blessed opportunities to minister the grace of God.

Since being ordained in the UCC, I believed that I should participate in whatever opportunities for fellowship and/or service that came before me. I attended monthly meetings of the association's ministers. I also went to the spring and fall meetings when all the churches of the association would gather for business and learning. I was also nominated to become a synod delegate for the meetings gathered in St. Louis, Missouri, in 1970 and Grand Rapids, Michigan, in 1972. By this time, I was also the moderator of the Essex South Association.

Moving to West Church would soon bring the congregation face-to-face with a decision they had dodged back in 1961. *West Winds*, the church's newsletter, gave the background of the issue.

> In 1957, the Congregational Church joined with the Evangelical and Reformed Church to form a new denomination, the United Church of Christ. Because we are congregational, the final decision of whether or not to join had to be made by us. In 1961, we voted "not to vote at this time." Although we never voted to join, we still partic-

ipate at the local level. This semi-attachment has continued for twelve years.

Denominational Affiliation

Over the years, West Church attracted many seminary students. Several were ordained into the UCC, even though they were not members of a UCC church. This practice was questioned in 1973 when a West Church member, Ms. Jeri Kroll, requested standing in the UCC in hopes of becoming ordained. She was told by Rev. James C. Marshall, a member of the association's Committee on Ministry, that the past practice of ordaining students from West Church has changed. He continued, "In a way, you are being penalized for the church's stand, but the church has coasted along now for some years, and we feel that it is about time it declared itself. A church that expects to share in denominational benefits should also be willing to share in denominational responsibilities."

This decision by the association forced West Church to either join the denomination or declare itself independent. Three separate meetings were announced, each describing one of three options. We heard from the UCC, from the Conservative Congregational Christian Conference (CCCC), and from Pastor Gordon Macdonald, pastor of Grace Chapel, an independent congregation. At a congregational meeting held on November 6, 1973, the motion was made to "accept the recommendation of the board of deacons that West Congregational Church become independent of denominational affiliation to be effective as of his date... On written ballot, the vote was ninety-six in favor, one opposed [that was me!], and three abstentions. It was *so voted*." West Church has been unaffiliated ever since.

Land in Maine

When we moved from Magnolia to Peabody, I received a raise in pay. We figured that this was a good time to plan for our future, perhaps some land in Maine for a retirement home.

Somehow we heard of Leisure Living Estates in Waterboro, Maine. They called it Lake Arrowhead. The advertising said that we could drive to Maine, be given a motel room for the night, and then be driven to Lake Ossipee to view some lakeside property. Much to our surprise, we decided to purchase a lakefront piece for $100.00 down! Arrangements were made for us to pay the balance of the down payment over a couple of months. The total cost of our investment was $10,000.00. We were faithful with the monthly payments, but after a year or two, we were informed that the Saco River Commission had rendered our plot nonbuildable. The slope of our plot toward the lake was too steep and the property itself not deep enough to construct a home, allowing for the necessary setbacks from the lake and the street.

To compensate for our loss, the company gave us two lots in another part of the development. We had to keep paying the mortgage of course, but at least we had something. Leisure Living Estates went bankrupt as a result of the Saco River decision and was eventually purchased by General Acquisitions.

We were not the only people whose land was nonbuildable. Many stopped paying their monthly fees. They just took the loss. Their land reverted back to the town of Waterboro. Eventually we were able to purchase the two lots contiguous to ours from the town for back taxes. I think it cost us about $1,500.00 each.

We now had three lots having over four hundred feet of lake frontage. This arrangement provided one spot where a house could be built! We sold the two back lots to a builder for $8,000.00 each and dreamed of some sort of place when the time came. We made our last payment in October 1981.

Pat and I continued to vacation at Moosehead Lake every August and would often stop at our land at Arrowhead on the way home. I remember one sunny August afternoon we went down to the lake and spread out a blanket for a picnic. We prayed that God would do something with the land.

It hadn't yet occurred to us that our son David and his wife Sharon would show interest in moving from their Pennsylvania home, but they became excited about the possibility.

It was in 2000 that he and Sharon sold their house in Warrington, Pennsylvania, and bought a mobile home, which they towed to Maine. They parked it in Walnut Grove Campground while Dave drove to our site by the lake. He cleared the land and pretty much by himself built a home from a log cabin kit from Moosehead Cedar Log Homes. Pat and I tried to help on the weekends. We drove up after church and stayed over, sometimes till Tuesday. We truly enjoyed working together, and I am happy to say that I was able to capture much of his progress on video.

Ron and Betty Kent

Before we arrived at West Church, the leadership anticipated the possible need for a pastoral assistant. I was told to pray for God's guidance and begin looking for a candidate.

While in Magnolia, I met Ron and Betty Kent. They came to New England from the Midwest. The guest book at Union Congregational Church indicated that Ron and Betty together with Ron's parents visited on August 24, 1969. I assumed that the family came east to help Ron and Betty settle in before seminary classes started.

Betty came from a farm in Wisconsin and Ron from Des Moines, Iowa. Betty attended Fort Wayne Bible College in Fort Wayne, Indiana, where she graduated with a bachelor of arts degree in Christian education and missions. Ron attended Gordon College for two years and then transferred to Drake University in Des Moines graduating with a degree in philosophy and history.

Betty worked for three years as a church secretary in Des Moines where she and Ron met and married. Ron and Betty came back to Massachusetts so Ron could attend Gordon-Conwell. Ron and Betty attended Union Church regularly, and Pat and I developed a relationship with them. Although he would not graduate till June 1972, I asked him to consider coming with me to West Church. They discussed this possibility and then consented to the church's offer.

God was gracious in providing just the right couple at just the right time. Our partnership would grow into a wonderfully complementary relationship. Our friendship matured over the six years we were together. Not only did Ron and I see ministry through a very similar lens, but also Pat and Betty developed a mutual friendship as well. And to make things even more satisfying, Ron's bass voice and Betty's soprano made a quartet when joined with Pat's alto and my tenor!

Razing the old Building

Before I write more about Ron's ministry, there was another major issue that concentrated our attention. It centered on the question of what to do about the church's original building.

When the second addition was built 1967–1968, it was attached to the old building by a covered walkway. Because of the deteriorating condition of this older building, our insurance company required the church to do one of two things—either repair the old structure or tear it down.

The board of trustees called for a special congregational meeting for December 4, 1972.

There were many who loved the old white church and thinking of removing it was a painful thought. The structure stood for many years as a witness to Christ in the community—memories filled many hearts. Nevertheless it was voted 70 to 2 to spend $4,500.00 to raze the building, remove the refuse, fill the remaining hole, landscape the property, repair the new building where it joined the old, and establish some kind of permanent memorial for the bell, salvaged from the steeple.

It required almost a year, but on Sunday, December 2, 1973, the congregation gathered in the narthex after morning worship to celebrate the placing of the bell in the Taylor Street entrance and to rededicate ourselves to God's will and service. Mrs. Mary McIntire, our oldest member, age 105, pulled a string unveiling the refurbished bell. A separate committee announced the renaming of our fellowship hall to honor Rev. Chris Lyons and old fellowship hall to honor Rebecca Goodale, and the multipurpose room became the Upper Room.

Ron graduated from Gordon-Conwell in May 1972. On Sunday night, June 18, he was ordained as a minister in good standing in the UCC. The service, held in our sanctuary, was memorable as several ministers from the area were called forward to lay hands on Ron, setting him apart for a particular purpose and to publicly recognize his calling and giftedness for his special task. Dr. William Nigel Kerr, professor of church history at Gordon-Conwell Theological Seminary, delivered the ordination sermon. The choir sang a deeply moving arrangement of "When I Survey the Wondrous Cross." A reception followed.

Ron wrote his response,

> How can we thank you for your part in my Service of Ordination last Sunday night? Betty and I have come to love you dearly, and we in turn have felt your love for us. For your prayers, your gifts, your friendship, we thank you and we truly thank God. I was glad to have my family out from Iowa for the weekend and I would thank you also for your hospitality to them. We look forward with great expectation to ever deepening fellowship with you and a mutual ministry that's fruitful in the service of our Lord Jesus Christ.
>
> Ron Kent

Ron was an excellent preacher, but his main responsibilities centered on Christian education. There were two initiatives that he started that were quickly adopted by the congregation and contributed greatly to the growth and maturation of the church family.

Summer Adventure, School of Christian Living

Summer Adventure was a program designed to breathe new life into the traditional Vacation Bible School. It began in 1972 and was an effort to minister to the social, physical, emotional, and spiritual needs of the youth of the community. The program was centered on workshops that were designed to provide new and exciting experiences for both the leaders and participants. Workshops included such interests as nature study (ocean, forest, animals, hiking and camping, rock collecting, and fishing), sports (soccer, swimming and diving, sailing and canoeing, bicycling, and kite making and flying), homemaking skills (sewing, knitting, crocheting, cooking, cake decorating, woodworking, and candle-making), music (singing and guitar lessons), and arts and crafts (model making, painting and drawing, and photography). We charged $1.00 per student for the week.

Each workshop had its own Bible study presented from an interdenominational perspective. It was our prayer that each student would come to know Christ in a personal way and find that the Bible is relevant to all areas of life.

Obviously such a program required a great deal of planning and coordinating. The committee consisted of Marge Fecteau, Mary Stockwell, Heather Ensworth, Charlie Barker, and Pastor Ron. They did a fantastic job!

The program was repeated in 1973 and this time with an enrollment of over 330 and staff punching leather, pounding nails into soapboxes, painting, bicycling, beaching, etc.

Our newsletter *West Winds* for August 19, 1973, outlined our upcoming fall schedule.

> Morning worship: 9:30 and 11:00
> Sunday school: Classes for nursery through college age at 9:30 to 10:30
> Adult classes: 6:30 to 7:30, taught by Ron and Rich [me] plus professors from the seminary.
> Senior choir: Starting with a swimming party and potluck supper at the Ensworths
> Youth choirs: Jesus Explosion (grades 5 to 8), children's choir (grades 1 to 4), Dawn Treaders (senior high to college)
> Youth groups: Ambassadors (grades 5 to 6), Crusaders (junior high), senior high

Pioneer girls: Four clubs that started in 1972 for
girls (grades 2 to 9)
Boys' brigade: The stockade (for younger boys)
and brigade (for older boys)

Ron wrote a summary of Summer Adventure for the July 7,
1974, *West Winds*.

Summer Adventure is a perfect description
for what happened last week at West Church
when 270 children and sixty-six staff members
got together for fun and spiritual growth. The
response from non-West Church folk was grat-
ifying, as close to half the enrollment was from
other churches, or unchurched families. Students
came from eleven different communities.

One of the many positive results of this
new-style VBS is the personal relationships that
develop through the week between leader and
children. In a relaxed atmosphere of fun, activity, and learning, children are able to pick up
through the attitudes and actions of the leader an
example of Christian living. The spiritual input
was therefore a continual process rather than
confined to just thirty to forty-five minutes of
formal Bible study daily. This means that every
child is exposed to the Christian faith from two
directions. Devotions are part of every one of
the twenty-three workshops. And in addition to
hearing the gospel, they get to see it displayed
in the behavior of their teachers. Biblical truth
needs flesh and blood examples and that is what
is presented.

Special effort has been given by every member of the staff, but Marge Fecteau outperformed
us all. She is so capable and so quick to share

with all of us. We all owe her our hearty thanks, and spread some of that gratitude to her husband Phil.

Won't you pray that the seeds of spiritual truth sown in young lives last week will be able to grow and bear fruit? Follow-up will be made with each child who attended, before the fall programs start.

Both Pat and I believe that Summer Adventure taught many children of the church and community valuable lessons. We trust that there has been many lasting positive experiences as a result of this very special program. Pat helped in the canoeing department. I can't remember what I did. I must have helped somewhere!

West Church was particularly blessed by Gordon College and Gordon-Conwell Theological Seminary. Our bus made two round trips to the college every Sunday morning bringing students, many of whom took up ministry opportunities. Then there were six seminary professors and one from the college who attended regularly and were willing to teach an adult class. We took full advantage of their knowledge and generosity. So in 1973, we inaugurated the School of Christian Living.

Each semester, we would offer two courses at 6:30 p.m. on Sunday, beginning in January. Over the years, Dr. Gordon Fee taught "1 Corinthians," while Dr. George Ensworth taught "A Christian and His/Her Emotions." "Relating to Your Jewish Neighbors" was offered by Dr. Marvin Wilson, while Dr. Ramsey Michaels taught "the Gospel of John." "The Dynamics of Spiritual Life" was taught by Dr. Richard Lovelace. Our church treasurer, Angelo Constantine, taught a class entitled "Managing Your Money." Pastor Ron offered a class on "the Minor Prophets," and I shared my ideas on the subject of "the Christian Way of Death." Each year approximately seventy-five people strengthened and expanded their faith through these courses. All three youth groups met at the same time, and at 7:30 p.m., we gathered in the Sanctuary for a brief service of singing, prayer, and sharing. Babysitting was provided (25¢ per family).

Along with the six professors from the seminary, there were several seminarians who chose to fulfill their supervised ministry requirement at West Church. Ron and I were approved by the school to meet weekly with these students, checking on their responsibilities, progress, and results. Over the years, almost twenty seminary families labored together with us. It became a very special privilege to play some small part in their education.

Added to our weekly ministry together, I was asked to preach the ordination/installation sermon of at least five of these men after they had graduated and had gotten a call to a local church.

Worship Committee

The Sunday morning worship service should be of primary importance to any minister and it always was to me. It is such a privilege to gather in freedom with like-minded brothers and sisters and exalt the name and character of Jesus Christ. Jesus said that if we lift up His name, He would draw others to Himself (John 12:32).

While at West Church, five of us were able to develop a small group to pray and think about each worship service in a creative way. With the help of a product offered by Rev. David Mains called Step Two, we worked together to plan every aspect of the service to, in Reverend Main's words, "say one thing well"—announce the theme at the beginning of the service through the hymns and special music chosen; through the various prayers of invocation, offertory, family prayer, and benediction; and of course through the sermon.

Once a week, Ron and I drove to the home of Kathi Ensworth to be joined by Dick Sanderson and Midge Little. Kathi generously provided a delicious lunch, and then we would sit on the floor of the living room and begin to brainstorm various ways to hammer out a theme and how to incorporate that theme into the various parts of the service. The ideas that emerged guided Kathi, our minister of music, to select hymns, special music, and choir anthems to enlarge whatever the theme of the day might be. This method of planning became a great assist to the preacher too. I believe that the hours we spent together enhanced the worship experience for the congregation during the years of our ministry.

When we left West Church and moved on, I tried to keep these ideas in mind. Sadly I was never able to duplicate the West Church model in the succeeding churches, but building a worship service around one key idea, one character of God's nature, has remained in my planning ever since.

Not only did Kathi provide a meal and meeting place for our worship committee, but also, as minister of music, she led the senior choir, the men's choir, and the teen choir who took their name the Dawn Treaders, from the novel *the Voyage of the Dawn Treader* by C. S. Lewis.

Dawn Treaders was a West Church-sponsored group of young people from the North Shore of Boston. Twenty-seven of the forty-seven-member group was part of West Church. Kathi started the group in 1971. As far as I know, it produced and performed over a six-year period. The group sang musicals and incorporated lighting, narration, choreography, drama, costuming, color slides, and five instrumentalists lending support. All this required a crew of seven headed by Bill Fisher. I was the narrator for a few years presenting our program in local churches to over two thousand people every year, and this entire ministry effort was financially self-supporting. I know from personal experience that Kathi's efforts, supported by her husband George, provided a blessing to all who presented or attended each performance.

Kathi was also responsible for the church's purchase of a $10,000.00 Allen Organ. She wrote in the January 1973 *West Winds,*

> A recognized need, which began as a dream in the hearts of a few over four years of age, became a beautiful reality for all of us in March 4, the first Sunday after our new Allen Organ was installed.
>
> This instrument was dedicated at a special service on April 1, 1973. I presented a plaque on

which was inscribed, "This memorial organ, dedicated to the *glory of God* through the ministry of music this first day of April 1973, is a gift of many in the family of God at West Congregational Church… 'Praise ye the Lord, praise God in His sanctuary, Praise Him with the sound of the trumpet, Praise Him with the psaltery and harp, Praise Him with the stringed instruments and organs'" (Psalm 150:1,3,4).

The weekly participation of all the members of the Ensworth family in the life of West Church was a wonderful gift from the Lord. I have already mentioned the many ways that Kathi ministered. Dr. George Ensworth was professor of pastoral care at Gordon-Conwell and served as a deacon and chairman of the board. He also taught classes Sunday evenings in our School of Christian Living. Besides these formal responsibilities, he became a close friend and often gave helpful counsel during our years together. And all three children, Tim, Heather, and Gary, participated in Dawn Treaders and taught workshops at Summer Adventure. I can honestly say that the Ensworths were some of the special folks who kept me going while I labored as pastor at West Congregational Church, and I thank God for them.

Thoughts Church Finances

Around 20 percent of the recorded words of Jesus refer to material possessions, their use, their potential, and their danger. Jesus talked more about one's finances than He did about heaven or hell. I think Jesus saw material wealth as the source of His greatest competition. And I also think that it is God's blessing that most believers are not extremely wealthy, since most believers do not have the necessary discipline required to handle great wealth.

My parents were not stingy, but they were frugal—they had to be. Neither of them had formal education beyond the ninth grade. As a consequence, Dad had a reputation as a trash-picker. People threw out perfectly good stuff, and Dad would spot it along the road and bring it home. My first bicycle and countless other items found their way onto Dad's workbench where they were straightened out, repainted, recovered, or repaired. All three of my brothers have taken after Dad in this regard.

Back in October 2002, I wrote the following for the church's newsletter:

> When I think about my giving habits, I think of the right side of the mantelpiece in my childhood home in Southampton, Pennsylvania. Every man has a place where he empties his pockets after work; my father's place was the right side of the mantelpiece. Each night Dad would put his watch, ring, wallet, change, pen, keys, and other valuables on that convenient shelf. Then he'd rest for twenty minutes before dinner.
>
> My brothers and I were taught that that place was private. We could look but we could not touch. That place was where important and valuable items were kept. After Mother wrote the checks, they would be placed there, ready to be mailed. And every Sunday morning the check for the church would be there for dad to put into the offering plate.
>
> Dad had difficulty verbalizing his faith, but he clearly demonstrated it through his kindness, honesty, and generosity to God and others. He and Mother had given ten percent of their income to the church for as long as I can remember. In the 1950s, that meant $16.00 every week; in the 1960s that meant $37.00; in the 1980s, that meant almost $80.00, every week.
>
> That impressed me. When Pat and I married, we too agreed to tithe our gross income to the church. We had read from E. Stanley Jones

that a Christian's tithe is like paying the rent. We owe our tithe to God for the gift of life while on this planet, the air, the water, etc. It is our weekly recognition that the sights and sounds, the smells, and tastes of life are all gifts from a gracious hand. And above all, our tithe is our response to the indescribable gift of Jesus Christ upon the cross for our salvation.

Of course this is a challenge but let me quickly add that the rewards of this discipline far surpass the "security" the world offers. No bank is as safe, no luxury brings more joy, and no possession is as fulfilling.

Giving is not a matter of the pocketbook. It is a matter of the heart. The love of Jesus Christ urges me to respond in love. No force is as compelling. You may have learned this in church, or from reading your Bible. As for me, I learned it from the right side of the mantelpiece.

The issue is *stewardship*. Every minister and every church member and attender must face and deal with this call from the Savior. I tried to raise the consciousness of the congregation any way I could. I wrote articles in newsletters, I shared our family habit from the pulpit, I preached on the subject during the month of October, and I introduced the tradition of Tithe Sunday. I challenged everyone to tithe their income on the first Sunday of November. I figured there were a few members who already practiced tithing, but I wanted everyone to try it at least once. "Do this out of love for your Savior!"

Our first effort was on November 7, 1971. I failed to record the total of the offering that day, but the next year, our total was over $4,000.00. I wrote the following in *West Winds*:

Despite a cloudy, damp Sunday morning, the members and friends of West Church contributed $4,557.00 on this second "Tithe Sunday." This is almost double last year's total and more than three times the usual weekly offering. What does this mean? For one thing, it indicates a potential budget of substantial proportions and a reasonable goal toward which to press. Secondly, many families and individuals invested special thought and planning in their own family stewardship. This is certainly encouraging. We recovered two-thirds of our $6,000.00 deficit in one week. Praise the Lord!

There was one other issue surrounding the question of stewardship that I faced in the churches I served. In congregational churches, the annual budget is formulated by the board of trustees. The congregation usually elected men with some background in business to serve on this board. Starting in May or June, the board would invite the various other committees to submit their financial forecasts for the coming year, and the board of trustees would add them up.

Usually in October or November, a financial canvas of the membership would be conducted. Pledges of support would be requested and tallied. The total pledged amount would be placed against the plans of the committees, and the challenging task of reconciling the two would begin. After a total was found, the board would usually subtract an amount—$3,000.00 to $5,000.00—for those who would falter on their pledge; people move, people encounter financial trouble, and people are hurt or discouraged by a decision of the congregation or action of an individual and choose to leave the fellowship.

You don't have to be a genius to conclude that the requests always surpassed the amount the board expected to receive. This meant that the plans for growth and possibilities for something new were usually put on hold. The trustees held that it was irresponsible to plan to spend money that wasn't going to be received. "First determine your income, then match the budget to it." This is the way West Church operated before I arrived.

Of course, there is another way of looking at the issue. It was famed China Inland Mission founder Hudson Taylor who said,

"God's work done in God's way shall never lack God's supply." He believed that people would give to God's work when they were motivated by the spirit of God. I believe that too.

When a congregation believes that the only resources available to them are the promises of their brothers and sisters, they limit God's activity in their midst. Planning for the future with only these promises in mind can be a suffocating experience. How often we fail to remember that God can add to the congregation's income in at least four ways.

There are always folks in a church who do not pledge but who give regularly. This income is usually called loose offering. The amount expected in this column is never more than an educated guess.

Second, there will always be new folks who become part of the church during the coming year and they will, out of their enthusiasm, probably begin giving. Again, how many people we are talking about is unknown.

Third, I believe that the spirit of God will move within the hearts of faithful members during the year who will increase their contributions. Then there is always Tithe Sunday.

Add to that the fact that there are usually one or two families in every church who possesses more wealth than the average member. Usually most of the congregation has no idea that such people are part of their fellowship. An unexpected gift is received or a challenge gift is announced. This often occurs when such people see that their congregation is seeking to do something special, something out of the ordinary, something not attempted before, but something desperately needed. They are moved by the Spirit to support that project, program, or outreach effort.

Changing one's attitude regarding one's stewardship is almost always slow. Sometimes members get upset at what they see as irresponsible planning, and they may resign from a committee or even stop attending and giving. But God is faithful in speaking to open hearts. Attitudes and habits do change. God did surprising things at West Church in the area of stewardship. During our six years, income increased from $71,892.67 to $91,317.00. Missions giving grew from $11,840.91 to $43,852.00. *Praise the Lord!*

In the summer of 1975, Pat and I took advantage of a generous offer from Ted and Bonnie Smith to spend a weekend in their cottage at Alton Bay, New Hampshire. One morning, I experienced a grand mal seizure. I had to take this seriously because Dad had suffered seizures most of his life as well as Bill's son Matthew and brother Dave's daughter Brie, who both died from complications of the disease. I saw a neurologist right away and he administrated an electroencephalogram. He concluded that I indeed "had a seizure in the temporal lobe but electroencephalograms of May 5 and July 1 have not confirmed or demonstrated the diagnosis... The cause of these spells remain undetermined. Neurological examination has been normal up through May 21, 1975. Treatment is Dilantin, 100 mg, TID."

I took the pills for a few years I guess. I actually don't remember. By God's grace, I have never had a recurrence.

According to my records, I was called to conduct thirty-one funerals during our years at West Church. There were two that touched the congregation in a very profound way.

The first was the death of Nadine Chapman. The Chapman family lived in West Peabody but were not a part of the West Church family. When Nadine got sick, her husband Ed dropped by the church one day asking that we might pray with him for a miracle for his very sick wife. Nadine was a patient at Peter Bent Brigham in Boston suffering from leukemia and not given much hope of surviving. He told me later that he went into our sanctuary and fell prostrate before the altar begging God for that miracle. Then he went the North Shore Shopping Center and bought a Bible at Jordan Marsh.

I visited Nadine several times but sadly she died, and I conducted her service at West Church on May 25, 1972. Ed, now the single father of three, began to attend church.

As time went by, he shared that while visiting Nadine, he met a woman named Charlane LeTarte. She was visiting her husband Steve who was suffering from the same fatal disease as Nadine. They developed a friendship, and to make a long story short, on September 22, 1973, I conducted the marriage ceremony of Ed and Charlane at West Church.

Ed accepted Jesus Christ as his savior and became an active and generous member of our congregation. He began a ministry to the local nursing homes in the area. He was soon conducting services in eight different homes every week.

Ed and Nadine grew up in Millinocket, Maine, and married as teens. She hoped that her final resting place would be in her home state. But she did not want to be buried or cremated, so the only option left was a mausoleum. There was only one mausoleum in Maine, Gracelawn Memorial Park in Auburn. Ed bought the place and moved his family north.

While there, he developed a unique ministry at Gracelawn, by employing ministers who would counsel grieving families. This was a great blessing to those many part-time ministers in the Auburn/Lewiston area.

Pat and I continued our friendship with the Chapmans through the years, enjoying their generosity. He owned two condos along the slopes of Mount Abram Ski Area in Bethel, Maine. Our family used one of them several times. Sadly, Ed died on April 11, 2007. We have continued to keep in touch with Charlane at least once a year on our way home from our annual vacation spot at Moosehead Lake. God's grace in Ed's life remains a bright testimony in my memory.

The second special funeral was occasioned by the shocking death of Bill Fisher. I described the event in our newsletter.

> The entire West Church family was shocked to hear of the untimely death of Bill Fisher. Bill and the family were at the Advent Christian Campground at Alton Bay again this year where he managed the food service. On Friday, August 16, 1974, he wanted to try his hand at waterskiing. After several attempts to get up, he finally decided to rest and let someone else try. It was then that he suffered a massive heart attack while still in the boat. He was rushed ashore, and strenuous efforts were made to revive him, but within a half an hour, Bill went into God's presence.

The sanctuary was filled to near capacity on Tuesday, the 20th, for the funeral service. God's presence was sensed from the very outset. The victory God offers to His children, even in the face of death, was clearly demonstrated.

Bill was thirty-six years old. He leaves his wife Joan and five children—Mark, Stephanie, Dean, Diane, and Troy. In the light of this tragedy, the church has established a fund to help with their needs. You are encouraged to contribute what you can.

Many are the places where Bill's ministry will be missed. He was our full-time custodian, our Junior High Youth Group leader, chief cook at the Men's Breakfast, operated the lights for the Dawn Treaders, and was the self-appointed ambassador of good will through the generous distribution of chewing gum. Bill's life was simple, honest, and genuine, filled with the graces of humor, hospitality, and generosity. Most of all, Bill loved Jesus Christ and sought to love Him more. We are all grateful to have known Bill Fisher and pledge our prayers and support to the family he leaves behind.

The church hired Joan to replace Bill as our full-time custodian. She, with some help from her older children, met our needs. I remember the times Joan and I would take a break from our tasks at hand to chat for a while.

I remember one specific time when I was sharing my frustration over a recent committee meeting. She put down her mop and asked me if I knew why some meetings became frustrating. "Rich," she said, "sometimes you have the charm of a train wreck." She went on to warn me about my short fuse. "Some people know just what buttons to push to make you lose your self-control. Don't let them do that to you." I will never forget her words to me that afternoon. She spoke the truth in love to me (Ephesians 4:15). I am forever grateful to her.

After a few years, she moved away and took a job at Gordon-Conwell. I would see her once in a while when I was on campus for a class or program.

Her daughter Diane called me in October 2016 asking if I was available to conduct her mother's funeral. "Of course," I replied, "it would be a privilege." The service was held in the sanctuary of West Church followed by a reception in Lyons Hall. It was so good to be with all five of Joan's children. I hadn't seen them in thirty-nine years.

Emphasis on Mission and Community Outreach

As I have indicated earlier, Pat and I have always tried to use whatever opportunities arise to emphasize the Christian church's obligation to share the gospel, heeding the command of Jesus Christ in Matthew 28:18–20: "All authority in heaven and on earth has been given to me. Therefore go and make disciples of all nations, baptizing them in the name of the Father and the Son and of the Holy Spirit. And teaching them to obey everything I have commanded you. And surely I will be with you always, to the very end of the age."

Our decision back in 1966–1967 not to pursue becoming missionaries ourselves did not mean that the urgency of sharing the gospel message would ever take second place in our ministry. It became clear therefore that raising the mission consciousness of the congregation was of extreme importance.

Response to this challenge appeared in Magnolia and grew dramatically at West Church. God prompted many families and individuals to give and some to go.

The congregation was always aware of the Great Commission of Matthew 28, but they admitted in their profile that the issue needed greater emphasis.

The Missionary Committee of West Church organized a two-day mission emphasis weekend for at least ten years before our arrival. In the fall of 1971, I made a suggestion to the committee that we might expand that two-day experience to a full week including two Sundays.

While in Magnolia, I had developed a relationship with Betty Vetterlein, the missionary chairperson of Boston's Park Street Church. This church, pastored by Dr. Harold J. Ockenga, was known for its annual missionary conference and the amazing missionary family they supported. In the 1970s, their mission budget came close to half a million dollars.

Through Mrs. Vetterlein's contacts with various mission leaders, we were able to invite those same leaders to our congregation. Our first "Missionary Week" was in May 1972, and it ignited within many hearts an increased interest, involvement, and participation in this critical aspect of Christian church life. Most importantly it resulted in an increase in giving. In 1970, missionary giving amounted to $10,700.00. After our first conference, giving leaped by 60 percent to $17,000.00. After our second in May 1973, we had received faith promises totaling $23,600.00. This enabled the church to take on a portion of the monthly support of new mission families and organizations.

I addition to the yearly conference, Ron and I preached a three-part series, "Why Missions?", "What is Mission?", and "Who Missions?" In 1975, we prepared an eight-week series entitled "Gaining a World Perspective." There were many Sundays when the congregation heard from a mission guest or mission agency representative. Most encouraging were the times we heard from our own young people sharing their growing desire to spend their summer on a mission trip. All this exposure added to the congregation's awareness of how a church ought to function.

By 1974, the missionary family of West Church included eight missionary families and twenty-two agencies. The budget required $24,360.00.

Ron and Betty had been considering overseas service for months, so he wrote to the congregation, explaining his thoughts in March 1976.

> A few years ago I went rappelling with some friends. I had never done it before. I got all harnessed up and watched several other guys disap-

pear over the edge of a sheer cliff. Then it was my turn. I'll never forget the churning feeling of fright and exhilaration as I planted my feet on the edge of that cliff and then leaned back and trusted my entire weight to that rope. With sweaty palms and pounding heart, I descended until I reached the bottom.

The idea of becoming missionaries produces that very same mixture of feelings in us—fear and excitement. And the analogy of approaching a cliff with the idea of going over the edge is not too far off. I suppose it's true that the closer one gets to the edge, the sweatier one's hands and upper lip become. Some weeks we want to charge ahead; other weeks we want to run in the other direction.

Yet our confidence in taking this step comes from one source—we know Who's holding the rope. Our loving Father has never left us alone; we've never needed anything He hasn't provided. Being weak and vulnerable has been the occasion to showcase His strength and grace. And we believe that God holds the rope not only through His character, but through His people. We are grateful for your words and actions of support, encouragement, and your prayers. Please know that we count on your prayers and are certain that they will be answered in the most perfect way possible.

In Christ's love,
Ron and Betty Kent

Kalihi Union, Church, Honolulu, Hawaii (1977-1983)

Final Goodbye to West Church, Background of Kalihi Union,
Installation, Leper Colony, Fuller Theological Seminary, Kwajalein,
Micronesia, Gay and Randy Hongo, Hawaii Congress of Christian
Discipleship (HCCD), Recall Vote, Resignation, Memories

As I trudged through the snow to check the mail on Monday,
January 5, 1976, I was curious about the arrival of a letter from
a church in Honolulu, Hawaii. Their pastor, Rev. Stanley Johnson,
had resigned in August 1975 to serve a congregation in Saratoga,
California. This letter was from the Pastoral Search Committee who
were in the process of seeking a successor.

The church was a member of the UCC at that time and had
asked the conference minister, Dr. Chet Terpstra, for his help.

Since the gospel was introduced to the islands by congregational
missionaries from Boston, Massachusetts, in 1820, the majority of
those serving congregational churches in Hawaii in the 1970s were
New Englanders.

Dr. Terpstra asked Dr. Avery Post, conference minister of the
Massachusetts Conference of the UCC, for his suggestions. The
committee received thirteen potential candidates, of which eight
were reviewed and evaluated. I was one of the eight.

I was not looking to move from West Church at that time, especially since I knew that Ron and Betty were contemplating ministry
overseas. But I had always believed that I should seriously consider

any new opportunity that came my way believing that God was guiding my life and any open door set before me could always be closed. After a serious time of discussion and prayer with Pat, I responded to the church's invitation with a willingness to be considered but rather certain that Hawaii was not my next place of ministry. However I must add that ministering in a congregation with an Asian majority piqued our interest.

In February, I received an application form for senior pastor. I filled it out and sent it back and didn't hear anything till August when another packet arrived requesting my views, beliefs, and convictions concerning the following doctrines and subjects.

The packet listed twelve subjects—sacraments, gifts of the Holy Spirit, neo-Pentecostalism, dispensationalism, and eschatology. They were also interested in my strategy for evangelism, my personal devotional life, where I find professional support, and what my attitudes are toward drinking, smoking, marriage, and divorce. They also requested a tape recording of my sermon for the upcoming Sunday. They wanted all this material by August 16! I worked on that application and was able to return it to the church on time.

Again I heard nothing till 10:12 p.m., Tuesday, September 28. It was Mr. Tom Masaki, the chairperson of the Search Committee in Honolulu. I was informed that I was the first of three candidates they wished to meet in person, and they asked me to fly out ASAP. Their suggestion was for me to travel alone and if called to candidate at a later date to come a second time with Pat. I was not comfortable with that arrangement; I did not want to make such a major decision without Pat's knowledge and support. I suggested switching the plans. Pat would join me on the first trip, and then me alone if I would be called to candidate. He said he would take my request back to the committee.

Pat and I left Boston on Friday, October 15, 1976. After a stop in Chicago, we landed in Los Angeles at 5:45 p.m. The Barkers met us and took us to their home for dinner and overnight. On Saturday, we flew to Honolulu and were met by the committee chair who took us to the Pacific Beach Hotel, 2490 Kalakaua Avenue. Our room overlooked Waikiki Beach and had a kitchenette and lanai. The cost was $32.00 per night—this was 1976 remember. Every morning we were welcomed with sweet-smelling floral leis and began an experience like no other. If the committee was hoping to win us over with the beauty, weather, and food of the islands, they accomplished their goal!

The committee had plans for every day except Sunday when we simply attended the worship service incognito. Every day we had lunch and dinner at different restaurants with a different member of the committee. We also enjoyed a tour of the island and an opportunity to view the parsonage and the elementary school. On Wednesday, October 20, we departed at 4:45 p.m., arriving home at 10:05 p.m. It was an amazing six days.

About a week later, I received another call saying that the committee had decided that they didn't need to talk to the other two candidates and asked, "Would you come to candidate?"

Pat's brother Tom was married to Jacki Rupert in Cincinnati on Friday, October 26. We drove to the wedding and flew to Los Angles Saturday afternoon and then on to Honolulu. I preached from Luke 24, "God on a search," and then remained for a question-and-answer session responding to questions that members of the congregation had written and submitted. Things went very well with an affirmative congregational vote to call me as their pastor (209-9). We were then taken to another restaurant in Waikiki to work out the details with the committee.

We left Honolulu and flew to San Francisco and then on to Philadelphia. Pat's parents had driven our car and children back from Tom and Jacki's wedding. We probably spent some time with the family and then drove north to Peabody, Massachusetts.

I shared with the congregation our plans that led to my resignation from West Church on Sunday, December 5, and on Monday wrote to the chairman of the Search Committee of KUC.

Dear Tom,
It is with a mixture of confidence and fear, joy and sadness, peace and confusion that I accept

the invitation to become senior pastor of Kalihi Union Church.

Thank you for your many hours of work that have been used by our heavenly Father to draw us together over such a great distance. You and the committee have helped me discover God's leading in my life; I am very grateful.

I look forward to a time of growth and fruitfulness for the glory of God.

In His care,
Richard A. Weisenbach

Final Goodbye to West Church

Pat and I have often reflected upon the sacrificial love of the West Church congregation as they were challenged to say goodbye to both of their pastors within two months. The tone and example of the leaders were truly a gift from God. I think particularly of George Ensworth; his counsel was so helpful in this regard.

Our parents never once indicated disappointment, confusion, or sadness at our announcement that we would be taking their grandchildren six thousand miles away. We were nourished by their strong support of what we believed to be God's will for our family. We are so grateful for their faithful love. We did, of course, provide them with a reason to vacation in the islands!

In the September *WestWinds*, Ron shared with the congregation,

Betty and I have made formal application to Overseas Crusades, complete with medical forms, references, and two nine-page questionnaires. Now it's a matter of waiting, probably until later this fall for a decision from OC about us. We want all of you to know how very grateful we are for your continuing prayer support and personal encouragement. And we understand

well your expressions of both sadness and joy. We
share those feelings too.

Ron and Betty Kent were formally accepted as members of
Overseas Crusades on October 20, 1976. He resigned as associate
pastor on Sunday, November 14, to be effective on December 31,
1976.

The Kents' decision to serve the Lord through Overseas Crusades was a major boost to our church's missionary involvement. The
budget for 1976–1977 jumped to $43,852.00.

West Church was connected to twenty-six mission families
and sixteen mission agencies. I wrote in the Missionary Committee
report for 1976, "This was the year that seven of our members left
for fields of service. Our participation moved from simply sending
money, to sacrificial sending of our loved ones. Missions became personal in 1976."

I am very grateful to see that West Congregational Church has
continued its active involvement in the Great Commission over the
years.

The time had come to write a letter of resignation to the board
of deacons, to the congregation, and a final annual report. I have
included a paragraph or two from that report.

> How do I write my last annual report? I'm
> tempted to go through the stack of back issues
> of *West Winds* noting all that God has enabled
> us to do since I've been with you. But I'm think-
> ing that such an exercise would be yielding to
> my pride more than to the Holy Spirit. Actually,
> what has really happened isn't written in *West
> Winds* anyway. The significant events in the life
> of West Church do not concern the razing of the
> old building or the purchase of a new organ or
> choir robes, or even whether or not we became
> independent of all denominational ties. The real

events took place within our hearts, within our families, within our community.

As I look back upon the years of our relationship together, I am most heartened by the signs of "Body Life" I observe within each of you. Your genuine and dependable love for each other, your willingness to widen the doors of the fellowship to include an exciting mix of backgrounds and persuasions, your thirst to worship God in new and deeper ways, and your personal involvement in missions, these all speak of real Christian growth.

When a minister leaves a church, people often look at those years as a self-contained unit with clear starting and stopping points. I really don't see it that way. The Christian ministry occurring in West Congregational Church has been a continuum for almost a hundred years and is deeply rooted in the people of the congregation, not in the several pastors who have served them. I prefer to say that ministry began here a long time before I came and will continue a long time after I have gone. It has simply been my special privilege to be a part of that exciting tradition during the 1970s. I don't want to underestimate the strategic place any pastor fills in the life of a congregation. God's work is never the work of one pastor and his family, but rather of the total fellowship. It has been my joy to be included in that fellowship for these past six years and to remain a part of your lives for many years to come.

I concluded with a special tribute to Pat, Ron, and Betty and Shirley Young, our very capable secretary of West Church.

Goodbye. God bless you all. I love your dearly.
Pastor Rich Weisenbach

Our last Sunday was on January 30, 1977. The board of deacon planned a farewell reception and buffet supper in our honor. It was a happy/sad evening. I remember the choir singing one of my favorites, a barbershop quartet trying their best, and a group of teenage boys dressed in hula skirts made from shredded newspapers doing a "dance."

Here is a copy of the program:

> Barbershop quartet
> Some slides
> Dick Sanderson from the Worship Committee
> Angelo Constantine from the Board of Trustees
> A taped greeting from Pastor Ron Kent
> Special music from Ken and Cathy Campbell
> Betty Robinson from the Bible Study Groups
> Bonnie Smith from the Ladies' Aid Society with gifts for the children
> Sister Mary Grace McCullough from the Peabody Clergy Association
> George Ensworth from the Deacons
> Words from Rich and/or Patty
> Choir: "Canticle of Praise"
> Prayer: George Ensworth

The highlight of the evening were the remarks by George Ensworth and the presentation of an original oil painting by Wayne Morrell, a Rockport artist. He named it "Clamming," but the Ensworths renamed it "Memories." It hangs in our condo today. I imagine it to be quite valuable.

I was encouraged to read in the order of worship for that last Sunday that Dr. Carlyle Saylor of Gordon-Conwell consented to be interim pastor and doctors Ensworth, Michaels, and Fee, all part of West Church, would be filling the pulpit till Dr. Saylor arrived.

We began the big chore of deciding what to ship, what to sell, what to give away, and what to store. Looking back, we should have stored most of our furniture; after all we were not going to live in Hawaii for the rest of our lives. But not thinking that far ahead, we shipped most of our furniture in a container that went through the Panama Canal and on to Honolulu.

We attended Union Congregational Church in Magnolia in February 6 and hosted a farewell party at my parents' on Friday, December 11. Then we attended Wycombe Baptist in December 13, where Pat's father pastored.

It was on Valentine's Day that we aimed our 1972 Chevy Suburban westward, visiting friends along the way.

It must have been our first or second night out that our son David had a grand mal seizure. We were very nervous as to what to do. He said he couldn't see or move his left arm. We prayed of course and drove to Des Moines, Iowa, where we visited the Kents who took us to see a doctor. Dave was put on Dilantin and was steady till we were able to get him the necessary care at Queen's Hospital in Honolulu. Thank you, Lord!

It was at the Kents that we delivered our dog Missy for safekeeping. So sad.

We didn't make too many stops along the way, but I do remember Albuquerque, New Mexico, a gondola up Sandia Mountain, the purchase of a genuine Indian rug, and a stop at the Petrified Forest.

We visited the Barkers in Pasadena, California, and saw the first *Star Wars* movie. Then we took our Suburban to a port and then flew to Honolulu on Monday, February 28, arriving at 7:50 p.m. I still remember coming off the plane at gate 9. A crowd of almost two hundred church members greeted us with a huge banner, posters, and scores of leis. Pictures were taken and many have made it into Pat's albums. The chair of the Search Committee gave me a key to KUC, and this was followed by a prayer of thanksgiving and the singing of "To God be the Glory." (These were the days when anyone could go right to the gates without going through security.)

Our furniture arrived in March 15 and our Suburban about a week later. We had great fun filling the parsonage—five bedrooms and three full baths—with our furniture, pictures, and music. Another blessing came when the church provided a new 1977 Buick

Century, insurance package, and a credit card for gas and possible repairs.

Background of Kalihi Union

In August 1982, I compiled the following information about KUC:

1. History. Kalihi Union Church is located in a residential, light industrial district called Kalihi (edge) on the western edge of the city of Honolulu. About fifty-five thousand people reside in this area.

   The church began as a settlement near the turn of the century, and on September 21, 1913, it was organized into a church with 180 members. They met "to found a church in Kalihi for the glory of God, the service of our fellowmen, the mutual assistance of Christian life and the upbuilding of the Kingdom of God on earth."

   The Rev. Horace Chamberlain became the first pastor. Ten other pastors have followed him.

2. Covenant. We are united in striving to know the will of God as taught in the Holy Scriptures, and in our purpose to walk in the ways of the Lord, made known or to be made known to us. (As you can tell, this covenant is identical to the covenant of most New England Congregational Churches.) We hold it to be the mission of the Church of Christ to proclaim the gospel to mankind, exalting the worship of the one true God and laboring for the progress of knowledge, the promotion of justice, the reign of peace, and the realization of human brotherhood. Depending, as did our fathers before us, upon the continued guidance of the Holy Spirit to lead us into all truth, we work and pray for the transformation of the world into the kingdom of God and we look with faith for the triumph of righteousness and the life everlasting.

3. Polity, affiliation, and theological position. KUC is congregational in polity (government) and affiliated with the Oahu Association of the United Church of Christ. It is evangelical in perspective.

4. Physical plant. The church property consists of approximately six acres. A new sanctuary and one education unit were constructed in 1957. A gymnasium and a second education unit were built a year later. A larger education building built in 1937 is still in use but scheduled for replacement in 1984–1985. Plans for new construction and a million-dollar building fund were approved by the congregation in November 1981.

   A three-bedroom cottage is located on the church campus and houses a part-time custodian. A three-bedroom cottage to house the Japanese language pastor was constructed in 1977. A second parsonage is located at 1461 Lalamilo Street, about three miles away from the church premises. This houses the senior pastor.

5. Staff. The present church staff consists of the senior pastor (full-time), an associate pastor (full-time), director of Christian Education (half-time), minister of Music (three-quarters time), two organists and two custodians (full-time), a church secretary (half-time), an accountant (full-time), a preschool administrator (full-time), and six preschool teachers (seventeen in all). In addition to the English-speaking pastor, there is a full-time Japanese pastor, a part-time Laotian pastor, and three part-time Filipino pastors. The Gospel of Jesus Christ is preached from the campus in four different languages every Sunday.

6. Membership. The active membership of KUC is about five hundred. It ministers to a church family of about 750. Members represent various ethnic cultures—Americans of Japanese ancestry, 65%; Caucasian, 15%; Chinese 10%; and Filipino/Hawaiian mixed 10%. There is also a broad financial spectrum represented at the church as well as great freedom of theological opinions. Four families speak

in tongues privately. Both modes of baptism are respected. An average of 435 persons attend Sunday morning services at 8:00 and 10:30 a.m.

7. Ministry. A Sunday school program, children through adult, has an enrollment of about five hundred with a staff of sixty-five teachers. The church conducts preschool and childcare with ninety children is attendance. Several Bible studies are available. A men's prayer group meets in the pastor's office at 6:00 a.m. every week. Midweek prayer and praise fellowship. Boy Scouts, college and career group, intermediate and high school groups, athletic activities, and leagues gather in the gym. A choir program for children through adult involves about one hundred persons in three choirs. A "summer fun" program is conducted during the ten weeks of June, July, and August. Pastoral counseling is offered along with the distribution of clothing, food, and furniture to the needy of the community.

8. Finances. The church is in a stable financial condition. The proposed budget for 1982 is $320,686.00. There is approximately $75,000.00 in the savings/checking accounts presently.

9. Japanese department. The Japanese ministry began about forty-five years ago with a membership of fifteen. Pastor Paul Waterhouse, pastor of the English-speaking congregation, became the first pastor. He had been a missionary in Japan and was fluent in the Japanese language. Over the years, the group grew to eighty-eight members and approached the English-speaking department for help in finding a full-time pastor. In 1977, Rev. Toshioki Kegeyama was found and hired. He and his wife Ayako served for five years, leaving in August 1981.

I wrote this nine-part description of KUC as part of my initial dissertation required by Fuller Theological Seminary for the DMin degree.

In order to meet as many members as possible, I asked the congregation to wear name tags in the worship service for our first month together. Then we organized small groups to come to the parsonage for fellowship and food.

At West Church, we did the same thing but met in the homes of church members. At KUC, we invited everyone to our home to let them see how we had furnished their parsonage with New England furniture. They were quite interested in the differences they saw.

The congregation was already divided into sixteen flocks, each headed by a deacon. We met together on Tuesdays and Fridays for two months. Each deacon took responsibility for light refreshments. We took all who were interested on a tour of the house, and then we gathered in the living room where I asked a few questions. How did you first start coming to KUC? Why do you keep coming? How are you involved? This was always enough to precipitate a discussion that would fill the evening.

Our relationship with the members was almost always warm and honest. One family in particular, the Chinen family, was especially loving. They realized that we were far from home and could not enjoy our families, especially during the holidays. Their acceptance and generosity made our transition much easier. Other families offered the same welcome, but the Chinens were special.

Other *haole* (Caucasian) families and anyone who had been in the military seemed confident enough to entertain us. But there was always the notion that the minister and his family were different. We never felt rejected, but there was always a distance between us due to our different cultures. Faithful church members and friends were always accepting and respectful, but I sensed a definite dynamic between me and a few of the leaders. I'll reflect more on this issue a little later.

Installation

We made things official by asking the Oahu Association of the UCC in Hawaii to conduct an Ecclesiastical Council and Installation service for me and Kageyama Sensei, Pastor of our Japanese Language

Department, on Sunday evening, May 22. The service was conducted in English and Japanese. Rev. Jay Jarman, my associate, led the congregation in a call to worship. Bob Yuen, church moderator, read a statement of our purpose. David Yamashiro, chairman of the board of deacons and deaconesses, read from 1 Corinthians 12:27–13:13. The choir sang "Eternal Life," and greetings were brought by Dr. Chester Terpstra, conference minister of the Hawaii Conference of the UCC. An installation litany was conducted by Genevieve Eggleston, former chair of the Church and Ministry Committee of the association. Jay and Rev. David Hosomi, pastor of Honolulu Holiness Church, shared in an installation prayer. Mrs. Dorothy Shimer, moderator of the Oahu Association, read a declaration from the association. Rev. Michio Oyakawa, pastor of Manoa Valley Church, and Rev. Philip Tsuchiya, pastor of Makiki Christian Church, gave charges to both me and Kageyama Sensei. The service concluded by giving both me and Kageyama Sensei a brief opportunity to make a few remarks. We ended by singing "the Church's One Foundation" in two languages. It was quite a start for both of us.

The next Sunday was Pentecost and we marked it in a very special way. Acts 2:1–13 describes the coming of the Holy Spirit, freeing the gathered believers to declare God's glory in many languages. Hawaii is a melting pot of cultures and languages, and the membership of KUC reflects the mix. On that Sunday morning, I asked five members who were fluent in their native tongue to help read the scripture. I asked Winifred Dow, who was born in England, to stand in her pew and begin reading the text of Acts 2 in English. When she got to verse 3 or 4, I instructed Leonard Chun to stand up and begin reading in Chinese. The congregation, who was not aware of my plan, began to wonder what was happening. While Win and Len were reading at the same time, I instructed Evelyn Tashima to stand and begin reading in Japanese. By this time, there were three readers all speaking at the same time. A few faces reflected an understanding of what the first Pentecost must have been like. Next came George Arlantico reading in one of the Filipino languages, and then George Ahuna stood and added Hawaiian. The scripture reading that Pentecost Sunday was quite similar to what the early church must have experienced. It was a wonderful illustration of the very special birthday of the church.

A typical schedule of services on a Sunday morning began at eight thirty with Sunday school, English language worship at ten o'clock, Japanese language worship at one o'clock, and Lao and Filipino worship services in the afternoon and evening.

After four months, I announced a membership class, and we welcomed sixteen new members on June 26, 1977. I conducted fourteen membership classes during our six-year stay for a total of 160 members added to the congregation.

We also conducted baptismal services in the ocean on Thanksgiving and Easter Sundays, and 140 took this very significant step. Our daughter Pamela Lynne was one of that number, and much to my joy, my parents were visiting during this very special event in Pam's spiritual journey.

My parents wasted little time in their plans to visit us. They arrived on October 15, 1977, and stayed until October 30. They helped celebrate my thirty-sixth birthday in October 24. We tried to squeeze in visits and activities for them, and I think we were pretty successful. During their fifteen days in the islands, they attended two worship services at KUC, ate at several very nice restaurants, and visited Paradise Park, the Bishop Museum, and the Punchbowl (National Memorial Cemetery of the Pacific). They also spent time and money at Ala Moana Shopping Center. They visited Pearl Harbor and got to see the Pali—a high cliff formed by the chain of mountains dividing the island. They were even able to see the neighbor island of Kauai. They enjoyed themselves so much that they came back five years later!

One lasting effect of their visit was a special breakfast I arranged. A Swiss-born, French-trained chef named Gerhard Tschanz was cooking his way around the world. When he stopped in Hawaii, our associate pastor Jay Jarman met him on Waikiki Beach and invited him to church. He became a faithful church member, so I asked him to come to our house and prepare breakfast for the family. What he cooked was fabulous and became an immediate favorite. The children named this egg, bacon, cheese, and onion dish "super egg." We enjoy it at every holiday gathering of the family to this day.

Ron and Betty Kent stopped in Honolulu for two weeks in the middle of July, when they were on their way to the Philippines as missionaries with Overseas Crusades. We had a good time together, and I invited Ron to preach in July 17. It was a special treat to sing once more in the pastor's quartet that Sunday. We enjoyed each other, played, prayed, and sent them on their way.

One of the realities of living on an island six thousand miles from New England is missing important family events. The time and the price of airline tickets made for some sad misses. I was however able to be present for my brother Bill's marriage to Cynthia Stuen. It was in New York City on Saturday, on May 28.

Our hope was to allow each one of our children to spend a summer with their grandparents sometime during their eleventh or twelfth year. (Now that I am writing this, I don't recall ever discussing this plan with our parents.) Bill's wedding gave me the opportunity to enjoy this special family time and deliver Pam to Mother and Dad. I'm sure she enjoyed her summer, and Pat and I remain thankful to our loving parents for accommodating their schedule to her. She returned home that September traveling with Pearl, Pat's younger sister who lived with us for a year or two.

Leper Colony

I received a letter from Rev. Jim Drew in April 1978 inviting me to preach at his church, Kanaana Hou, on the island of Molokai. His ministry was to the people of Kalaupapa, a leper colony. I felt this was a privilege and agreed to fill the pulpit on July 23, 1978. He arranged for the special permits and filled us in on a few details. The congregation was small of course, but we were warmly welcomed, well-fed, and given a tour of their part of the island. We were welcomed back in December 10 and spent a few extra days.

We had read about the sad history of leprosy in Hawaii and had gotten a firsthand account from Margaret Zamora, who as a teenager was taken by members of the Board of Health to a facility that deter-mined that she was a leper. She was taken to the colony on Molokai. After several years, and with the fear of the disease no longer threat-ening the population, Margaret came home and became a part of our church. She was a courageous older woman who was welcomed into the fellowship of the congregation. Our son David was able to invite her to his class at school so others could hear her story. It was a privi-lege to know her. Dr. Mel White wrote a book, *Margaret of Molokai*, chronicling her experience.

Pat found time to arrange activities for the children, classes at the YMCA, and participation in the Honolulu Children's Opera Chorus. Both Pam and Kim had to audition before Charlotte Roth-schild, a scary experience to say the least. We did attend a concert or two on the stage at Ala Moana Shopping Center.

Fuller Theological Seminary

As I wrote earlier, it was Dr. Barker who urged me to consider pursuing a DMin degree. I'm not a scholar, but he got me thinking. I'm pastoring in Hawaii, the church has provided me with a two-week study leave every year, I was invited to stay with the Barker family while at school, and the classes were held during two-week periods three times a year.

After prayer and a conversation with Pat, I made my application on March 30, 1979. Judging from my academic record at Muhlen-berg and Gordon-Conwell, the admitting committee was willing to accept me as a special student on the proviso that I earn a B+ or bet-ter in my first two courses.

I remember shopping in Pasadena and buying a very classy brief-case, which I still use, and spying a beautiful watercolor painting of the Royal Hawaiian Hotel with Diamond Head in the background. It cost $58.00. Today it hangs on the wall in our condo.

I remain very grateful to KUC for providing those two-week study leaves. This gift made the degree program possible.

My brother Bill and Cynthia visited us for about two weeks in July 1979. He was willing to preach in July 8, and he did a very good job, but my most vivid memory of their stay was the morning he invited the whole family for a sailboat ride from Kailua on the north shore back to Honolulu.

We arrived early enough to have breakfast on the boat, and so far so good. As we headed out of the harbor, the waves began to pick up. I was feeling very queasy, and within minutes, I got really seasick and went below deck. I thought I was going to die, and then a few moments later, I wished I would!

Bill quickly realized that his plans were not going to work out. He was able to get the boat turned around and safely back to our mooring. Then he called the company who had rented him the boat. We later learned that during the company's effort to get the boat back to Honolulu, they had blown out the mainsail. Other than that, we had a marvelous time.

Bill bought a summer place in Bayside, Maine, which we try to visit each year on our way home from Moosehead Lake. He had a sailboat but we weren't very keen to be passengers.

While we were serving West Church, I joined the Barbershop Harmony Society—the Society for the Preservation and Encouragement of Barber Shop Quartet Singing in America (SPEBSQSA). We met weekly in a room at the First Parish Congregational Church in Wakefield. (Little did I know that I would become pastor of this church in about five years.)

When we arrived in Hawaii, I soon discovered and joined the Hawaii chapter. The chorus eventually moved to KUC for rehearsals and sang in our worship service once or twice. In addition to the chorus, I was in a quartet with three other Christian men. I enjoyed the music and the connection with those outside the church. It was through the Barbershop connection that I was introduced to Larry McCracken who eventually joined KUC and became a faithful member along with his wife Lois. When we left Hawaii, I decided that I had enough barbershop singing.

In the spring of 1980, I began studies at Fuller Theological Seminary for the DMin degree. I had to do well to remain enrolled in the program. I signed up for two courses, Building Christian

Community through Small Groups and Issues in First Corinthians. By God's grace, I was able to earn a B+ in one course and an A in the other. I was informed that I was no longer a special student. In my enthusiasm, I called the office asking that if I continued earning good grades, "Might I graduate cum laude?" I'll never forget their response, "Reverend Weisenbach, everyone graduates cum laude!"

I stayed with the Barkers for the two weeks and felt so privileged to be welcomed into their family. As we had learned a few years earlier, Marge was struggling with cancer. She trusted the Lord through the whole ordeal and continued to maintain her home, but she was often exhausted at the end of the day. At one point, I asked Glenn about Marge's condition and his reaction to it. He shared his struggle and his faith. I believe he really appreciated my interest. It was so special to listen to my dear friend share with me his deepest fears, feelings, and faith.

At the end of May, I was awarded a three-month sabbatical, from June 1 to September 1. May 25 was Pentecost, so I preached from Acts 2, and then we went to an all-church Memorial Day picnic on Monday.

The next day, we boarded our flight to Philadelphia arriving at 8:25 p.m. with all thirteen pieces of luggage and David's bike! We crammed in more than twenty visits with seminary classmates and friends from Union Church, Magnolia, and West Congregational Church, Peabody. I think it was Kim who finally complained, "I do not want to meet any more people who knew me when I was a baby!"

Then there was Granny and Poppy's fortieth wedding anniversary, a Weisenbach family reunion, a weekend at the Adcocks in the Poconos, and six days in Maine including Camp Cherith and Moosehead Lake. We made more visits in New Hampshire, New York, and New Jersey. Then we left Dave with our parents and boarded our flight back to Los Angeles. We spent the night with the Barkers and the next day at Knott's Berry Farm. We landed in Hawaii on Thursday, June 26, just in time to put Pam on an Aloha Air Flight to Kauai on Saturday where she spent the next two months working at a stable and living with a Hawaiian family.

Kwajalein, Micronesia

The next two months found Pat, me, and Kim in Micronesia, the atoll of Kwajalein to be specific. I learned from Rev. Philip Brink that Rev. Elden Buck, Protestant chaplain at the Island Memorial Chapel, was taking a choir of Ponapean young people on a tour of mainland United States. He needed someone to replace him for three months. As it worked out, Phil filled in for the month of June, and we took responsibility for July and August.

Chaplain Buck wrote to me saying that we were an answer to his prayers. He had made all the necessary preparations for our flight in July 2 and our return to Hono in September 1. Reverend Brink wrote to me with lots of details concerning our quarters and that I be prepared to give the chapel secretary my text and sermon title the moment we landed. She was eager to print the order of worship for the upcoming Sunday.

My main responsibilities were to conduct and preach at two worship services, 8:00 a.m. and 11:00 a.m., and to fly every Sunday night to Roi-Namur, a neighbor inland, to lead a group of four or five in a half-hour time of worship and discussion. That was the extent of my duties outside of any emergencies that might occur.

From 1942 to 1944, 6,200 US soldiers would die and 22,800 would be wounded as Americans battled the Japanese for control of Micronesia in the Western Pacific. US forces captured Kwajalein Atoll in 1944. We saw the remains of Japanese bunkers as we walked around the island. They were Quonset-shaped buildings made of concrete. They all had huge craters in them from the American bombing. One of our children found several bullets and shell casings littered on the ground.

From 1945 to 1980 tells a sad tale of American abuse of the islands and its inhabitants. Nuclear bomb testing continued from 1945 to 1954. People were displaced from their homes, and thousands suffered the results of nuclear radiation.

Then in 1970, the Pentagon decided that the location of the islands was an ideal place for a permanent military base. Kwajalein

Missile Range (KMR) was negotiated and in 1976 agreed on a payment of $704,000.00 per year. (I'm certain that this amount has been increased since then.)

The chapel was built by the military and dedicated on February 11, 1945. A memorial reads, "This chapel is dedicated to the memory of the gallant officers and men of the Armed Forces of the United States who gave their lives in the capture of Kwajalein, February 1–5, 1944." In 1975, the chapel was rebuilt, adding air-conditioning and a new roof and interior laminated beams.

When we were there, a few signs of all the horror that took place could be seen. The island had been enlarged to provide a long runway for large military aircraft, and scores of trailers were provided to augment the existing naval housing. Every building was air-conditioned, and it reminded me of California. There were a few Step-Vans available to deliver groceries and run errands, but everyone rode a bicycle most of the time.

Today Kwajalein is an active Army base with a population of 2,688 (as of June 1980). There were only sixty-seven military on island; civil servants who work for such companies as Bell Labs, MIT Lincoln Labs, RCA, Sylvania, TRW, GE, Raytheon, McDonnell Douglas Astronautics, and Kentron International composed the majority of the island's population. They were engineers, mostly married and usually from Massachusetts or Alabama. These families made up the great bulk of the chapel's membership. We obviously had much in common with these folk and still, after many years, remain close to John and Barbara Wallace whom we met on the island. They are in Florida now and we see or hear from them enough to remain current.

The highlight for me was the opportunity to organize and lead two small group Bible studies. At the first Sunday service, I asked if anyone would be interested in such a small group. Thirteen came to our trailer that Monday evening indicating their desire. I decided to put my recent Fuller classes to good use. Twenty-seven signed up to study 1 Corinthians on Monday or Thursday evenings. I was delighted with the response and so grateful for God's timing that equipped me to organize the group. I later discovered that there were several women's groups that met in the afternoons but nothing that afforded men and women the opportunity to study the Bible together. Reverend Buck wrote to me when he returned to say that the groups are continuing. Praise the Lord!

Of course, I did enjoy preaching, and since I had the time, I decided to write new sermons rather than use material I had preached previously. I focused on the gospel message for the first three weeks and then preached a series on the last six commandments. I am humbled to say that the church on Kwaj. appreciated these weekly sermons very much.

Pat kept herself very busy watching over ten-year-old Kim, teaching the fifth-grade Sunday school class, singing in the choir, and taking active part in both small groups.

Then there was the sand pile. After the island was enlarged to make way for the runway, large piles of sand, coral, and shells remained on the tip of the island. When it rained, which was often, many shells and corals were exposed. This pile became a spot that Pat visited often. She would ride her bike down the street that ran alongside the runway and spend hours collecting treasures.

I took some time to snorkel and discovered some shells myself. Mine had creatures inside, and fortunately folks taught me how to clean them. Many of these shells have decorated our homes ever since.

Besides the boxes of shells and corals that we sent home, Pat made candles, mobiles, and collages and gave them away to Kwaj. friends and some to KUC folks.

While there, we attended three special events, Kim's synchronized swimming show, the Continental Singers and Orchestra concert, and a dance performed by eighty-five Marshallese celebrating the opening of the Likiep airstrip. These very unique opportunities added to our two-month stay.

My salary was more than I was earning at KUC. Purchases at Macy's (the local department store) were tax free since we were not in the United States. Since Kwaj. was considered hardship duty, there was a variety of perks all free of charge—snorkeling, scuba, boating, fishing, waterskiing, movies, bowling, and several classes on a variety of subjects were offered. It was relaxing to ride our bikes everywhere, no gas to buy. We never had a fear concerning the children. Anyone who created a problem was simply taken off the island. When a family received a permanent change of station (PCS), there would be a patio sale, which were great bargains. The sunsets were beautiful, so were the sunrises.

And there was a downside—minimal healthcare and dentistry, and anything serious required a trip to Hono. There was very limited fresh fruits and vegetables. Television was offered on only one station and only reruns. It was hot and it rained at least three times a week.

When we left, I wrote a goodbye letter with a picture of us three in the corner.

> August 30, 1980
> Dear Friends,
> How can we express our thanks to God for bringing us here and to you for receiving us so warmly? Words are not able to capture the joy and fulfillment we've experienced while among you. There are so many fond memories, which will always be ours when we think of our summer on Kwaj. Faithfulness at worship, eager participation at the Bible studies, delicious dinners and the potluck at Emon Beach, Micronesian handcrafted gifts, our airline tickets and delightful quarters, the choir, and your flexibility with all the changes. These times will remain with us always.
> May God grant us more!
> Aloha,
> Rich, Pat, and Kim Weisenbach

A sad letter awaited us on our return. It was from Bill Keyes, director of Personnel for Overseas Crusades (OC Ministries). It was dated August 11, 1980.

> Due to some personal circumstances in the lives of Ron and Betty Kent, it has been necessary for them to return from the Philippines.
>
> We thank you for faithfully supporting the Kents during their time in the Philippines. They were a vital part of the Mindanao Team.
>
> We trust that you will be in much prayer for them these days as they seek the Lord's direction for their lives.

We later learned that Ron had divorced Betty and married Cita, their live-in housekeeper/cook. Ron wrote us a heartbreaking letter in October explaining just how alone he felt.

We heard little until 1983 when we stopped by Ron's house in Comfrey, Minnesota, on our way across the mainland, headed for Wakefield, Massachusetts. He had just taken up a part-time pastoral ministry in the congregational church in that community. We also stopped to see Betty in Mount Hebron, Wisconsin. She was married to Bob Becker, and we later learned that she had died of cancer.

Ron and Cita moved to Hawaii after a few years, thinking that Cita, who was Filipino, would feel more comfortable in that culture. Sadly, Ron divorced Cita and married Priscilla Lee. He pastored a UCC church on the Big Island for several years and then did some interim work. I will often call him on his birthday (4/4/44—easy to remember). He is doing very well now and is planning his retirement.

We loved Ron and Betty Kent and have such fond memories of ministry together at West Church. He is a gifted writer and preacher, and we find it challenging to understand the choices he has made, but we still love him and are grateful to God that he has found a good place.

In 1980, Jay Jarman, associate pastor at KUC, began thinking and praying about leaving our church to start another. On September

14, 1980, the congregation sent out about twenty-five of our members to plant a new church in Mililani, "the Church at Our House." Here is the opening paragraphs of my sermon on that morning. My text was Acts 13:1–5 and 14:26–8.

> There is never a good time to send our friends away. "Away" means separation, distance, sorrow, grief, and loneliness. Yet today, according to God's direction and timing—which are always prefect—we at KUC will send away some of our best friends! Today is the day that we separate the Jarman family and other members of our church family for the work to which God has called them. And, because He has called them, we can rejoice, for His call is always good.
>
> Jesus has promised to build His church and He has been doing that here at Kalihi Union in several ways. We recently had to expand our Sunday worship schedule to two services because of the size of the congregation. Add to this the fact that there are now four congregations that meet on this campus every Sunday, each speaking a different language: our English department, the Issei department (Japanese), the Cosmopolitan UCC (Filipino), and the newly formed Laotian Fellowship. These are signs of God's blessings. We will take another step this morning; we will seek to release several of our members to plant a new church.
>
> Praise the Lord!

At the conclusion of the service, I called forward those who were leaving, several KUC members came up behind them and laid their hands upon their brothers and sisters, and a prayer of dedication and blessing was shared.

On April 7, 1981, the Church at Our House became a member of the Oahu Association of the Hawaii Conference of the UCC. On

Pentecost Sunday, June 7, we marked the occasion with a special service at Mililani High School cafeteria. Six clergy and eleven laypersons participated in the celebration. Jay gave a history and I preached. It was a great day! We received a progress report in March 1983.

In October 1980, we had one house church with seventeen adults and eight children. Today we have six house churches with 109 adults and seventy-one children. Around 50 percent of our regular attenders had no previous church experience. Forty-five people have been baptized. New Christians for a new church.

As I mentioned, Jay left KUC in the fall of 1980 to develop a new work in Mililani. During the spring of 1981, the KUC church was able to hire two very capable partners on a part-time basis. Dr. Kathy Wilson brought new direction and energy to our education efforts, and Randy Hongo and his wife Gay brought new life and joy to our music ministry.

Gay and Randy Hongo

Randy was an amazing pianist, composer, vocalist, organizer, and all-around humble servant of Jesus Christ. He played the piano at most of our worship services and would often sing something that supported the sermon theme or an original composition with his wife Gay. He directed the senior choir and organized a youth choir. This group performed several major events, "Celebrate Life" (1981), "Backpacker's Suite" (1982), and "the Cross and the Switchblade" (1983). He gathered a choir of forty-five teens plus six musicians for his first effort, and by 1983, the production required close to a hundred. We were always so proud of our daughter Pam who was in all three productions.

Gay and Randy went on to found Christian Vision, a ministry to support their worldwide ministry. They did in fact tour the world, singing Hawaiian songs and Christian hymns along with several of his own compositions.

He and Gay visited us at First Parish several times, giving concerts—indoors and on the common—and ministering in our Sunday worship services. It was always a special treat to have them.

One of our great privileges came in 2007 when we joined Gay and Randy and a small group of travelers on a tour of Japan. They were experienced tour guides. They had visited Japan more than twenty times on previous occasions.

We rode the bullet train and luxuriated in an *onsen* (hot baths in the nude; Pat has her own story to tell about her experience). We visited several ancient castles, attended a sumo match, benefitted from my first and only acupuncture treatment, ate incredible food, bought several gifts, and visited three Christian churches where Gay and Randy shared their testimony and music. The highlight for Pat and me was their invitation to sing with them in a quartet, "Great is Thy Faithfulness." This was truly a memorable experience.

In December 2011, Randy was diagnosed with multiple myeloma and was admitted to City of Hope Hospital in California. The skill of the medical staff gave him six more years to share his love and gifts. Sadly he suffered a heart attack on December 16, 2017. A celebration of his life was conducted at KUC in December 23.

During the summer of 1981, I was reading up a storm in preparation for two more classes at Fuller, "Church Organizational Structure, Administration and Management" and "Conflict Management."

Getting ready for any course in the DMin program required a great amount of reading before arriving on campus. I usually took two courses during each two-week session. One seminar (worth eight units) required reading three thousand pages and writing a one-page summary of each book read. A course (worth four units) called for 1,500 pages and summaries of books read. Seminars were taught in the mornings (eight o'clock until noon), and courses were in the afternoon (one to three o'clock).

Anyone taking the DMin degree program had to complete forty-eight units earning a B+ or better. There was also the requirement of a dissertation, which is to be designed to benefit the candidate's place of ministry, and it was worth eight units.

The sign on the door of the DMin office said, "This way to DMin possession." That about sums it up! By God's mercy, I was given an A in both courses.

On this visit, I again stayed with the Barkers. He had always wanted to visit the Chrystal Cathedral, so one Sunday morning, he and I traveled to Garden Grove. We found seats at about row 3.

The service began when Dr. Schuller entered, strode across the dais, turned toward two floor-to-ceiling windows, and thrust his arms into the air. At that point, the large windows swung open giving the people parked in the lot partial access to the sanctuary. (You might remember that Dr. Schuller's ministry began at a drive-in theater.) At the same time, two long fountains running up the aisles shot up streams of water. At this point, Dr. Barker leaned over and whispered, "Jesus has a long way to go to beat this!"

I returned from California on Saturday, August 15, just in time to join the family for a two-week vacation on the neighbor island of Kauai. We divided our time into two parts. The first was at a house-keeping cabin available at no cost to all UCC clergy. It was in the mountains and was called Kokee. It was a great place and we were able to take advantage of the offer at least two times.

The area was filled with wild chickens and David was determined to capture one. They ran all over the place, so getting one didn't seem too hard. He planned to make a bow and arrow and bring it home for dinner. Good luck, Dave.

Another memory was a hike we took up into the mountains; there were many well-marked trails. Somehow, we lost David for a short time, but he reappeared, having blazed his own path. I took a picture of him with his arms folded across his chest and mud up to his knees; the expression on his face told us not to ask any questions.

The second week took us to Anahola. Peter Galuteria, a member of KUC, owned a cottage right on the beach, and he invited us to use it for the week. We were greeted by this note.

> August 18, 1981
>
> My dear friends, The Weisenbachs
>
> Aloha and welcome to Anahola Beach Cottage! How truly wonderful to have you here to experience a week of rest and recreation together as a family. Feel free to use whatever foodstuffs

you find in the cupboards and refrigerator. They
are there for you to enjoy. Please do me a favor
and see that the plants are watered each evening
and given your tender, loving care.

God bless you each one!

In Christ,
Peter

We were right on the beach and enjoyed walks and swimming.
Pam jogged the beach, and Dave tried his hand at surfing.

The highlight was a visit to a farm that raised pigs. We arrived
just as they were about to uncover their *emu*. Hawaiians would dig a
hole, line it with smooth stones taken from a roaring fire, and then
place a prepared pig into the hole. The pig was usually wrapped
tightly in chicken wire after placing a few hot stones inside the pig's
cavity. The animal was then covered with banana leaves and left to
itself for the night. In the morning, it was uncovered, and that is
when we arrived. It didn't take long for the men to wrestle the carcass
out of the pit and start separating the meat from the bones, which
were thrown into a wheelbarrow. We were all fascinated to watch
something we had heard about but never witnessed. Then the best
part, we were all given a taste. *Ono* (Hawaiian for delicious)!

By September 3, I was back in the saddle after our month's study
and vacation. I began a preaching series from the book of Psalms that
took us to the Advent season.

I often arranged my preaching schedule into a series built
around a topic or book of the Bible. My preaching record for those
years includes the following, among others: The Beatitudes (5), The
Return of Jesus Christ (4), The Seven Last Words of Jesus (7), The
Christian Family (6), The Purpose of the Church (9), The Life of
Joseph (5), The Gospel of Mark (12), The Book of I Corinthians
(18), When God Says 'No' (8), and from the book of Psalms (12). Of
course there was always an Advent series and one during Lent.

Because it is easy to get preachers, missionaries, and seminary
professors to visit Hawaii, we had our share of guests. Over the years,
we were treated to Moishe Rosen, founder of Jews for Jesus; Pete

Hammond of InterVarsity; Frank Severn of SEND; Ray Haley of World Vision; Arsenia Banaga, Siegfried, and Gudrun Neumaier of the Liebenzell Mission; and Mark and Suzanne Jacobsen of Wycliffe Bible Translators. The Covenant Players made four visits. Four professors from Fuller preached from our pulpit—Dr. Lewis Smedes, Dr. Newt Maloney, Dr. Orlando Costas, and Dr. Roberta Hestenes. We also invited the missionaries that KUC supported to bring a word whenever they could, Yokichi Suzuki, Ken Takushi, Henry Ayabe, Ada Lum, Jim Kakamatsu, David Hall, and Geraldine Hinote.

Hawaii Congress of Christian Discipleship. (HCCD)

Because special speakers always add to the ministry of a local church, I realized that we were located in the perfect place to invite major leaders to come to Hawaii in February all expenses paid! I contacted the pastors of three other evangelical churches, First Chinese, Makiki Christian, and First Presbyterian, suggesting that the four congregations might combine our resources to present such an opportunity to our congregations and community. They agreed and we began the Hawaii Congress of Christian Discipleship (HCCD) in February 1980.

Our first speaker was Elisabeth Elliot, missionary, author, and radio speaker. Dr. David Hubbard, president of Fuller Theological Seminary, was our scheduled speaker for 1981 but he had to cancel. Rev. Bill Steeper, former pastor of KUC, was able to take his place. In 1982, we had Rev. Gordon MacDonald, pastor of Grace Chapel, Lexington, Massachusetts. Dr. Mel White, pastor and author, came in 1983.

This yearly event continued after we left Hawaii for a year or two and then took a break. Fortunately, Rev. Dan Chun, a product of KUC and pastor of First Presbyterian, organized a similar and much larger gathering called Hawaiian Island Ministries (HIM). I'm grateful that a program similar to HCCD continues today.

As I wrote earlier, my parents visited twice, Pat's parents came also, and in November 1981 Pat's mother came alone (November 17 to December 1). She spent much of her time with Pat, visiting the school where Pat taught in the Title 1 program, or visiting Lao women trying to learn English. She was invited out to dinner to restaurants or member's homes, went shopping for gifts to take home, and attended the Thanksgiving baptismal service on the beach. She made a special trip to Molokai to see a missionary friend named Donna who lived "topside." She also visited Kalaupapa and met Jim and Sally Drew and toured the colony. Just before she left, we celebrated Kim's eleventh birthday, four days early. I'm sure she was grateful for the opportunity and rather tired when she arrived home.

One of my favorite memories of Hawaii was Wednesday afternoons, I called them "special days." Each week I would spend three or four hours with one of the children. We went wherever they wanted to go, and in Honolulu, there were plenty of places to go. As the kids grew older, shopping became their first choice followed by a stop at McDonald's. I want to believe that those hours spent one-on-one helped to build strong relationships.

I do not recall how we were invited back to Kwaj, but we served for just three weeks—this time with Pam and David. It was Kim's turn to be with our parents in Pennsylvania.

We arrived on Friday, August 6. After worship, the congregation had a nice welcome back/happy wedding anniversary reception; it was our eighteenth. Pat's card was a keeper.

> In these eighteen years, we've made it through seminary days and hospital hours, growth with the Barkers, youth groups and beach walks in Magnolia, our three beautiful children and pastoring our congregation, refreshing trips to Moosehead Lake, the big change to West Church, sharing with many seminary couples, learning to deal with differences, enjoying gardening, canoeing, apple picking, Marriage Encounter, Ron and Betty, the huge move to Hawaii, learning to be quieter and indirect, special times with our families, private getaways, and lots of guests, the joys

and struggles of teenage children, the constant challenge of sharing every day for eighteen years. I'm so grateful for your faithfulness, sacrificial love, and supportive friendship and look forward to another eighteen years.

With my loving respect,

Me

Because Kwaj was a relatively safe place, Pam and Dave felt a sense of freedom, and this required a talk. Generous members of the chapel had provided them with bikes of their own, so a curfew was needed—10:30 p.m. on weekdays and 11:00 p.m. on weekends.

We went fishing together and snorkeling, enjoyed picnics, and long walks.

I tried to keep some order to my days and was able to write a paper to fulfill my class requirements for Conflict Management. Colonel Banks, the officer in command, was a believer, and he attended worship and was eager to chat with me over coffee or lunch. It was a special privilege. I honestly cannot remember if we led a few small groups, but we were not there long enough to provide lengthy Bible studies like we did during our first stay.

On our last Saturday, the chapel organized a picnic on Emon Beach. About eighty-five people showed up, and we had a delightful and delicious time together. More than one person drew me aside urging me to consider becoming their permanent chaplain. I guess I thought about it for a little while but soon realized that I was called to pastor a local church. But it was pretty flattering to receive their invitation.

Our last Sunday was August 22. The choir gave us a gift and signed a card expressing their love and gratitude. I distributed the following letter to everyone:

August 22, 1982
Dear Friends,
It has been a real joy being among you all again. The last time we were here, we wondered if

God would grant us the opportunity of a return visit. He did.

We have all felt your love and acceptance through your many expressions of welcome and support.

Thank you for your cordial invitations, generous provision, delicious dinners, loving gifts, and faithful prayers. We sincerely hope to see you when you come through Honolulu and would be delighted to welcome you some Sunday morning at worship. Be certain to let us know if you must be in the hospital, we would make an effort to minister God's grace to you.

May God continue to bless all the families and individuals of the Island Memorial Chapel.

Aloha,
Pastor Rich, Pat, Pam, and David

Recall Vote

While in Kwaj, the church council back home met to discuss the matter of pastoral recall. KUC, like most congregational churches in Hawaii, hired their leadership for a specific time, usually three years, after which the congregation voted whether or not to renew the contract for another three years. We began in March 1977 and was, in 1980, recalled to serve a second three years till 1983.

In August, the council met and voted to set October 3, 1982, as the time for a recall vote. However, the council vote to do so was twenty-four in favor of recall and thirteen against. Two council members abstained. The results of this vote came as a shock to the membership of the council. There was no hint of dissatisfaction, nor public complaint or controversy. "Why?" was the question on many hearts.

Subsequent council meetings voted to work through whatever differences existed, to discuss them openly and find reconciliation.

I was grateful for the council's decision to press toward unity, but sadly that did not happen. There were many reasons for the deterioration of my relationship with a minority of the leadership. Unfortunately I was ignorant of the distance that was growing between us.

I believe that cultural differences played a part. There is a reluctance to confront conflict within the Japanese, and there remained such reluctance among some in the congregation. Some folks consider conflict, or any difference of opinion, to be a sign of the lack of love and therefore sinful. Discussion of difference will only make matters worse. There also developed theological differences between me and a few within the leadership, but we never had opportunity to discuss these.

During my second three-year term of ministry, there had to have been several signals that I missed, misunderstood, or refused to take seriously—signals chiefly from the chairman of the Search Committee who invited me to KUC in 1977. As time went on, I disappointed him, but out of politeness, he didn't say anything to me.

I remember one conversation we had when he wanted to give me some advice about ministering in Hawaii. He said that he was highly invested in my success, as I succeeded, he would too. He said, "When you look good, I look good." Obviously, I do not remember any specific tips he might have shared that afternoon, but I listened and told him I would consider his counsel. All I can conclude is that my less than enthusiastic response to his advice sent the wrong message, and I'm sure that other things I said or did over the next months and years came as another cause of frustration to him.

I also had a hunch that the chair, who was an extremely intelligent man, perceived that I was leading KUC in a direction he believed was dangerous. He assumed that what he had discovered about me from the interview process was all there was to me. I am theologically conservative but seek to remain open to the opinions of others, and this openness made the chair uncomfortable and, I believe, fearful for the future of the congregation.

The chair worked behind the scenes, taking certain people to lunch, talking to staff members and church leaders, and planting seeds of doubt about my fitness to continue. I'm sure that he had spoken to council members prior to their vote back in August, suggesting that there should not be a recall vote that fall. He told the council, "When you buy a car, you should always look under the hood." I remember that one council member spoke up saying that that was an unkind remark. This was very unusual, and rare for anyone to speak back to the chair. His belief was that I had completed my second three-year contract and should move on. I believe that he was probably aware that a recall vote would go in my favor, making it more difficult for him to achieve his goal.

The church council did go forward with the calling for a congregational vote on recall to be held in October 3. After worship, a special meeting was convened by the moderator, and the recommendation of council to recall me was moved and seconded. A secret ballot was called for and the results tallied—227 votes cast, 163 in favor, 61 opposed, and three abstentions, 71.8 percent. The following Sunday, during the announcement period, I spoke to the outcome.

> Last week the congregation voted to retain me as senior pastor for the next three years. To all those who voted to recall me, I offer my gratitude for your support and trust. Pat and I have been encouraged by your calls, cards, and conversations. To those who voted against recall, I am sorry that I have not met your expectations. Please forgive me. I depend upon your love and patience. Please speak to me of your ideas and suggestions. I am eager to hear from you. Finally, to all members and friends of KUC, the vote is over. God's will is clear for the next three years. Let us all seek to be loving to one another.

Here are two paragraphs from my annual report (1982).

> [About the recent recall vote] Let me mention two things: first, a comment from one of you. "I never realized that the work of the church could

be so hard," he continued. "I guess I'll pray more from now on." That brother's comments really encouraged me and I believe his prayers for his church will be more serious and regular. That is a great step in spiritual growth. I believe he represents many of you.

Secondly, someone else pointed out how important relationships are, far more important than programs. I've always believed that. I believe this more firmly now. Our ministry for God's glory grows out of our relationships. Jesus said it long ago in John 13:34–35. I will continue to seek to develop honest, loving relationships with each and every member of the KUC family during the coming years and will depend on you to seek to do the same. Ephesians 4:15 must be our standard, "Speaking the truth in love." How wonderful, how challenging, how rewarding!

Let us move ahead. God has opened the way for us. Let us walk on together.

Pastor Rich

As you can tell, I anticipated three more years as pastor. Sadly, it was not to be.

Mother and Dad had visited us for a second time during those challenging and stressful days. They were there when the vote was taken and were relieved at the outcome, but they both sensed an undercurrent of restlessness in the congregation.

On February 3, 1983, the ceiling caved in. Three leaders came to my office saying that because of continued murmurs and some dissatisfaction among a few staff members—none of whom ever tried to talk to me—I should resign as soon as possible. I was shocked, angry, and fearful about our future. I also had a strong belief that these three came to me because they were forced by strong pressure from one or two other leaders.

During the months since our return from Kwaj, one leader persisted in calling for my resignation. Surprisingly, this call came from the chair of the Pastoral Search Committee who had worked so hard to attract me in the first place.

I have observed, in more than one occasion, that the chair of a committee charged to find a new minister often becomes personally involved in the results of the choice. The chair is tempted to take credit for the new minister's success or blame for the minister's failures. The chair deserves neither, but the fact remains that our spiritual adversary often finds opportunity to plant certain thoughts that become very destructive.

I immediately shared the freighting news with Pat and we decided that I would resign. I did not want to ignite a congregational fight if I decided to remain. I had a strong belief that conflict would arise within the congregation between members who would criticize me and others who would feel the need to defend me. This would be very destructive.

After our decision to leave, I called my parents. Mother and Dad wrote to me in February 5.

> Dear Rich and Pat,
> I have had you on my mind since your call last night and just thought that a word of encouragement would be in order. I'm sure it has been and is a difficult time right now, but I'm also sure that as long as you seek God's guidance along the way, you will know of a surety what God wants for you.
> Keep seeking and asking and don't tire, constant, fervent prayer will ultimately give you the right answer and you will have peace about whatever decision you make.
> I know you must feel rejected—I know I would—but this is all for your good whatever the outcome. I certainly don't have any real wisdom

to give you… I just know that we are praying on this end that God's will may be done.

May God bless and strengthen you both for what is to come. It will be the right thing!

Our love and prayers to all.

Dad and Mother.

Dad added his best,

Some news! I cannot put into words the feeling I have in the pit of my stomach. I know the feeling you two have is much worse… In the days of selling I found that once you sell it—shut up. I truly don't know the answer… I don't know what Mom and I can do but count on us. Keep us informed.

Dad

The following week was Valentine's Day, so Pat made me a card, shaped as a heart, with her picture on the front. "Darling, thank you for working so hard to maintain our love and unity in the Lord. And we'll trust Him for a future full of loving service together." Then she added this verse from Philippians 2:2, "Make my joy complete by being of the same mind, maintaining the same love, united in spirit, intent on one purpose."

The support the Lord provided from my parents and wife was invaluable. Praise God for such loyalty.

In February 25, I wrote to the moderator.

Dear Ken,

After considerable thought and prayer, my wife Pat and I believe it would be best for me to tender my resignation as senior pastor of Kalihi Union Church effective Saturday, June 11, 1983.

A major factor leading to our decision was the recent recall vote of October 3, 1982. Although the percentage of support at both

175

council and congregational levels was adequate in terms of constitutional requirements, it falls below what I would desire and need to continue to serve with joy and confidence.

May God guide you, Ken, as you seek to lead Kalihi Union Church in her search for new pastoral leadership.

Aloha in Christ,
Richard A. Weisenbach

I read the following statement on Sunday morning and included it in the next edition of *Ike Pono*, the church's newsletter.

Resignation, Memories

Dear members and friends of KUC,

Yesterday, February 27, 1983, was my sixth anniversary as pastor. This is a time for reflection, to note with joy, certain steps we've taken together these last few years.

Over 160 have joined our church, 140 of you have been baptized. We have given birth to two congregations, "the Church at Our House" and our Lao Fellowship. We became grandparents with the birth of "the Church at Our House: Aiea."

Another deep joy is to recount those who have gone into full-time service for our Lord, a full dozen: Gail and Dexter, Teruya, Lisa Reh, and Tomi Gibo, all with Liebenzell Missions and Nina Lau-Branson, Scott Tamaoka, and Gay Akamine all in campus ministry. Leonard Leong with Language Institute for Evangelism and Linda Mitchell in Bangladesh. Three others, Gerald Chinen, Carl Imakyure, and Dan Chun, have all taken up pastoral ministry here in Honolulu. God has blessed us and used us. To God be the glory!

Other signs of growth, "inside growth," have also taken place. Many demonstrations of patience, forgiveness, flexibility, sacrifices, generosity, faith, long-suffering, and hope have been evident. God has stretched and refined our faith and I know there are many areas in which He is well pleased.

This is not to say that all that has happened among us is Godly. We know better that that, don't we? The church is a collection of sinners. We are all sinners, from our most mature leader—and only God knows who that is—to the newest baby believer. We are all sinners and we always will be. There has been struggle, disagreement, and tension among us of late. Several of you have sensed it and told me about it.

Ever since our return from Kwajalein last August, there has been a growing sense of uneasiness and dissatisfaction among some of you. The October 3 recall vote invited me to stay for three more years, but I must confess that the results of that vote saddened me. It hurt when I realized that I had disappointed some of you. But I decided to remain among you for three reasons: I felt it was my duty to God to remain at my station; second, I wanted to meet my obligation to all who voted their support; and third, I believed that those who voted otherwise would come to agree with the majority, would yield their desires to the will of God as expressed in the church as a whole. Unfortunately this didn't happen. I have remained a source of pain, disappointment, and embarrassment to some of you. I don't want to be but I know this is the case.

So, as I complete six years of ministry among you, I must also tell you that I cannot accept your kind invitation to continue as your pastor. The vote of last fall indicated a lack of support, which is below what I and the family would need and desire in order to serve you with joy and confidence.

I will be in California for most of March as formerly scheduled and return to the office on the 28th. We will remain here till Monday, June 13, when we will fly to the mainland to take up a new ministry on the East Coast.

I realize that this comes as a shock and cause for anger among some of you. Please trust me in this decision and pray for my future as I will pray for yours.

There is something else you can do—please communicate with your flock leader. He/she has some answers to your questions and an open ear to your complaints. And please speak with compassion to one another. I have sought to do so in all my actions, please seek the same.

Aloha,
Pastor Rich

First Parish Congregational Church, Wakefield, Massachusetts (1983-2013)

Memories of Hawaii, Final Goodbye to KUC, Chronology
of First Parish, Installation, Membership Class, Outreach/
Missions, "Four Seasons," Graduation from Fuller, Stephen
Ministry, 9 a.m. Worship Service, Free Masons, Trust
Funds, Sharing Inc., Thoughts on Baptism, Passion Play,
Serious Conflict, Pastor's Prayer Group, 911, ALPHA, New
Hymnal, Community Dinners, Clothing Closet, Abram
Kielsmeier-Jones, Retirement, Interim Ministry Training

In my message to the congregation on the February 27, I said, "We will remain here till Monday, June 13, when we will fly to the mainland to take up a new ministry on the East Coast." I said that as a step of faith, on February 27, I did not have a clue as to where I might be. It never occurred to me to seek a new position in Hawaii, the East Coast was uppermost in my vision.

I went to our conference minister, Rev. Terry Kawata, asking for his help in finding something. He told me, "Sit down, Rich, and take a number. Six of your colleagues have been looking and waiting for one to two years." He explained that since the Gospel of Jesus Christ was brought to the islands by congregational missionaries from Boston, Massachusetts, the majority of congregational ministers in Hawaii have roots in New England and a few have been waiting to return. This was not very encouraging, to say the least.

I was previously scheduled to take another two courses at Fuller during two weeks in March, but I was too stressed to prepare. I was forced to put my progress toward the degree on hold till I found another position. I tried to think of ways I might use the time to investigate future possibilities. Through friends, I heard of three churches who were looking for a pastor, one in Pennsylvania, one in Connecticut, and one in Massachusetts. I would try to make a contact and maybe even fly east for an interview.

One of the churches was First Parish Congregational Church in Wakefield, Massachusetts. My friend Rev. Westy Egmont told me about the church and their search. In God's timing, they had received my profile back in the fall of 1982.

A member of the First Parish Search Committee had been a minister and was asked to contact his college friend who was now the president of Gordon-Conwell Theological Seminary. The president gave the committee member several names, mine among them. The committee thought I looked interesting, but I was six thousand miles away. "Can't we find someone east of the Hudson River?" They put my name on the bottom of their pile. (I realize now that if the committee from Wakefield had approached me in the fall of 1982, I would have turned them down; after all I had just been recalled at KUC and not looking for a move.)

While in Pasadena with Dr. Barker, I sent my profile to the three churches, telling them that I was planning to fly to the East Coast and was available for an interview if they were interested.

When First Parish received my packet of information, they soon realized that this was the interesting pastor they had encountered back in the fall of 1982 and he wasn't in Hawaii but coming to Massachusetts. They sent me their profile, and in March 16, while sitting at the dining room table in Pasadena, California, we shared a phone interview. It was an extraordinary moment.

On an impulse, I suggested that before the interview proceed, we might pray together. This was an important step for them and me, and we needed God's presence and guidance. I later learned that a member of the committee could not be present, so they taped the interview. Here is the text of my prayer.

Dear God, we are very grateful that you have invited us to be a part of your church, and it is such a privilege to be able to invest our efforts in the work of your Holy Spirit in this world. With all that there is to do and all that we could be spending our time upon, we are grateful that you have given us this chance to deal with important issues, serving your glory and your will in the world.

I thank you for each one of these people, Horace, Ralph, Jean and Jeannette, Ed, and Connie and I thank you for their work in the Wakefield Church. I pray that you will guide our conversation tonight, give us openness, a pursuit of the truth, and a sense of your will. Grant us the courage to proceed in the task you have given to us of finding important leadership for the future. Father, hear our prayer that we pray to you in the name of Jesus. Amen.

I learned later that my suggestion for prayer sent a very powerful message to the committee. It seemed that no other candidate had prayed for them, and they were very touched. I think I was actually pastoring them at that moment. After our conversation, which lasted for over an hour, I ended the conversation saying that I had a ticket for the next morning for the East Coast and that perhaps we could get together.

Within twenty-four hours, Mr. Horace Hylan, committee chair, called to say that the committee was sending me $200.00 toward the cost of my flight, and they wanted to talk as soon as possible.

I flew to Boston that Friday, March 18. Horace met me at the airport and fed me lunch and then a brief visit to the parsonage. Through the kindness of Pastor Greg Meserole, the committee had arranged for me to preach at his church in Dunstable, Massachusetts, that coming Sunday, March 20. God's spirit was evident that morning, and I was grateful to God for the opportunity and the committee was pleased with my manner and preaching. As the committee chairman left the church, he said, "I'm shaking your hand now and won't let you go!" Another committee member, Dick Bryant, the one who missed the interview, said, "Regardless of whether or not you come as our pastor, you have really ministered to me." I was so pleased and grateful to God to hear from these two members.

I drove that evening to Portland, Maine, to attend Tim Ensworth's ordination service. Many were surprised and happy to see me, especially Tim's parents, George and Kathi. I returned to Honolulu, and on Pat's birthday, the chairman called saying that "a call to candidate" was in the mail. About a month later, Pat and I flew back to Massachusetts.

Horace met us at the airport and fed us lunch and then a visit to the parsonage. We had dinner with Ralph and Lennie Peterson and then to the church to meet the committee and other church leaders. I preached that Sunday, April 24.

After the service, Pat and I were escorted to the Fireside Room to wait with Charlie Willis while the Search Committee presented their choice for the new minister of First Parish Congregational Church. The vote of the congregation was unanimous, and we returned to the sanctuary greeted by a standing ovation. I spoke briefly expressing our gratitude to the committee and then quoted Psalm 34:3, "Glorify the Lord with me; let us exalt His name together," the verse Pat and I had inscribed inside out wedding rings. We returned to KUC, eager to share our good news.

Most everyone was grateful and happy that we had found a new ministry, and even those who believed that we should leave were relieved, for they were certain that God would provide for our future. These few never thought that I was a poor pastor, but they were certain that I was no longer the best fit for KUC.

I wrote updates in the April, May, and June in *Ike Pono*. Here is a summary.

April

I was able to meet with three churches in the New England area who are presently looking for new pastoral leadership. It would be presumptuous to speak too soon but, Lord willing, I'll have good news by the first of May.

Meanwhile, back here at home, Pat kept me posted on how kind and considerate so many of you were with your visits, calls, and letters. Thank you dear friends for your kindness and understanding. Your prayers for us are being answered. God is providing and exchanging our pain and fear into joy and hope.

May

I am happy to report to you all that while in Massachusetts, on the weekend of April 24, I received an invitation from a congregational church in Wakefield, Massachusetts, to be their pastor. We will begin ministry on August 1.

June

I've been sending boxes of books to the East Coast for about a month now, and Pat is preparing for moving day, Friday, May 27. We plan to take six weeks before August 1 to camp across the mainland.

To give you a better idea of where we will be living and serving, I'll be sharing some slides of the church and parsonage on Wednesday, June 8, during our regular prayer and Bible study hour. Please come if you have the time.

Our last Sunday was June 5, and it was very special with a full sanctuary sharing communion and expressing grateful praise. The leaders called the family up to the dais and presented us with a financial gift ($4,000.00) to cover about half of our travel expenses. Then an invitation was extended to the congregation to come forward and extend their hands toward our family as a symbol of unity and love. The service was followed by a delicious luncheon.

I wrote the following thank-you note for their newsletter:

> Dear friends,
> My entire family joins me in expressing a deeply felt thank you for your generous gift toward our travel and moving expenses. The service of worship last Sunday will remain in our memories for many years to come. Special thanks to all who provided their favorite food for such a delicious luncheon. I want to mention Tomu Nakamura who was responsible for the whole event and Larry McCracken who planned the service with me. I am also grateful to Vernon Von for his challenging words and thoughtful prayer of farewell.
> May God continue to watch over us all whether we are near or far away.
>
> Aloha,
> Pastor Rich, Pat, Pamela,
> David, and Kimberly

It is truly a sign of God's grace that we were able to secure a place of ministry back in New England in such a short amount of time. It was just fifty-six days between the Sunday I resigned from KUC and the receiving of a call to First Parish (February 27-April 24). This transition from KUC to First Parish was extraordinary and served as undeniable evidence of God's hand in leading our lives. Because of this expression of God's faithfulness, we were fortified to face any future challenge.

Our departure in June 13 was very memorable. I couldn't count how many were there at the airport to send us off that afternoon, but our necks and arms were draped with leis, both floral and seed. We also received many cards and financial gifts. We spent hours on the plane ride opening and recording all the greetings.

As Pat and I left, we experienced such a mixture of feelings. There was relief from the criticism of a few, sadness for the many who felt deserted and confused, excitement about our new call, and eagerness to see the sites as we drove across the country.

Memories of Hawaii

As the years passed, God has cleansed our minds of those dark times. Our present memories have centered on the uniqueness of the islands and her people. As we look back over the years, smiles of gratitude fill our hearts, as God did have another opportunity for us. Our years at KUC did prepare us for a thirty-year ministry among a new congregation needing what we could bring.

Hawaii will always fill a special place in our hearts, and we are so grateful to God for allowing us to live there for six years. The weather, the music, the flowers, the food, the floral leis, the rainbows, the colorful clothes, and all the loving people add to the joy of the place. And the special memories of visiting some of the world's most beautiful hotels, resorts, beaches, and attractions.

Then there were the trips to neighbor islands to attend the annual *Aha Mokupuni*, the gathering of all the churches on Oahu, and the annual *Aha Paeina*, the gathering of all the congregations in all the islands.

Most memorable were the few times Pat and I escaped to special places on neighbor islands. We were so privileged to spend a few days at Kuilima on the north shore, the Kahala Hilton, Hale Koa, Halekulani, and of course the Royal Hawaiian where we were treated to the best room in the house, really! It was complete with the seal of Hawaii carved in the door, a huge lanai, Jacuzzi, and towels that had to be two inches thick.

Pat and I have often remarked that one of the many benefits of ministering in Hawaii was the opportunity to share our great country with the children. We drove west in 1977 and east in 1983. What a treat! After our arrival in Pennsylvania, I sat at the picnic table in Mother and Dad's porch and wrote a letter to KUC recounting our cross-country adventure.

Final Goodbye to KUC

Dear Friends,

It is a beautiful July morning here in Pennsylvania, and I'm reflecting back to just one month ago. How busy we all were as we anticipated the big move to our new place of ministry in New England. We are so grateful to God for His superintendence of every detail of the move and trip.

After a very exciting and somewhat confusing three hours at the airport in Honolulu, we boarded the plane with your floral leis up to our noses and draped on our arms. We all felt so rushed as we said our final farewells to so many of you. Our love and gratitude for each other had to be spoken without words; there wasn't enough time. But your presence, your gifts, your letters, and your eyes told us what was in your hearts. We found our seats on the plane and opened your cards and read for hours. We all thank you for a memory which will remain with us always.

After two days in California, retrieving our Chevy Suburban and spending a final day with Dr. Glenn Barker, we headed northwest to Yosemite National Forest. Here is an abbreviated list of the highlights: the California gold rush town of Columbia, the Grand Tetons, Jackson Hole, Wyoming, a raft ride on the Snake River,

Yellowstone and "Old Faithful," Custer State Park, Wall Drug, Mount Rushmore, the Corn Palace in Rapid City, Iowa, then friends in MN, WI, OH, and PA. Then a tour of Gettysburg National Monument. Our final stop was at Hershey Park in PA. Pat announced that because she was tired, and she would stay in the car. I said, "Nothin' doing!" "We are going to have some family fun!" And we did. After twenty-seven days and four thousand eight hundred and twenty-two miles, we arrived at my parent's home.

God's protection and provision were evident throughout every mile. We were sideswiped by a hit-and-run driver, had to buy a new battery when ours exploded, and finally were forced to replace our fuel pump. But each event was cushioned by God's care and became a reason to pull to the side of the road, join hands and say, "Thank you, Lord."

We will drive to Wakefield, MA, at the end of this month and begin unpacking. Our furniture shipment arrived ahead of us and awaits our attention. Fortunately we'll have lots of help.

Please know of our deep and enduring gratitude to each of you for the six years of ministry God granted us—to God be the glory! May God bless you this summer and fall as you seek His will for the future by loving each other for His sake.

Aloha in Christ,
Pastor Rich, Pat, Pam, Dave, and Kim

In May 15, Horace wrote a letter reflecting on our weekend together, the congregational vote, and his joy and excitement. He concluded, "Twenty-eight more days and counting! May the sorrow of your leaving be tempered by the love of God and a host of new friends. May your journey across this great land be filled with joy and wonder. And may your arrival here be another glorious beginning in His service. Love, Horace."

Horace was so excited about our arrival that he went ahead and had my name carved in the oak panel listing the names and tenure of all twenty-one previous ministers. Seeing that was very humbling to say the least. I wept tears of gratitude.

I'm certain Horace's joy and enthusiasm waned a bit over our thirty years at First Parish, but he remained a very faithful member of the congregation, contributing his time and talent in many ways. His vision for the church to present a *Passion Play* during Holy Week has remained for almost thirty years. He was also the main force behind our memorial garden. I was very grateful that he did not fall to the mindset other Search Committee chairs suffered.

After seventeen years, Dr. John Prescott Robertson resigned from his position as senior pastor on Easter Sunday 1982. The council appointed seven members to serve as the Search Committee and elected Horace Hylan to be their chair.

During the first few months of my first year, Horace confessed that he had become very concerned about the future of his church. He shared that on one particular Sunday morning, as he served as usher, he glanced over the congregation and said to himself, *There are too many gray heads. We must do something, something major.*

Dr. Verne Henderson, interim minister, had written in *the Church Herald*, "There is some danger that First Parish will become a church *of* retired people run *by* retired people *for* retired people… There seem to be large numbers of young people floating in and around First Parish but it is not so clear that we have woven their presence and interests into the fabric of our life."

Both Verne and Horace were reflecting on the last decade and a half of the church's life. A few facts include church attendance slipping from 374 to 192, income growing but less that one-half the rate of inflation, and membership sliding from 1,333 to 728. In the seventeen years of Dr. John's ministry, only two years showed growth. Deacons, trustees, and pastor were all frustrated and unable to determine what needed to be done.

Dr. Verne Henderson served First Parish as interim minister from May 1982 to August 1983. In his last, "From the Pastor's Desk," he shared his thoughts on how to welcome a new minister.

> As you prepare to establish a helpful and happy relationship between yourselves and your new minister, may I suggest a few ideas.
>
> One, pray for him and build spiritual power for you both. Two, be patient in your hopes and expectations of him and anticipate the same patience from him. Each of us has a history which explains our thoughts and actions. We do not really know each other until we know something of that history. Three, get to know him and his family. Four, build his leadership and morale by supporting him with your presence at worship, your faithfulness to the covenant you share, your pledges of time, talent and treasure. Five, pray, always, that you may find additional ways for your relationship to be a helpful and stimulating one.
>
> May God be with you in your new adventure,
> Verne Henderson

I did have opportunity to spend some time with Verne before he left. He passed on three issues that I would have to deal with as soon as possible—first the custodian was an alcoholic, second one of the ushers was a thief who enjoyed touching young girls, and third a bossy woman in an effort to "help" tried to control wedding rehearsals and wedding ceremonies.

After a few visits to a rehabilitation facility in October 1983, we had to retire the custodian in May 1984. At offering time, the usher would grab a plate and race to the balcony to gather the collection. On his way down, he would help himself to some cash, but he was exposed and removed from the usher committee. In May, the "helpful" lady resigned to care for her aging husband. Thank the Lord!

While still in Honolulu, I began work on a DMin degree at Fuller Theological Seminary in Pasadena, California. This course of study required the writing of a dissertation on a subject pertinent to the congregation of the student.

I had planned to investigate the possibility of developing a multiethnic congregation on the campus of KUC. We were already welcoming four distinct congregations every Sunday, English, Japanese, Lao, and Filipino. Could a structure be formed combining these four into one congregation, sharing facilities, staff, finances, and constitution? This was my original hope when I began the program.

When I left KUC, that vision had to be set aside. Arriving in Wakefield, Massachusetts, a new subject had to be developed. First Parish was 339 years old when we arrived. The 350th anniversary was not too far off. Why not dig into the history of this historic church and plot a plan for a fitting celebration?

Ordinarily the school expects the DMin student to complete work in five years, but exceptions are made when a student leaves his church and takes up ministry at another. I requested an extension of my time due to our move and introduced a new dissertation topic. Thankfully, both requests were approved.

I took three more courses during the summer of 1985 and the winter of 1986, "Church Growth I and II" and "the Training of the Laity." My dissertation topic dealt with the history of First Parish and how we might prepare to celebrate our 350th anniversary.

Because the church's history is so long, I will highlight just a few events. (For anyone wanting a fuller account, they might read my dissertation; a copy is the church's library.)

A Selected Chronology of First Parish

> 1644 First Parish organized by forty-one men and women and Rev. Henry Green called and ordained
> 1645 First meetinghouse built, corner of Main and Albion (served for forty-four years)
> 1648 Pastor Green dies

1679 The Cambridge Platform affirmed by First Parish

1689 Second meetinghouse erected (building served for eighty years)

1692 Four women accused of witchcraft

1713 Decision to "free all citizens of the community from required support of the church"

1720 First daughter church planted (present-day Lynnfield); second daughter church planted (North Reading)

1729 Third daughter church planted (present-day Stoneham)

1733 Fourth daughter church planted (present-day Wilmington)

1734 The Great Awakening

1741 George Whitfield preaches on the common

1751 Pastor Hobby rides to Northampton to defend Jonathan Edwards

1769 Third meetinghouse erected (served for 122 years)

1770 Fifth daughter church planted (present-day Reading)

1775 Pastor Caleb Prentiss shoulders his musket and marches to the battle of Concord and Lexington

1818 Sunday school started

1839 Women allowed to listen in at church meetings

1860 Church purchases first organ

1892 Fourth meetinghouse erected—large stone structure

1909 Meetinghouse burns, Sunday, February 27 (served for seventeen years), only stone walls remained

1912 Fifth meetinghouse dedicated

1919 Mortgage burned, February 21

1940 Women allowed to attend and vote at church meetings

1944 300th anniversary

1949 Women's Guild formed

1953 Church addition including Covell Chapel dedicated

1983 Rev. Dr. Richard A. Weisenbach installed as twenty-second pastor

1984 Council votes "with deep regret to eliminate all financial support to the Mass Conference of the United Church of Christ"

1988 Board of deacons and board of deaconesses combine forming a diaconate

1990 Church unity disrupted by the request and behavior of members of the Masonic Lodge

1992 First *Passion Play* presented to the community

1994 350th anniversary

1997 Petition to remove the pastor

1998 Congregational vote sustains the pastor

1999 Second attempt to remove the pastor, but congregational vote sustains the pastor again

2006 First Parish becomes dually affiliated with CCCC and the UCC

2015 Congregation votes to leave the UCC

2013 Reverend Weisenbach retires

2018 Congregation votes to honor Reverend Weisenbach as Pastor Emeritus

2019 Congregation calls Rev. John Dale as twenty-third pastor.

I said there was a lot of history!

The Church Herald is the name of the newsletter of First Parish. Here is what I wrote after one month into the job.

"O magnify the Lord with me, and let us exalt Him together!" (Psalm 34:3)

This verse from scripture comes so quickly to my mind as I consider the leading and blessing of God in my life over the last six months. God has indeed shown great care and love toward me and my family and I would heartily call each and every one of you to join me in praising God together!

He has brought us back to New England, back to the north shore, back to so many people and places that mean so much to Pat and me. The safety we experienced over the eight thousand plus miles, the financial support we received from First Parish, the generous gifts from so many of God's children in Honolulu, the safe and timely arrival of our furniture, and the gracious welcome we received from all of you, the full pantry, the new refrigerator and garbage disposal, the home-cooked meals from the Board of Deaconesses, and of course your open-hearted reception of us all this first month here in Wakefield. Truly, "Our cups overflow" and we thank God and you.

As at KUC, we held "cottage meetings" hosted by members of the board of deacons and board of deaconesses. This along with name tags for a month or so and a church pictorial directory, initiated by seminary student Robert Woodward, helped us to get acquainted.

Installation

Arrangements were made to have a service of installation scheduled for Sunday, November 27. I wrote about this special event in *the Church Herald*.

Next Sunday evening people will come to First Parish from most of the churches here in Wakefield, folks from several sister UCC congregations in the Metropolitan Boston Association and lots of guests and friends. We haven't had a service like this in almost twenty years. The choir will be singing two special numbers. Ed Nutting and Forrest Musser will join us along with Robert Woodyard and Dennis Carter. [Reverend Nutting and Reverend Musser were former members of the First Parish Staff, and Robert and Dennis were students at GCTS who were serving in the church.] The preacher is Dr. George Ensworth, long-time friend and professor of Pastoral Psychology at Gordon-Conwell. Rev. Dr. Westy Egmont, pastor of South Church in Andover, will pray the Prayer of Installation. Rev. Bill Keech of First Baptist, Wakefield, will bring a personal challenge to me, and Rev. Chuck Harper, the UCC Associate Conference Minister, will represent the denomination. It will be a great night! Members of our family will be attending, including my mother and dad. I sincerely trust you will come. It all begins at 7:00 p.m.

It was a very special evening and timed to begin the new church year the next Sunday.

We ended our first five months with an invitation to come to the parsonage for a Christmas open house. Pat had been preparing for days and offered lots of goodies, many with a Hawaiian flavor. We continued this tradition for the next twenty-nine years enjoying the fellowship of the congregation. Such events provide a great opportunity to build greater closeness among church members and friends. Of course we could never do this without the planning and work of Pat. As the years passed, many of the congregation began bringing personal contributions to the table and even lingering to clean up.

A significant sign of growth occurred in January 1984 when the results of the stewardship drive were announced. Our pledges totaled $108,000.00, an increase of $14,000.00 (18 percent). The average pledge increased from $4.73 to $5.63. The budget that year was $164,000.00; building rental, the church fair, and trust fund income made up the difference. The $14,000.00 increase that year was equal to the increases over the past ten years. We were experiencing God's blessings! During those first two years, I felt as though I was walking through the congregation with a watering can. Everywhere I looked, I saw positive signs.

Membership Class

I also announced that in January, a class leading to church membership would be offered. Before the class began, I raised a few questions with the board of deacons about the way members were welcomed. I learned that there wasn't any formal class. The board said, "Dr. John took care of that." I reminded the board that according to their constitution, they, the board of deacons, were responsible for how new members were to be prepared and welcomed.

I suggested that a class taught by me might be the best way to proceed. This class would stretch over four weeks, ending with the candidates appearing before the board, each sharing something of their Christian beliefs and reasons for choosing First Parish as their new spiritual home. The majority reaction upon hearing of my plan was immediate rejection.

"Pastor, we need more members. You would be making it more difficult by putting up hurdles! Do you expect that people will actually speak out loud about their faith?"

Some discussion followed of course, and then Deacon Matthews Jacobs said, "The pastor has used this plan in his previous churches. Let's try it once." They agreed and I was much relieved.

As you might figure out, there were a sizable number of folks from the community who were actually waiting to see who the church would hire as their new minister. A number began attending and remained once they realized the direction the church might take under new leadership. Several of those joined that first class.

When the class ended, the board gathered after morning worship in the Fireside Room and were joined by the candidates. I had prepared them to answer two questions, "What does Jesus mean to me?" and "Why do I want to join First Parish?" I went around the room giving each candidate the opportunity to share their answers. As the discussion continued, the board heard very heartwarming testimonies from those who spoke. Tears began to flow from the speakers and even from a few deacons. After the sharing ended, a deacon had to make a motion to welcome the candidates as new members, have it seconded, and then voted upon. That motion passed unanimously, and the candidates were welcomed the next Sunday. The board became convinced that this was a very good way to prepare and welcome new members.

It was a moving moment and I believe a critical corner was turned. Scores of classes and hundreds of members were added during the thirty years that followed.

Over the years, the class format changed to a single Saturday, 9:00 a.m.–3:00 p.m., with personal sharing, teaching, a tour and some history of our building, lunch served by the board, and a concluding session.

Dr. John Robertson participated very little in the activities, meetings, and workshops of the UCC while he was pastor. I was unaware of that when I arrived. I assumed that a church the size and reputation of First Parish would keep abreast of denominational doings.

I attended monthly meetings of local UCC clergy, both spring and fall meetings of the Metropolitan Boston Association, and the Annual Meeting of the Massachusetts Conference. I reported back to the leadership concerning the decisions of the denomination, thinking that they would appreciate an update. Upon hearing of the recent motions and directions of the conference, they were surprised and disappointed.

This disagreement led to a major decision of the church council to withhold and redirect all missions dollars, about $12,000.00 at the time. We would continue to pay our dues but nothing more. This action led to a significant boost to the congregation's need to reestablish a committee to investigate new outreach opportunities. It also initiated a string of letters from fellow clergy who were highly critical of this decision.

I remember our moderator, Bob Sproul, telling me of his desire to reestablish the Outreach Committee. Years earlier, the church voted to disband the committee because funds were sent to the UCC. "How the money is spent is out of our hands." There seemed to be little effort to investigate how the church might reach out to the local community.

With new energy and financial resources, an Outreach Committee was formed with Ann Ludlow serving as chair. I started introducing possibilities for ministry, and this of course was another crucial step in our growth.

There were staff changes that first year too. One of the two secretaries left in January, and the custodian was dismissed in May. Interim personnel were appointed, and by the fall, we were back to a full complement.

A more significant change occurred when Robert Woodyard graduated and left to pastor a church in Wisconsin. Robert had come to First Parish in 1981 as assistant to the minister. He told me how privileged he felt during the three years he was there. He said, "I got to observe a pastor's resignation, a search committee working, the functioning of an interim minister, and finally the installation of a new pastor."

He and his family left us in July and I was invited in October to preach the sermon at his installation as pastor of First Presbyterian Church of Cedar Grove, Wisconsin. He has since served congregations in Oklahoma City, Oklahoma, and he is now serving in Lynden, Washington. Their son Todd was born while they were with us, and now they have five boys and a grandchild, with more on the way I'm sure.

I believe God used him to help prepare the way for the changes that would come when we arrived. I thank God for Robert and Phama and their witness while at First Parish.

There was little opportunity for adult Christian education, so we introduced a six-week opportunity to gather during Lent. Several families invited others to come to their living room, "Living Rooms for Lent." This helped spur expanded classes for adults in the future.

There were also changes in the order of worship. The announcements were moved to the beginning of the service rather than in the middle and the pastoral prayer and offering were placed after the sermon as an opportunity to respond to the Word preached.

A second change was the addition of a worship service on Wednesday evenings during the nine weeks of summer. Going away for the weekend is a New England custom. Wednesday worship, a repeat of the previous Sunday, would meet a need. These changes were kept in place for thirty years.

Each member of the family found activities to help them get settled into this new community. Pat began to teach ESL through the library, Pam won the lead in the senior play *Pippin*, Dave began working at Brothers restaurant, and Kim began studies in American Sign Language.

For the record, I performed twenty-nine funerals, thirty-two baptisms, and thirty weddings (including Ron and Pearl Geho, née O'Brien, in October 1) during my first seventeen months. Worship attendance hovered between 280 and three hundred.

We also were able to squeeze in two weeks for vacation at Lily Bay, Moosehead Lake, Maine. We rented a boat that year and also attended the Kiwanis Auction. Fun!

I have always strongly believed that the loving relationships a congregation forms will result in positive activities and programs. The annual meeting was such an opportunity. We ate together, we honored those of our church family who have been members for fifty years or more, and we publicly thanked those committee/board members who were retiring after their term of service.

I also began the custom of calling all the newly elected members forward on the Sunday after the meeting to place a cleaning cloth on their shoulder as a symbol of servanthood.

I always found this a clear demonstration of Jesus's action on the evening of his last supper. "He got up from the meal, took off his outer clothing, and wrapped a towel around his waist. After that, he poured water into a basin and began to wash the disciples' feet, drying them with the towel which was wrapped around him" (John 13:3–5). I looked each committee member in the eye, shook their hand, and placed the towel on their shoulder, trying to emphasize the servanthood aspect of their elected responsibility.

The church council voted to begin a search to hopefully hire a full-time associate by September. We went looking and seriously considered hiring Rev. Tim Ensworth. He was interested, but in the end, he chose to remain in Scarborough, Maine. He loved the outdoor opportunities the state afforded him, and he had become heavily involved in the Outdoor Ministries Committee of the Maine Conference of the UCC. The last I heard, he and Lynn were ministering in Waterloo, Iowa. Later we made contact with Doug and Teresa Tueting, and he was hired as associate pastor in September.

There were two more changes in the staff that year. After eight years at the keyboard, Alice LaFleur resigned in February as our organist and was replaced by Ms. Martha Sobaje.

Martha was the director of Choral Activities at Barrington College in Rhode Island. When Barrington College merged with Gordon College, she moved to Wenham, Massachusetts, and assumed similar duties at her new position. We were very fortunate to find and hire her. She is a very capable musician. Unfortunately she served us for only three years returning to her home church, Phillips Memorial Baptist Church in Cranston, Rhode Island.

A second charge was the departure of Dennis and Christine Carter. The Carters arrived at First Parish a few months before we did. Dennis led our worship services, preached occasionally, and conducted a few funerals. He was a great help, especially when Robert left. Chris was instrumental, along with Brenda Young, in the forming of the Wednesday Women's Bible Study. They returned to Cincinnati, Ohio, and their last Sunday was September 8.

In April 7, a fifteen-year-old high school student committed suicide. He did this terrible act in front of his best friend who was also a member of our youth group. The superintendent of the Wakefield Schools called me asking if I would be willing to conduct a funeral service for the student. He mentioned that he was planning to have the entire student body attend, and our sanctuary was large enough to accommodate the crowd.

I believe that the Lord enabled me to write and deliver a word of comfort and witness to all in attendance. It was a great privilege.

Outreach/Missions

The newly organized Outreach Committee realized that First Parish needed to be educated about the Great Commission. Jesus said, "All authority in heaven and on earth has been given to me. Therefore go and make disciples of all nations, baptizing them in the name of the Father and of the Son and of the Holy Spirit, and teaching them to obey everything I have commanded you. And surely I will be with you always, to the very end of the age" (Matthew 28:18–20).

To begin this educational process, we invited about a dozen men and women to our sanctuary and vestry on Sunday, April 28, to give us a clearer understanding of the need and opportunities to bear witness to the gospel in both word and deed. Each mission/missionary was given space in our vestry for a table to display information.

The preacher that morning was Rev. Mike Berg, general director of the Latin American Mission. I don't recall any specifics aside from the general belief that the day provided a strong boost to the congregation's understanding and responsibilities toward obeying an important command from Jesus Christ.

A second decision made by the committee and approved by the council was to distribute throughout the community of Wakefield the special offerings received at Thanksgiving, Christmas, and Christmas Eve. This was a big change since the money collected at these special holidays had always gone to the church's budget. I recall being strongly criticized by a member of the board of trustees for my leadership in this regard.

In June, I restarted my degree program at Fuller and was grateful that two of the courses I needed were offered by Dr. Peter Wagner at Eastern College, Philadelphia. I left home on Father's Day and discovered this note from Pat in my luggage.

> You are not my father, but you are an important man in my life. There have been times when you have patiently fathered me and I'm grateful for your commitment to me and our children. We appreciate your time and energy, often given sacrificially, and we thrive in your love. We all look forward to having you home again in several weeks... Life is never as vital with you gone.
>
> We're proud of your quest for excellence and hope you will be positively stimulated by your study.
>
> Missing you and loving you.
>
> Me

On Sunday, July 14, we received a call from the World Relief Commission (WRC) asking us to provide temporary housing and lots of love and support for two Cambodian families who, after six years in a camp in Thailand, were headed to New England.

Rita and Ron Messina, who have hosted and sponsored refugee families in the past, called Scott and Evelyn McCullough and Pat and me. The ten new arrivals were met at Logan Airport and brought to Wakefield. We kept one family of five for a few days till it was suggested that the families, who are related, might do better if they would be together. The move was made and all ten, four adults and six children, moved in with the McCullough family until September. Our Outreach Committee committed to pay $2,100.00 for a deposit and first month's rent for an apartment in Lynn. The deacon's funds were used as well to help with immediate needs. The congregation was becoming aware and responsive to ministry opportunities. Praise the Lord!

In September, I was surprised to receive a letter from James Morentz, editor of *the Minister's Annual,* published by Abington Press. Somehow he had gotten my name and invited me to submit a sermon for publication. I sent him a few and was informed that he was eager to print eight sermons in three editions of *the Minister's Annual* for the years 1988, 1989, and 1990. I felt very privileged. I am unaware of anything that ever came of this adventure.

By 1985, it became clear to me that there were scores of church members who understood very little about beginning and maintaining a personal relationship with Jesus Christ through the power of the Holy Spirit. I began to raise the issue as early as April 1984.

Here is part on an article I wrote for *the Church Herald.*

> Many today are converted to the phenomena surrounding Christianity, the music, the architecture, the ritual, the eloquence of the preacher, the community standing—"It's the thing to do." But despite these outward behaviors, there is no vital saving contact with the saving Person— Jesus Christ. It's all second hand and marginal. It's an echo instead of a voice. They haven't ever given themselves to God in confession obedience and trust... These are "half-conversions."

And again in November, I wrote, "We need to know what we believe and why we believe it."

I have often thought that what I began preaching was quite new to about 60 percent of the congregation. In my mind, I divided those folks into three groups.

- Those who said, "This is new and I want to learn more."
- Those who said, "This is new and I'm not sure I agree, but I'll listen for a while."

- Those who said, "This is new and I don't agree but this new minister won't be around for too much longer."

As the years went by, many responded to the gospel's call. Others realized that I was going to stay longer than they suspected and began looking for the opportunity to voice their opposition. By God's grace, changes were coming, and by God's grace, the changes occurred and brought blessings.

We got to Moosehead again, only that year we began going during Valentine's Day as well as our anniversary day. We tried Casey's Camps that year and the next two.

And for the record, I conducted eight weddings, twenty-four funerals, and twenty-seven baptisms.

I began 1986 by writing about New Year's resolutions, our goals for the coming twelve months.

> It is a great idea, but let's face it, we rarely follow through. But God has goals too and He has promised that He will complete what He has promised for His children (Philippians 1:6).

Then I listed six goals God is determined to fulfill.

1. To remove our sins from us as far is the east is from the west (Psalm 103:12)
2. To be with us forever (Matthew 28:20)
3. To protect us from all harm (1 Thessalonians 1:7)
4. To provide us with wisdom necessary for the moment (James 1:7)
5. To prepare a place for us for eternity (John 14:6)
6. To return to this earth and receive us unto Himself (John 14:3)

On Sunday, January 26, I flew to Fuller for my last class, "Training of the Laity for Ministry." Two memorable events are connected to that week. It was this class that introduced me to Stephen

Ministries. We would eventually enroll our congregation in this excellent program, bringing great blessing to our people.

The other event occurred on Tuesday, January 28. The NASA shuttle orbiter mission and the tenth flight of Space Shuttle Challenger broke apart seventy-three seconds into its flight, killing all seven crew members, which consisted of five NASA astronauts, one payload specialist, and a civilian schoolteacher from Concord, New Hampshire, named Christa McAuliffe. She was thirty-seven years old. This tragedy was caused by the failure of O-ring seals used in the joint that were not designed to handle the unusually cold conditions that existed at this launch. Space Shuttle flights were grounded for almost three years. One study reported that 85 percent of Americans had heard the news within an hour of the accident. I was in class when the news broke.

We continued to emphasize the importance of helping others and sharing the gospel message, so we established a food pantry and we offered another mission fair. The note in *the Church Herald* read,

> The Outreach Committee has invited several mission organizations to participate in the morning worship service in April 27. The following will be present to inform us of their work for Jesus Christ: Wycliffe Bible Translators (WBT), Central American Mission (CAM), Kingston House in Boston, International Students, Heifer Project, the Salvation Army, Wakefield Unit, and Bethany Christian Services. These missionaries will have a display booth in the vestry and would like to meet you individually prior to and following the morning service.

Rev. Chester Franz of WBT and Pat's brother Jack O'Brien of CAM shared the preaching.

It was announced in September that we were able to direct $3,000.00 toward the construction and furnishing of Kingston House's new conference room. Kingston House is in the center of

Boston and provides care for people living on the street. In November, Dr. Milton Friesen, who lived across the street from the church and was director of Kingston House, preached and thanked us for our gift. I remember that he informed us that one of the greatest needs of those they seek to serve was underwear.

One of the growing edges of any Christian is their relationship with money. A mature believer is naturally grateful for all of God's blessings and is eager to share those blessings with others. How First Parish dealt with money became a focus of my leadership at both the committee level and the pulpit. The fall was always the time to have a stewardship campaign and the ideal time to address the subject. I wrote the following for *the Church Herald* in October:

> I think that one of the greatest dangers that can occur around November is to think that First Parish is just raising money so she can pay her bills. That attitude is the worst possible attitude! If that is all we are about, we could reduce our bills real fast—stop a lot of what we are doing: reduce the staff, curtail our ministry and outreach, and just "pay as we go." But our calling from God to be the church is much more challenging, far more difficult and far more fulfilling than just financial survival. We are called to preach the good news of salvation, lift the fainthearted, heal the sick, train the youth, comfort the distressed, reconcile the stranger, reach out to the lonely, and announce hope to the despairing. Our task is to effect lives, and there are many lives that need the touch of God's love. We are all challenged at this time of year because the needs and opportunities are so great. And having received so great a salvation from the Savior, it is only natural to give back. "Love makes sacrifice a pleasure."

Albert & Ruth Weisenbach
April 15, 1939

The Weisenbach Boys 1952

Rich—Muhlenberg College Football 1962

Pat's graduation Germantown Dispensary and Hospital 1964

Our Wedding—August 8, 1964

Union Congregational Church, Magnolia 1966–1971

Kim, Pam & Dave—Magnolia 1971

Dick and Jean Cook
Our youth leaders

Dr. Glenn & Marge Barker—Gordon Divinity School

Pastor Abram & Sarah
Kielmeier—Jones—Union Congregational Church

Jane & Frank Severns Childhood & Phila. College
of Bible friends Missionaries with SEND

West Congregational Church—Peabody, MA 1971–1977

Ed & Charlane Chapman—West Church

Dean & Jane Pedersen, Sandy & Ed Whitmen "4 seasons" friends

On our way to HI '77

Off to HI

Arriving in Hi.—March 1977

Kalihi Union Church Honolulu, HI 1977-83

Rich at Kalihi Union Church 1977

Kim, Dave and Pam, 1977

Memorial Chapel, Kwajalein, Micronesia

First Parish Congregational Church—Wakefield 1983–2013

First Parish Parsonage—Wakefield

The O'Brien's 50th Wedding Anniversary 1990

Rich's graduation from Fuller Seminary—D Min
with Pat & Ruth & Albert Weisenbach 1987

The Weisenbachs—Rich, Bill, Paul, Dave & Mother and Dad. 2002

The Weisenbachs at Pete & Christine's wedding

Our Treasures—Brian & Kim, Pam & Gadar, Dave & Sharon

Gram Weisenbach with her grandchildren & great grandchildren 2007

First Parish Thursday Morning Bible Study Women

Pat Sharing scrapbooking & card making at the Topsfield Fair

The O'Brien Clan at Dad's 90th Birthday 2010

Magnolia Shore

Moosehead Lake 2018

Our family as of June 2019—celebrating Nate
& Marisa's Wedding, Saco, ME

On February 24, 1937, our church held a banquet commemorating the silver anniversary of occupancy of the fifth meetinghouse. The dinner launched a campaign to raise $25,000.00. They had several projects in mind, and new carpet in the sanctuary was a priority. It would cost $5,000.00. That was fifty years ago, and the carpet they laid needs replacing.

So in November 2, we launched our own campaign to raise $19,000.00 in sixty days, aiming to have the project completed by February of the next year, the seventy-fifth anniversary of the fifth meetinghouse.

The men of the congregation saved thousands of dollars by removing all the pews. It was a peculiar sight to see the sanctuary completely empty. By God's grace, we dedicated the new carpet on the seventy-fifth anniversary of our fifth meetinghouse in November.

By the middle of 1986, I had completed three years as senior pastor. The congregation was responding to my leadership, and things seemed very positive. Our attendance, membership, and finances were growing. We were developing healthy relationships, we were becoming more aware of the needs of the world around us, and folks seemed more open to the idea of gathering in small groups to study the Bible. We were welcoming visitors almost every week. And we had just hired a full-time associate pastor that past September. God was blessing!

But as any employer knows, hiring new staff is always a challenge, and one can never be sure of the choice. This was the case with our associate minister.

In our memory, the interview went smoothly, the references checked out, agreement was reached, and everyone was hopeful about the future. But after a few months, unexpected events occurred. A key relationship was harmed, strange habits surfaced, and professional counseling was recommended and engaged.

Soon the board of deacons appointed a special committee of three to talk directly about what seemed to be happening. Confidentiality was observed to protect those involved, but some in the congregation called it secrecy. Mistrust arose, and people started asking questions but did not receive satisfying answers. Finally an announcement was made, and a letter of resignation was written and read on a Sunday morning. People were surprised, some were shocked, and others were angry, especially parents of children who were in the youth group.

I have learned that when God blesses an individual or church family, Satan is not pleased and at an opportune moment will attack, sowing discord. I believe that is what happened that July when we were forced to remove our newly hired associate pastor after only one year.

Our associate resigned and left First Parish in September 14. It was a very difficult time. Our moderator resigned leaving us to find a replacement for his final four months. At least one family left the church. We lost the leadership of the senior high youth group. He was doing a good job and the youth became attracted to him and his wife. Our youth were hurt and confused by the action of the church leadership. We were attacked that year and would be again in the years to come.

We met the budget and ended the year with a $7,000.00 surplus. We were raising money to install a new carpet in the sanctuary, plans were being laid to enroll us in the Stephen Ministries program next year, and a second search committee was formed to find another candidate. We built a handicapped ramp to the entrance of the chapel, bought and installed a computer and printer, and were also able to attract Peter and Rhonda Kamakawiwoole, whom we met while in Hawaii and was now studying at the seminary. He took up the leadership of the junior high youth and began assisting in the pulpit.

And for the record, I conducted sixteen weddings, twenty-two funerals, and seventeen baptisms.

I began the year with two weeks of study leave, giving me time to put together a first draft of my dissertation, *A Strategy for the Renewal of Historic First Parish Congregational Church*. Everything was in place by May 11 with graduation scheduled for June 13. God was so gracious in providing me the time, energy, teachers, and finances to complete this very special program. And I must add that the time and skill of our church secretary Jane Wilkins, who typed the manuscript, made it possible. And by God's grace, First Parish was taking steps in the direction of renewal.

In February, we took advantage of the generosity of Ed and Charlane Chapman to use one of their condos right along the ski trails of Mount Abram, Bethel, Maine. As I remember the whole family was there along with some friends. Unfortunately Dave suffered a grand mal seizure early one morning. Dave had two normal EEGs in the spring of 1986 and was hoping to join the US Army, but this event required that he be put on 300 mg of Dilantin per day. He has been seizure free but his plans for the military were changed.

By March, I had noticed a few expressions of behavior that saddened me. There was a lack of unity among some and little regard or respect for the opinion of a brother or sister. One member not only disagreed with another but also felt compelled to speak against that other person in public. A member spoke cordially to another and then spoke critically of that same person behind their back. I witnessed church leaders shouting at various groups who rented our building and others who resigned their positions of responsibility because of a personal slight. Some have left our fellowship without any explanation and no desire to discuss whatever differences may have existed between fellow members.

I believed that such behavior could not be overlooked but had to be lovingly confronted. Sadly certain individuals did not listen or change their behavior. They continued in the church, rarely participating in any activities other than occasional Sunday worship.

It continues to puzzle me that a person can hear the teaching of scripture and observe loving behavior in others yet never humble themselves to consider the slightest need to reform. I slowly discovered that the only way to relate to such a person is to love them. Attempts to convince through talking are a futile exercise. Loving and praying works much better. Eventually I tried to treat others as I try to treat my own children who disappoint yet deserve my love and support.

"Four Seasons"

In June 7, Pat and I traveled to East Dennis, Cape Cod, where we joined Ed and Sandra Whitman and Dean and Jane Pedersen for the very first overnight together; we had dinner at Cooke's Seafood and spent the night in the Whitman home.

Ed, Dean, and I graduated together from Gordon Divinity School in May 1966. We went our separate ways for twenty years, but by 1987, we were in close proximity to one another and began getting together for fellowship. We soon decided to schedule four gatherings each year, once a season, "Four Seasons." We even have our own theme music written by Antonio Vivaldi.

At first we would gather on Sunday afternoon, share dinner, and spend the night in one of our homes. According to my records, we have met 152 times with our next time already scheduled.

Since 1987, we have enjoyed scores of fun activities, trips, meals, and special family events together.

We have skied, biked, hiked, canoed, taken a ferry, and crammed into "Eventually" (Dean's sailboat). We have visited country fairs, the Rose Kennedy Greenway, the JFK Library, museums, the Highland games, a field of lupines, Polly's Pancake House, and Strawbery Banke in Portsmouth, New Hampshire. We attended concerts at Gordon College, Shalin in Rockport, the New Hampshire Philharmonic, the Empire Brass, and *Forever Plaid*. We caught the Boston Marathon and the Patriot's Day reenactment. We endured Hurricane Bob, job losses, the passing of parents, and family crises. We played Golf (the card game), Five Crowns, Farkle, Quarkle, Rook, and Monopoly once! We traveled to England, Bermuda, Block Island, and Quebec, Canada. We celebrated installations, weddings, retirement parties, anniversaries, birthdays, first night, and our GDS fiftieth anniversary.

We have enjoyed the hospitality of Jan Martin's Rockport summer home, Ken Hodgon's "Owl's Nest" in Pittsburg, New Hampshire, Glenn Jamison's "Sleepy Hollow" in Naples, Maine, Ed Chapman's condo in Mount Abram in Bethel, Maine, and Pam and Gadar's "Red Door" in Rhode Island.

Four Seasons has been our unique and enriching source of support and encouragement, fun, challenge, and joy. All six of us love one another, respect one another, and enjoy our times together as a gift from our Savior Jesus Christ.

In May 7, I got a phone call from a North Reading Police detective telling me to pick up our son Dave and three of his friends. They had been kept in custody for four hours for destroying Barry's car with sledgehammers after driving it into the woods. After the hammering was finished, they thought that setting it on fire would be a good idea, these are three teenage boys remember. The flames brought the fire department. I picked them up, and instead of yelling at them, God's grace led me to take them to Burger King. It became a powerful lesson for the guys. We had to appear in Woburn District Court the next morning. This story has become part of Weisenbach legend.

On Sunday, June 7, the congregation surprised us with an informal party celebrating the completion of my DMin program. There was food, warm wishes, and a gift of $1,600.00. This was a very pleasant gathering that gave the people opportunity to express their support and love.

Graduation for Fuller

In June 12, Pat and I flew to Pasadena, California, for my graduation from Fuller Theological Seminary. This was the public conclusion of a very long journey. It was wonderful to have Mother and Dad join us.

Since we were so close, we flew on to Honolulu to visit KUC after leaving four years ago. We had a very enjoyable time despite some trepidation in the mind of the interim minister, Rev. Bill Steeper. All went well as we visited several faithful friends and attended the worship service in June 14.

On that Sunday, we were called forward by Reverend Steeper and were touched by his invitation to receive the blessing of the assembled congregation as they stretched out their arms in a symbolic gesture of love and unity. After worship, we enjoyed the reception line, receiving many loving greetings.

The few who had forced our departure acted as if nothing had ever happened. (I am always confused by this reaction. I guess if one believes nothing happened, then there isn't any cause to apologize.)

At our annual meeting back in January, the congregation supported a motion from the newly formed diaconate to enroll the congregation in Stephen Ministries.

Stephen Ministry

In August 2, we sent Jan Martin and Marianne Whitney to a twelve-day leadership training course held on the campus of Loyola College, Baltimore, Maryland.

When they returned, they made it clear that the pastor plays a critical role in a successful program. "You have to go to training, Pastor Rich." I did go the following January to Orlando, Florida, and returned ready to recruit our first class of caregivers. In February 6, we began our first training course, and we had ten folks enrolled. They were commissioned on Pentecost Sunday, May 22, 1988.

Over the years, we conducted the sixty-hour course several times, equipping over sixty church members to share Christ's care with their brothers and sisters.

The Assistant Pastor Search Committee interviewed Kevin Manley Leach in August 20. They had sifted through thirty-five profiles and conducted eight other interviews.

Kevin was born in Arlington, Washington, and attended Seattle Pacific University and recently graduated from Gordon-Conwell. Writing in *the Church Herald*, our moderator noted, "He is experienced as a preacher, teacher, counselor and visitor... He lists drawing, photography, computers, running, tennis and music among his interests." He preached his candidating sermon in September 13 and was warmly welcomed by the congregation that morning. Kevin proved an excellent ministry partner.

Our 343rd anniversary was extra special. We walked all over our new carpet and began a tradition of reading our original church covenant on the first Sunday of November. I discovered it in my research for the dissertation. It is a very serious expression of the heartfelt desires of our ancient forebears and serves as a timely reminder of our theological roots. It is divided into seven parts and is easily assigned to seven leaders. As it is read and reread every year, I never fail to thank God for such a rich heritage, which we must be preserved for future generations.

There was another surprise that Sunday. The church council presented me with a doctoral robe, complete with racing stripes. The attendance that morning was 350.

There were several other actions taken in 1987 that deserve mention. We began a monthly Men's Breakfast, a full breakfast served by the deacons followed by a Christian speaker, and Faithfulness Sunday, a luncheon served in May by the diaconate to our fifty-year members and all members and friends who are eighty years old and older. The entire meal and program was funded by a gift to the church from Ms. Mary Fairchild, a member and office volunteer who left her estate to care for older members of the congregation. We also reorganized the board of deacons and board of deaconesses into a diaconate. And finally we celebrated the fact that our finances had increased by 46 percent during the past four years. To God be the glory!

Other events worth mentioning include a contact from Paul Van Ness who was developing a videotape marking the hundredth anniversary of Union Congregational Church. Pat and I attended a special service in November marking the occasion. Then there was Dave's high school graduation and Pam's first job—after graduating from the Wilma Boyd Travel School in Pittsburgh—at Hertz Rent-a-Car; she was stationed at Logan International Airport. Pat began working for Gentiva, a respite ministry to children with special medical needs, and then she and I also took ballroom dancing lessons at the Stoneham High School. Dancing was frowned upon during our growing-up years, but all the wedding receptions we attended led us to get our act together.

And for the record, I conducted six weddings, twenty-nine funerals, and twenty-five baptisms.

The year began with a few changes in our staff. We hired Ken Wood as our custodian in 1988, and he is still there! I must say that Ken and I developed an excellent working relationship. He has a generous heart and in his position as custodian is in the perfect place to welcome those who wander into our meetinghouse or come as part of the many organizations that rent space during the week. He would often find "work" for those who needed financial help and were willing to give us a few hours for cash.

In May, Peter and Rhonda Kamawiwoole left to take up his ministry as associate pastor at Kaimuki Evangelical Church in Hawaii. That same month, we installed Kevin Leach as associate pastor/Christian education director. In June, Martha Sabaje returned to Rhode Island to become organist at her home church, and in August, we hired Dr. Fred Broer as our new organist/minister of music. I was very optimistic about all three of these additions.

This was the year I heard about Sharing Inc. from Rev. Burt Leno, pastor of Greenwood Union Church. Kay Doherty, a former Catholic nun, founded the organization to raise funds for the poor in the American South. She visited Burt's church hoping to recruit people who would be willing to walk on Good Friday. Jesus walked on Good Friday, so Kay figured that would be a good day. After hearing of this need, I committed myself to walk twenty miles, six times around Lake Quannapowitt.

Because our meetinghouse was located on the shores of the lake, we became the starting/ending point for the walkers. Much to my surprise, 180 people showed up that first Good Friday. They were from twelve different churches and twenty communities.

I started walking in 1992. I began at 7:00 a.m. and walked three laps, went home to soak in our tub, and returned to walk three more from 3:00 p.m. to 5:00 p.m. There were twenty-three others who completed the twenty miles that first year. Over the years, there were several First Parish members who would join me for a lap or two.

For the two Sundays prior to the walk, I would take my place behind a table in the vestry as soon as the worship service concluded. I called out to whoever passed me and invited them to contribute to my effort. They would sign-up and give me cash or wait till the next week. I did this for twenty years, relying on the kind generosity of my fellow members. Together we were able to contribute over $30,000.00 to Sharing Inc.

In 2003, I joined Rotary International and I described the goal of Sharing Inc. to them. Over the years, they contributed thousands. Rotarians are a very generous bunch!

9am Worship Service

In September, I suggested to the diaconate that we might try a worship service at 9:00 a.m. in the chapel. Our Sunday school was held during the worship service, requiring the teachers to miss their own opportunity to worship. I thought this was not good for the teachers, so would they respond to a 9:00 a.m. service?

As it turned out, the service attracted twenty-five to thirty each week. Several appreciated an early start, especially if they had plans in the afternoon. Others just enjoyed the intimacy of the chapel. The choir was not available, of course, so I invited the congregation to choose two or three favorite hymns we could sing. The diaconate took responsibility for providing an usher—usually Ed and Irene Schmidgall—and Ron Martin played the organ for us. It became a very enjoyable time, and I know that those who attended really appreciated the extra effort it took.

Those first five years were times of great spiritual and programmatic progress. A new pastoral associate, a new custodian, a new organist, new programs, Stephen Ministries, growing attendance, and finances—we were experiencing God's blessings.

I wrote my annual report for that year with optimism about the years to come.

> I really enjoy ministry here in Wakefield. In fact I look forward to many more years of service among you. It would be rather presumptuous to say that I will stay here for the remainder of my career—that could be thirty years! I believe much growth has occurred during these five years, and

it is just as true to say that there are countless opportunities that continue to surround us.

Yes, I was grateful and optimistic. But our archenemy was not pleased, and given time, we should expect his opposition.

We had a great trip through Western Massachusetts and Vermont in October, including a Shaker farm, Ben and Jerry's ice cream, Rock of Ages monuments, and Quechee Gorge.

We did get to Moosehead again that year, and this time we traveled to Spencer Pond and began seven years enjoying that quiet place, the abundant wildlife, and the friendship of Chic and Anne Howe.

In December 18, we dedicated a handicapped ramp at the Covell Chapel entrance. This was an effort of our board of trustees to be more inviting to those who found steps difficult to negotiate. A chair lift from the basement up to the second floor would come later.

For the record, I conducted ten weddings, nineteen funerals, and seventeen baptisms.

We began the year with a second trip back to Hawaii, in February 20 to March 2. We were invited by Peter Kamakawiwoole to preach at his ordination. Sadly that didn't happen. There were a few details that had to be worked out, and these postponed the service.

So we spent some time visiting friends from KUC and flew to the Big Island to visit Dave and Nita Shaw who had moved to a church in Kealakekua. We spent the week living in the vacation home of Dave's parents. Dave was not expecting us but arranged housing for us, and I preached for him on Sunday, February 26.

We enjoyed a trip to a farm that grew coffee and macadamia nuts and a brief stay at the Kona Hilton.

Back home, our Outreach Committee continued to bring before the congregation the critical needs of the world. Three of our members responded to these special opportunities.

Bob Tilton heard about Habitat for Humanity through a speaker at the Men's Breakfast Table. So he and his wife Donna felt led to join a work crew in the highlands of Guatemala (August 2–16).

Marcus Jamison served as a senior cabin group counselor for two months at New England Frontier Camp, a ministry of Christian Service Brigade. Our committee voted to support all three members.

In April, we drove to 610 Rising Sun Avenue, Holland, Pennsylvania, for my parents' fiftieth wedding anniversary. I have already referred to this event, which included an open house on their actual day and then a family gathering at Willow Valley, Lancaster, Pennsylvania. This started our annual tradition of family reunion.

In May, the following news was included in *the Lighthouse*, the monthly newsletter of First Baptist Church, Wycombe, Pennsylvania:

> Having come to know the Lord as Savior later in life, I had no aspirations of ever ministering the Word of God in any formal way. But the Lord had other plans, and at the ripe old age of forty-six, by His grace and the leading of this congregation, He called me here to Wycombe. These have been twenty-three plus years of great blessing for Gertrude and me and others of the O'Brien family… The last time when we felt that the Lord would have us move on and make room for a new shepherd, you honored us by recalling us for another four years.
>
> Once again we feel that in light of the gathering years and the firm foundation of God's church here in Wycombe, Gertrude and I believe time has come for us to pass the baton to a younger and more gifted shepherd. Therefore we submit our plans to retire as pastor and wife of First Baptist church Wycombe effective Sunday, August 9, 1989.
>
> Very gratefully yours,
Gertrude and Pastor O'Brien
[They were sixty-nine years old.]

They continued to serve the Lord in Morrisville, Pennsylvania, as an assistant to the pastor, adult Sunday school teacher, and leader of a group of seniors they named "Second Winders."

Granny and Poppy were very special people. The parents of eight, grandparents of twenty-seven, and great-grandparents of thirty-eight great-grandchildren. (The birth of great-grandchildren and the addition of others through marriage increases this total every year.) I have been enriched since joining the family in 1964. The support, generosity, and blessing of this Christian family have contributed immensely to my life.

The church Pat and I came to serve in August 1983 was an historic congregation. Dr. Austin Rice, the pastor from 1907 to 1944, preached an evangelical message drawn from the scriptures, and I concluded this after reading several of his printed sermons. The four ministers who followed were more liberal in their perspective—men who loved God and His church but believed that it would be prudent to avoid preaching too directly about sin and the need for confession and forgiveness. It was felt that too much emphasis on these issues would discourage attendance. I believe that this was a disservice to the Lord, His church, and the Bible.

When I sought to preach the Gospel of Jesus Christ, I knew that this would be an opportunity and challenge for the congregation, but I firmly believed that Pat and I came from Honolulu by the will and power of Jesus Christ. God wanted us here to give the people of this congregation and community an opportunity to hear a biblical message. If we were asked to leave, then that would be in God's plan too, and He would have another place for us.

Of course the startlingly message of God's love and forgiveness had to be introduced lovingly and gently. This I sought to do. I moved slowly, too slowly for some. These families eventually moved to other churches, and I never blamed them for leaving but missed their support.

I say all this because of a statement I overheard coming from an older and longtime church member. This is what I heard, "First Parish is a *congregational* church and that means that I can believe whatever I want." I knew that this person was speaking for many others in our church, and her comment received no question from those who heard her. After hearing this, I wrote the following for the next *Church Herald*:

> *Well, not exactly*, I thought to myself. There is much individual freedom within the congregational form of church government that is certainly true. But I wish I had the chance to jump into that conversation and remind the speaker that First Parish is a congregational *church*. And a church is a group of believers who have come to rock-solid unity about a few things.
>
> There is no debate whatsoever about the basics. For instance, we at First Parish don't question whether God loved the world and sent the Son to die for our sins. We don't debate that because the Bible, the Apostles' Creed, and the bylaws of our church state that doctrine rather clearly. Many people outside of the Christian church may debate that point but not a person who is part of the church of Jesus Christ. I could illustrate with another article of Christian faith, but you get the point, don't you?
>
> Now, even here, there may be some disagreement amongst believers because of what one might put on their "basics" list. It may be slightly different from the list of someone else. But what these two believers have in common—their loyalty and faith in Jesus Christ—is bigger than all their differences. It is that self-imposed unity that Congregationalists call "Covenant." When I confess, "Jesus is Lord," I am in covenant with everyone else confessing, "Jesus Christ is Lord." We are "stuck" with each other.
>
> Now we may disagree strongly, my Christian sister and I, over some issues, but because

of our covenant we are called to love and respect each other. These other issues can threaten the covenant but I am called to honor "the Covenant" for Christ's sake who loves us both.

Friends, from time to time the covenant amongst us at First Parish will be threatened. We should expect this; after all, our covenant in Christ is our strong defense in the midst of conflict. When disagreements come—and they certainly will—our covenant will hold us together, calling us to love, respect, and honor one another.

Parts of our large congregation are experiencing a threat to their healthy exercise of "the Covenant." There are differences among us, strong differences, differences that seek to destroy, even our covenant. Let us together do all we can to fortify the whole, to build the unity of the body, to stand squarely together upon our covenant in Jesus Christ. It is our only hope—and it is enough!

I wrote that "Raw Material" article in May for another reason; a simmering struggle had emerged within the diaconate over the presence of Freemasons worshipping with us on a Sunday morning.

Free Masonry

Back in February, the board received a letter from the Golden Rule Lodge of Freemasons requesting the opportunity to mark their annual observance of Saints John Sunday at our church. They had attended First Parish as a group to observe this special day eighteen times, beginning in 1910. (Saints John Sunday is in honor of John the Baptist and John the Apostle.)

In 1989, there were several deacons who were also masons. In fact I would guess that there were probably forty families—eighty plus people—in First Parish who were connected with the lodge.

My predecessor John Robertson was a member in good standing and past leader of the lodge and the district. In fact I was advised by a few masons that I should join the lodge and that this would help strengthen ties with many in the congregation. I declined realizing that I had little time for extra meetings! I was not, in any way, opposed to the lodge, but I was just busy with my ministry.

The diaconate extended an invitation to the lodge to attend on Sunday, June 3, as guests. The board requested that the members of the lodge not wear their aprons. (The Masonic apron is "a badge of fraternal distinction. During his first degree, each Mason is given a plain white leather apron. It represents the white of lamb skin, a symbol of innocence.") The motion passed 12-1. Sadly the diaconate chairperson, without my knowledge or agreement, allowed the lodge members to wear their aprons. (Her husband was a member of the lodge.)

On that first Sunday of June, four masons greeted worshippers at the doors, ushered, processed into the sanctuary as a group, provided the flowers for the pulpit, had a member read the Old Testament reading, selected the closing hymn, and processed out. Communion was served by six members of the diaconate, three women and three men.

As noted, one deacon was opposed to the invitation. He believed strongly that members of the Freemasons should not attend First Parish in order to mark one of their special days. Church members who were masons were welcomed as individuals, but attending as a group and participating as they did were very inappropriate. This deacon made his disapproval quite public through his letters to the board and the congregation.

The next year, 1990, the Masonic Lodge asked to celebrate Saints John Sunday again. This time they wanted to serve communion, and this caused quite a serious conflict (more to come on this issue, so fasten your seat belts).

I should also note that 1989 was the year that the board of trustees made our meetinghouse smoke free. We also announced and conducted a second Stephen Ministries class with six in attendance.

I became a member of the Board of the Open Church Foundation (OFC) that year. The OCF, founded by Roger Babson, of Babson College, was established with a sizable portfolio to develop and distribute Christian leaflets throughout the world. It was managed by George Rideout Sr., a close friend of Roger Babson. When George Senior died, his son George Rideout Jr. took the helm. We meet once a year at Longfellow's Wayside Inn in Sudbury, Massachusetts.

Another opportunity came in October, this time from Bibles for Africa. We collected over 120 Bibles and an additional $40.00 for postage to send them to Nigeria. That was also the year that Pat and I began thinking about buying a house in Wakefield, maybe even the parsonage.

And for the record, I conducted eleven weddings, twenty-three funerals, and sixteen baptisms.

At the beginning of the year, the congregation was told that we had received 218 pledge units totaling $139,000.00. This total was about $75,000.00 below what would be needed for the coming year. I wrote a congregational letter in January 5.

> I have an idea about the lower number or pledge units. I'm beginning to conclude that fewer of us believe that making a written pledge to the church is not as important as it once was. If my hunch is correct, there are about one hundred of you who plan to give and give generously to your church out of love and gratitude but have not told anyone but God.
>
> Since I arrived over six years ago, two facts are clear: the number of pledging units has gone down by 43.5% and the income of the church has gone up by 42.98%.

I was trying to help the church, especially the leadership, reduce the level of trust they put into the written promises members made and become more open to the financial blessings God might pour out upon those who would trust Him for the financial needs of His church.

I was trying to change the habit of the leadership to reduce their tendency of cutting the budget because they couldn't see anything that might give them hope about the future. In short, I was trying to help the congregation trust in God's provision. Over the years, and over the fears of some, the annual meeting voted to approve budgets that were beyond the pledge total. I believe that a congregation that trusts in God's provision will experience God's blessings.

In April, I drove to Lansdale, Pennsylvania, for a very special celebration planned by Bethanna. The board decided to honor Mother with a dinner and the establishment of the Ruth E. Weisenbach Volunteer of the Year Award, Mother being the first recipient. Mom was aware of the dinner, since it was the annual dinner of Bethanna, but she was unaware that she would be recognized with an award. To make the evening more special, all four of her sons were present. I still remember the look of surprise and delight on her face as the four of us entered the banquet hall.

Both Mother and Dad lived lives that were a consistent display of generosity toward others, and I believe that their sons have tried to follow their example.

It was a great night!

At their April 3 meeting, the diaconate received another request from the Masonic Lodge to celebrate Saints John Sunday in June 3, and this year the lodge expanded their request—"Could present and past deacons of First Parish, who are also active masons, serve Communion?" The diaconate responded positively but with the stipulation that those serving would not wear their aprons. The thinking was that Holy Communion is a Christian sacrament, not a Masonic ritual. To avoid confusion, the board wanted to keep the two organizations distinct from each other.

Fortunately, the Masons planning the service agreed with this request and accepted the fact that those serving the Holy Communion would remove their aprons while serving. The news of this decision was received by some members of First Parish as a serious error. Two letters were sent to the board. Here is a sample,

> Your decision to invite the Masons to our wor-
> ship service is forbidden in scripture... The ser-

vice is not and never will be honorable to the Christian God and His Holy Spirit... We are a Christian church not a lodge. We are believers in the one true God, not false gods... It is damming to any of our brethren in this church to sit and break the first commandment... Freemasonry is against God and His Holy Word... You must repent from this error so that this church will not be condemned with the world!

On Sunday, May 13, four Masons came to me sharing their deep concern that those deacons/Masons who would be serving communion in June 3 were not allowed to wear their aprons. They were angry, hurt, and threatened to leave the church if the decision of the board was not reversed. These four said they were speaking on behalf of many in the lodge. I tried to explain the reason why the board decided as they did, but I was unable to change any minds. At this point, I realized that the board would have to reconsider their decision. I told these four that if the board changed its mind, I would abide by their decision with reluctance.

These four quickly communicated with the chair of the board that I would concede the issue if the board so voted.

The next day, the chair phoned every member of the board and told them that I would go along with whatever decision they made regarding the wearing of Masonic aprons. The chair called me on Monday evening advising me that she had called every member of the diaconate and the members of the board had changed their minds—the deacons/Masons would be allowed to wear their aprons while serving the Holy Communion.

I was deeply distressed by the behavior of the chair. I figured that the board would be called to a special meeting to discuss the issue, and poling by phone was not a fair way to deal with a question as important as this one was.

At the church council meeting in May, the diaconate chair was instructed to call a meeting of the board to discuss and vote, and a poll was not a sufficient way of determining the will of the whole. A special meeting of the diaconate was called for May 28.

At this point, a second letter was sent to the board by another parishioner.

> Please do not reverse your decision of April 3. There is no question that the Masons are a religious organization. Their writings and ceremonies deal with the issues of deity, morality, worship and eternal destiny... What distinguishes Christianity from all other religions is the centrality of the person and work of Jesus Christ... Masonry identifies a god who is the Great Architect of the Universe (GAOTU). It is certainly clear that the centrality of Christ, the person of Christ, the power and beauty of His saving work on the cross, are remarkably and sadly absent from all Mason rituals and writings. Please reconsider.

I do not recall whether this second letter was ever read at that meeting on May 28. It was addressed to the diaconate and made some very clear and powerful points, but I don't remember any sharing of this letter.

About twenty Masons crowded the room that night of May 28. After discussion, the board took their vote and sustained their vote, which was taken over the phone (15-1), allowing the wearing of Masonic aprons by those deacons/Masons who were selected to serve. (Carlton Elliott was the sole negative voter.) I was very disappointed at this decision and especially the manner in which it was conducted. Their decision would perpetuate the confusion regarding the clear differences between Christian faith and Masonic ritual.

Here is a quote from a Masonic speech given to me by a Mason.

> Masonry is not a religion, nor a substitute for religion. It is religious in that it teaches monotheism. The volume of the "Sacred Law" is open upon its

altars whenever a Lodge is in session. Reverence to God is ever present in its ceremonials, and to its brethren are constantly addressed lessons of morality, yet it is not sectarian or theological. Masonry fosters a belief in a Supreme Being (this being a prerequisite for membership) and accepts good men who are found to be worthy regardless of their religious convictions and strives to make better men of them by emphasizing a firm belief in the Fatherhood of God, the Brotherhood of Man, and the Immortality of the Soul.

These tenets are the basis of the fundamental approach of Masonry as a builder of individual character, as an influence for humanness, kindness, gentleness, justice; those characteristics which constitute true fraternity, the full fraternity of all men, the Brotherhood of Man under the Fatherhood of God.

It is certainly easy to understand why so many men (and women) of First Parish would conclude that Masonry's goals are very close, if not identical, to those of the church they had grown up in. Why would any person criticize Masonry? "We are simply good men trying to be better men." "Our previous pastor was a mason. Need we say more?"

I heard these comments from a longtime church member, "Masons have been the backbone of this church and I have no sympathy for those who want to change it!" "Masonry was good enough for George Washington, so it is good enough for me!"

Any effort of mine or of the several who wrote letters trying to distinguish between the Christian faith and Masonry would be seen as a criticism, even rejection, of Masonry in general and individual masons in particular. There were a few masons of the church who realized that Christianity added a necessary dimension to their spiritual understanding, namely, their realization of their need of a savior, something Masonry never addressed. This key difference would eventually bring about a transformation within First Parish, but it would take years.

One of the reasons why a clear difference of thinking grew within the congregation was the fact that every person who became a church member during our first seven years had gone through a membership class that I taught. At the conclusion of the class, every candidate would come before the diaconate and bear testimony to their need of a savior. Over the years, every addition to the church rolls was a person who possessed a degree of understanding of the Christian gospel.

There were, of course, those whose understanding and acceptance of the gospel were less than complete. I realized this as I listened to their expressions of faith, but I didn't believe that it was my place to doubt them at that point. I was always optimistic about their spiritual potential if they worshipped regularly and especially if they became a part of a small group Bible study. My task as a minister is to explain the message, while their task is to open themselves to its truth and power.

Obviously, as the church added more and more persons of faith, certain aspects of church life would change. New programs would be added, Stephen Ministries, Alpha, forty-day programs, small group Bible studies, and the Men's Breakfast Table. Other programs would end, the Couples Club and the Women's Guild.

Add to this the fact that when I arrived, the majority of the church's leadership was composed of men and women who may or may not have fully comprehended the message of the Bible. In my judgment, they had little opportunity to hear biblical truth clearly expressed.

During those first years, the message from the pulpit was different from what most were accustomed to hearing. Eventually, everyone realized the differences. Some heard the Word and accepted its truth quite quickly. Others heard and were not sure what to think, so they would listen and wait. Sadly, others never seemed to hear or understand any difference at all. Still others did not accept what they heard but figured that I would leave their church in a year or two. I guess they never thought that we would remain for twenty-three more years!

What happened on Sunday, June 3, caused a serious division within the congregation and there were some who saw this conflict as an opportunity to test my determination to continue at my post. "Maybe he will leave. He has caused so much trouble."

The struggles within the church had been brewing long before they became public on that communion Sunday in June. For those first years, there was opposition but it rarely surfaced except from three or four members who, from the start, never did support the new direction of their church.

My relationship with one or two was a long series of battles—battles that were just about anything and everything. I remember describing it "as a long walk with a stone in my shoe." That walk would continue for all thirty years of my service.

In June 3, we marked Pentecost Sunday and baccalaureate it was also Saints John Sunday. Members of the Masonic Lodge greeted attendees, ushered, provided the memorial flowers, selected the last hymn ("How Great Thou Art"), read the Old Testament lesson (Isaiah 44:1–8), processed in and out, sat as a group, and served the Holy Communion wearing their aprons.

I preached a Pentecost sermon from John 7:37–44, "the Holy Spirit has come." We honored our graduates and then I moved from the dais to a place behind the communion table and spoke a word of invitation in preparation for communion.

As I invited the deacons/Masons forward to begin serving, a church member and former deacon who had previously protested the presence of the Masons walked down the aisle from his pew in the rear of the sanctuary and interrupted the service. The congregation was stunned, as was I.

He began, "Rich, I'd like to say something about what they are doing here. I want to speak for the Lord. If you want to remove me, that's fine." I was shocked and tried to silence the member. He continued, "This is an abomination." I pleaded again, "Please stop. You are doing damage. Please respect my authority."

Fortunately another member of the church, Dr. Glenn Jamison, a psychiatrist, who was sitting toward the front, was able to confront and calm the protesting member. The choir began to sing and the communion service began without further interruption.

Before the benediction, I spoke to the member, "I know you did what you did because you love Jesus Christ. It took courage but this is not the proper time or place."

I'm sure we could have found a better time and a better place to discuss the matter, but that never happened. Because I commended the member for his courage, some felt that I had arranged for the disruption. That was hardly the case!

Several church members and masons commended me, as they left the sanctuary, on the way I handled the situation. I received several letters and cards offering love and support.

> 6/10/90
> Dear Pastor Rich and Pat,
>
> We admire both of you for your peacemaking attitude and your patience. We are grateful that you are willing to hang in with us. God bless you and bring you His peace at this troublesome time.
>
> RR

> 6/12/90
> Dear Pastor Rich,
>
> I want to say I think you handled the conflict this morning firmly and with compassion. I thank God for you, for your sermons and teachings, but most of all for your example of God's love. I pray people will remember your great sermon instead of the outburst.
>
> JM

> 6/13/90
> Dear Pastor Rich,
>
> As the service proceeded, I felt deep repentance for myself and my church for disappointing

Jesus so; pain over the division which exists and which I know would widen because of what was happening, confusion about our fallen condition in which people who claim to love Jesus can hold such differing views. I know with certainty that God is in control and that out of this stress-filled situation, He can cause healing and growth.

TH

At the next meeting of the diaconate, a small group, composed of the diaconate chair, the pastor, and the moderator, were asked to speak to the dissenting member, seeking assurance that he would not bring any further disruptions or distribute unauthorized letters; otherwise he would be dismissed from membership at First Parish. Sadly the member would not give such assurance. "I must be obedient to the Lord," he said.

At a special joint meeting of both diaconate and church council, the member was dismissed from the church.

I spoke to the chair of the diaconate telling her that I believed that the congregation needed to learn how to better deal with conflict. She agreed and we appointed a committee of eight plus Pastor Kevin and myself. We employed Rev. Marilyn Rossier, the associate pastor of the Lynnfield Congregational Church (UCC), to chair our group.

The first action we took was to call for a congregational meeting for June 27. Our purpose was to listen to one another and have an opportunity to speak our thoughts and feelings concerning recent events. This was not a time for debate or discussion. We would stop for prayer whenever we felt it was necessary.

Two weeks later, I wrote for the *Church Herald.*

The discussions, decisions, and actions leading up to and following Pentecost Sunday have been a source of great pain for many of us. Words have been spoken by persons on both sides of the question concerning Masonic aprons and Christian Communion. Some of those words, and the attitudes behind them, have caused great pain to several members of the church family.

What do we do when we differ *strongly*? And I emphasize "strongly" because we all expect to differ over minor things, but how about when it's major things? When we are convinced that the other person or group is wrong—dead wrong? When their comments are harmful, hurtful, and misinformed, what then?

I'm sorry to say that what we are all tempted to do is to strike back. To label, mock and criticize, to withdraw within the ranks of those who think like we do. To gossip about "them" and wallow in self-pity concerning ourselves.

Friends, over the last six weeks, I have been saddened to hear and observe these kinds of behaviors from both sides of the issue. Fortunately, there are those, again on both sides, who are trying to be more positive. More able to listen to criticism without halting the conversation. Persons able, even eager, to put themselves in the other's shoes and look at issues from another's point of view. I praise God for each and every one of you who are seeking this path.

The event is now past but it has put one of our church families out of the fellowship and left others in a confused state about their future. I am concerned for First Parish. I long for all our members and friends to learn how to listen to another's words, even when we believe they are wrong. And I long for an opportunity for healing and reconciliation to take place within all of us so wounded by these events. I believe, with all my heart, that these days of pain can make us stronger, more open to others, more loving, more

mature in our faith. May we all, by God's grace,
grasp this opportunity.

I wrote, "The event is now past...." The committee, led by
Reverend Rossier, met eight times throughout the summer and
sought to provide an opportunity for folks to express their fears and
feelings. This exercise helped but, as I learned a few years later, differences persisted. The deeply held beliefs of many remained only to be
dragged up again eight years later.

Toward the middle of June, Pat and I along with two church
delegates attended the Annual Meeting of the Massachusetts Conference held at Mount Holyoke College. As usual it was a well-planned
series of seminars, business sessions, speakers, and worship services.
And as usual, we felt a bit out of step with the overall direction set
by the leadership.

Pat and I always admired the denomination's consistent desire
to meet the human needs of those about us, but there was always a
lack of a clear statement concerning our motivation. Of course there
will always be physical needs to be met, but in addition to compassion, there must be a verbal sharing of Christ's love and forgiveness
undergirding our actions; this clear statement was usually lacking.

Along with this difference, we were often in disagreement with
various resolutions coming from the meeting. Policy issues regarding
homosexuality, same-sex marriage, abortion, and government policy
would often present a serious conflict between the denomination's
direction and our understanding of biblical standards.

It goes without saying that the distance widened between the
conference and ourselves at First Parish.

In the fall, we were asked by the headquarters of Stephen Ministries to host an area-wide workshop held to introduce the ministry to surrounding local churches. We happily consented to their
request and worked hard to accommodate over a hundred interested
attenders. This event was a great boost to our own core of Stephen
ministers. We had grown to five leaders and seventeen ministers in
three years. I grew more and more convinced in the value of the Ste-

phen Ministries series. I'm sure this program contributed greatly to the changes taking place within our church.

At its December meeting, the diaconate issued a statement that they had printed in *the Church Herald.*

> According to our bylaws, the Pastor, along with the Diaconate are charged with the responsibility of determining how our worship services, including the observing of the sacraments, are to proceed.
>
> We are not under the illusion that a decision made by a majority of that Diaconate is guaranteed to be correct. It does, however, indicate how we will proceed in a particular instance. As such, it deserves the respect of individual church members whether or not they agree with it [ten in favor and six abstaining].

Again I wrote in the December *Church Herald,*

> I am convinced that forgiveness is our only hope for unity, growth and fruitfulness... Forgiveness is a very simple sort of miracle. It is a new beginning, starting over and trying to relate to the person who caused us pain. Forgiving doesn't take away the hurt, it doesn't deny the past injury it merely refuses to let those feelings and memories stand in the way of a new start. We need a new start friends and by God's grace we are offered one. Let's take it!

This was the year that Pam started at TGI Friday's, and I think she really enjoyed herself. She knew the menu so well that she never had to write down what a customer ordered, and she could carry four full-water glasses in one hand! Our son Dave moved to

Pennsylvania to work with Uncle Ron Markloff, and Kim transferred from Northern Essex Community College to Gordon.

We did get back to Moosehead Lake to mark our twenty-sixth anniversary. We returned to Spencer Pond enjoying the quiet and the fellowship of Chick and Anne and the wildlife. We were in Skip Wiley that year.

For the record, I conducted seven weddings, twenty-three funerals, and twenty-two baptisms.

As one might imagine, the trauma of June 3 was a serious blow to the exercise of our stewardship. I addressed the issue at the annual meeting in January and had my comments reprinted in the *Church Herald* as well.

> The Bible makes clear from the words of both Jesus and Paul that if Christian believers and churches are faithful to the gospel, they will be at war with the world around them (John 15:18–17:26; Ephesians 6:10–20). But the fact of this warfare isn't always recognized. Some may even be surprised to hear me talk this way. But in 1990 it became very clear.
>
> Over the last eight years, we have grown and changed rather dramatically. In 1983 our average attendance was 194 per week and our income $147,300.00. In 1990 our average attendance is 223 and our income is $248,600.00, a 15% increase in attendance and a 68.7% increase in income, more than three times the rate of inflation.
>
> But because the Christian church is at war, we should expect to be attacked by our enemy when progress is made. Last year we were attacked by individuals expressing their impatience with the pace of our growth and by others expressing disagreement with the direction of our growth. I

believe we sought, as best we could, to deal with these disagreements through personal conversations and several small and large group meetings

By the grace of God I believe we are going in the right direction. I believe the pace of our growth is about right, and I pledge, as long as you allow me and as long as God sustains me, that I will continue to lead First Parish in her present direction. [At this point in my annual report, the majority of the group that night stood and gave me a rousing round of applause. I said the majority, not everyone stood.] I have no plans or desire to leave First Parish. I love the ministry and I love you—each of you.

We are presently wincing from our wounds. Scores of our brothers and sisters are in pain. They are confused, fearful, and in agony; consequently, they are not expressing the joy, confidence, faith, and peace of the Holy Spirit which is their spiritual heritage in Jesus Christ.

Others of us, the vast majority I believe, have endured the pain and confusion and are growing stronger as a result. But the withdrawal of a few has left our church council with a sizable financial shortfall of about $37,000.00.

Some say we should cut our financial expectations by that amount. Others say we need to increase our giving.

Let me remind you of what Stephen Grey, UCC stewardship director, told us last February. He calculated the net worth of First Parish. He did that by adding the number of adults, children, and friends—787—in our church family then multiplying that number by the annual income of every man woman and child in Wakefield, $14,177.00. He came up with the surprising total of $11,300,000.00, the net worth of our church.

If you divide that eleven million by what we gave last year—$191,000.00—you will conclude that we gave 1.7% of our net worth to God's work. Our denomination's percentage nationwide is 1.8%. There is plenty of room for growth, friends. God has given us the resources to do the job!

I leave you with this challenge. Go home and prayerfully seek to see things with this per- spective in mind. If one-half of our pledging fam- ilies raised their pledge by $5.00/week, we would raise $39,000.00. Do this as an act of love for your Savior Jesus Christ, your church, and your brothers and sisters.

Thanks for reading.
Pastor Rich

To help mark the 347th anniversary of our congregation in November, this suggestion appeared in the October *Church Herald*. I honestly can't remember who was behind this effort, and I don't think I ever knew.

Tithe noun (1) "a tenth part of one's annual income, contributed voluntarily for charitable purposes." (2) A small amount. (The American Heritage Dictionary)

Tithing to our church is a difficult thing to do for most of us. Ten percent is a lot of money and we need a lot just to pay the bills and help out a few charities. As much as we'd all love to tithe on a weekly basis, it seems to be an impossi- bility. Therefore, we the Close the Gap Commit- tee invites you to tithe to First Parish for just one week, Sunday, November 3, our church's anni- versary. Instead of your normal pledge, calculate

one-tenth of your annual, income divide that by
fifty-two and give that amount. Thank you very
much.

The GAP committee

As I noted in my annual report for 1991, we not only ended the
year in the black but also had a $17,000.00 surplus. Praise the Lord!
I also included the fact that our diaconate was able to distribute more
than $10,000.00 to needy church members from the income earned
from the trust funds allocated to the board.

Trust Funds

First Parish is the only church I was able to serve that possessed
trust funds. Because the congregation was established in 1644, there
was plenty of time for members to leave part or all of their legacy to
the church.

It began in 1715 with a gift in pounds and shillings, "for the
needy of the congregation." Usually the gift was designated for a specific purpose and only the interest would be available for distribution. Every board and most committees have a generous and growing
sum of money to use for their special projects. The diaconate had
funds for needy members.

There were also funds under the authority of the Outreach
Committee that were put at my disposal for the needy of the community. And you can easily understand that because of our stately
building, located at the intersection of two interstate highways, we
had "needy" visitors—some who were passing through and others
who were local.

It is always a challenging task to determine the worthiness of a
person or family who comes knocking on our door. I was reluctant
to give cash, so I had an arrangement with a gas station for those
who needed gas money, a pharmacy for those who needed money for
medicine, and a restaurant for those who were hungry. I would give
my card to the person, sign my name with a dollar amount, and tell
them where they could redeem it. I would later visit the gas station,

pharmacy, or restaurant to reimburse the owner. I was always grateful for generous merchants.

Sometimes the person would ask if there was work around the church in order to earn some cash. Our faithful and generous custodian, Ken Wood, would patiently find some task that needed doing. When the job was complete, I would give our custodian enough money to pay the worker. This system worked well, I think. I'm sure we were fooled once in a while, but we felt that was okay.

At present, First Parish has trust funds totaling almost $3,000,000.00. What a resource!

After four full years, Pastor Kevin Leach left us. He started in September 1987 and announced his resignation on September 22, 1991. His last Sunday was November 17. He was loved and respected by our congregation. Not only did he meet Michelle Sebastian at First Parish, but I conducted their wedding on August 19, 1989.

He was a wonderful associate who responded positively to any request I would make of him. He nurtured the youth of the congregation and started a young adult group. According to my records, he preached more that forty times, about 20 percent of the Sundays he was with us. He left us to pastor a church in Middletown, New York. I preached at his installation in April 1992. He remained there till he took the pastorate at the CCCC congregation in West Newbury, Massachusetts. He now pastors in Arlington, Washington.

For the record, I conducted six weddings, twenty-eight funerals, and nine baptisms that year.

I suppose most everyone has heard of *Aesop's Fables*, "the Tortoise and the Hare." It tells the story of a race between unequal contenders—the sleek and swift-footed hare and the slow and stumbling tortoise. At first glance, the hare should be an easy winner, but we all know that the hare fell asleep and the tortoise won. The lesson? The race is not always to the swift, slow and steady often wins. Throughout the next few years, I felt like the tortoise. I understood my task to be "slow and steady," and that was my constant prayer.

Of course Scripture said it long ago, "But God chose the foolish things of the world [the tortoise] to shame the wise [the hare]. God chose the weak things of the world to shame the strong. He chose the lowly things and the despised things—and the things that are not—to nullify the things that are, so that no one may boast before Him" (1 Corinthians 1:27–9). And again in 2 Corinthians 12:9, Scripture said, "My grace is sufficient for you. For my power is made perfect in weakness." I certainly felt my weakness.

We had weathered the conflict and confusion of June 3, 1990, but as I have already stated, there remained a small group of members who were waiting for another chance to raise major questions about my qualifications to be their pastor. There was opposition, in one form or another, for the next eight years.

For example, with the leaving of Pastor Kevin, we voted to form an Associate Pastor Search Committee, but two members of the group proved problematic. They realized that I was conservative, so they figured in order to bring some "balance," we should hire a liberal associate.

We actually interviewed a candidate they hoped might fill the bill, but he quickly saw the theological differences between himself and me. After the interview, he wrote a letter to the committee stating that it was utterly foolish to expect him to labor alongside a senior pastor who believed as I did. He withdrew his name from contention. The two committee members resigned and were replaced. We did hire an associate but it wasn't till October of the following year. "Slow and steady wins the race."

During these stressful years, God sent me letters, notes, gifts, prayers, and conversations by way of faithful church members. Here are a few samples.

> 8/14/92
> Once again we are thanking you for your love and generosity. We are so grateful to have been led to First Parish and to get to know you and Pat. It will be a long time before we find another church like First Parish. I already miss your sermons! I desperately need to hear God's

word each Sunday and you always communicated it to so clearly!

SD

4/15/92

You and the church are in our daily prayers, knowing your work load is heavier without an assistant. We love First Parish and we pray that it will grow and prosper. We feel very close to you and Pat. We love you both.

DT

1/8/93

So often, during my first Sundays at First Parish and since then, your sermons have comforted me and given me hope. You have often challenged me to be a better person, more like the person God wants me to be. For all the gifts you've shared with me through your sermons on Sunday mornings and for our one talk this past spring, I am very grateful. I'm praying that God will return to you tenfold the kindness that you have shown me and that you will be surrounded by supportive friends and family during this new year of 1993.

BF

11/14/92

I know you are frustrated with the progress of the Search Committee. I prayed again that God would protect us against Satan's captivating guile, that He would show mercy on us and send us another man like you—a man devoted to the Lord who longs to serve Him according to His ways and that He would open the hearts of our congregation to recognize and receive this person when he comes.

I can't tell you how much I appreciate your continuing ministry among us. In your latest letter in *the Herald* you mentioned your "great job" and I marveled again at your determined optimism while enduring such back-stabbing opposition.

I thank God that He has sent you here. We need you. You have blessed us from the moment you arrived. You were a major influence in my coming to know the Lord as more than just a far-off "master." I pray that He will strengthen you, inspire you, encourage you, and comfort you in the challenging months and years ahead.

Your faithful friend,
TH

3/8/92

May God return all you have so generously given! We love you dearly and are grateful for your ministry to us at First Parish. Consider your self hugged.

CL

11/25/92

I have seen more clearly in the past year the spiritual war that continues. I never knew it existed! May you bloom where God has planted you. May you grow in love and wisdom on your holy walk. Rich, you and Pat are shining examples of God's light. Shine on!

RR

6/12/92

This letter is to let you know once again how much I love you and appreciate the struggles you are feeling every day. I feel the pain at times when you are in the pulpit and certain folk choose to look upon one of God's faithful servants with disdain and contempt. It is at those times, if you see me with my eyes closed, that I pray that you would feel God interceding from my pleas of strength for you.

MF

4/28/92

Watching you has made me ever more aware of the pain that comes from being a pastor. I have learned to appreciate that sacrifice that you make every week for the sake of your love for Christ's church.

DL

These letters kept us going, and now you can understand more fully why we stayed.

Of course, there were high points. The Men's Breakfast Table had been going for five years. I tried to end each season with someone special. On Saturday, May 9, our speaker was Irving Fryer, wide receiver and punt return specialist for the New England Patriots. Irving, the first player picked in the 1984 draft, shared with the crowd of 130, the highlights of his personal and professional life.

He was raised in a Baptist church in Mount Holly, New Jersey, but in high school and college wandered from his faith in Christ. After a series of disappointments and struggles, God's grace renewed his life and he now seeks to be fully Christian in all aspects of his life. All enjoyed hearing and meeting this well-known athlete.

In succeeding years, we heard from Ray Berry of the Baltimore Colts and Rico Petrocelli, shortstop and third baseman for the Boston Red Sox. These gatherings were attended by men and boys from many north shore churches.

Sharing Inc.

Another step in our mission awareness came on Good Friday. As I mentioned already, I heard about Sharing Inc., so in 1992, I finally decided to take my first steps. I walked around the lake six times to raise money for poor black children in rural Mississippi. The organization was founded by Mrs. Kay Doherty, and she believed that Good Friday was the perfect time to walk for others. Jesus walked carrying His cross, so we walk. He hurt, so we walkers hurt, to a very small degree. His pain is felt as we walk in His name.

Because of the need for a youth leader, the church hired Jim Watson in September. He was a student at Gordon-Conwell, planning to graduate in 1994. I knew Jim from West Church, the fourth child of six, born to Bill and Sandy. He graduated from Gordon College and after a year in Cincinnati, Ohio, enrolled at Fuller Theological Seminary in Pasadena, California. He then transferred to Gordon-Conwell.

Jim met his wife Kristin while in college. She graduated as a mechanical engineer from the University of Lowell. She worked at Hermeneutics in Braintree. Jim and Kristin have a son Christopher and live in West Newton. The Watsons were with us for just one year, and he preached twice and led our youth groups.

This year marked the twenty-fifth anniversary of my ordination. The church was very kind to remember and celebrate with Pat and me. Cards, gifts, and letters again came across my desk.

> 10/4/92
>
> *Congratulations* on twenty-five years of dedication. You are a wonderful pastor and wonderful person, and a wonderful friend.
>
> PC

> 10/5/92
>
> I am so glad and proud to be able to express my best wishes to you on your twenty-fifth anniversary of your ordination. You have helped me

in so many ways in your sermons and just talking with you. I am sure I am not the only person who feels that way.

JW

10/8/92

This day is a wonderful day in remembrance for you in serving our Lord with love and dedication. I am glad you have shared some of those years with us at First Parish. God bless and congratulations!

ML

10/6/92

No amount of money can pay for the amount of caring you give, but we wanted to say thank you and we sure do appreciate you!

With love,
JM

PS. And congratulations on your twenty-five years in the ministry. [Enclosed was a check for $100.00.]

10/7/92

Warmest congratulations on the twenty-fifth anniversary of your ordination to the ministry of the Gospel of Christ.

The Lord has wonderfully used you in His service, preaching the Word, "in season and out," counseling, caring, long-suffering, and wise. We thank you for the blessing you have been to us. We are truly grateful to you and to Him who sent you to us. We pray that the Holy Spirit will continue to lead you in green pastures and beside still waters. Much love to you and Pat.

R+L P

I also received a letter of love signed by seventeen Stephen ministers.

In November, I was invited by the congregational church in Somerville to help them decide whether or not to become Open and Affirming (ONA).

Back in 1984, each local congregation of the conference was strongly encouraged to consider becoming a church that would welcome LGBT persons and affirm their lifestyle.

I was always open to welcoming anyone to the churches I served, but because of the clear teaching of scripture and the traditions of church history, I could not affirm a homosexual lifestyle. I was one of a very few ministers who was willing to share my reasons. So I was grateful for the opportunity to explain my position to a relatively small group of church members in Somerville. They listened and raised their questions, but later I learned they voted to be ONA.

Checking the Mass Conference website, there are 251 UCC churches in the state, and 110 are ONA, less than half. There are one thousand ONA churches in the nation, and 10 percent are in Massachusetts. The MAUCC is more liberal than those further West; after all the ONA movement began in Massachusetts.

On the last Sunday of the year, I preached from Psalm 111. It is a psalm of praise and took a page from that Psalm to compose a psalm of my own to conclude the sermon and to conclude the year.

> Parents carrying their children forward for baptism,
> A sanctuary altar filled with Easter lilies and Christmas poinsettias,
> Children on Christmas Eve and canned goods on Thanksgiving,
> Church officers draped with towels over their shoulders,
> Stephen ministers waiting in the chapel after worship to offer loving care.
> And loving Father,
> I remember moments of distress that proved groundless,

Imagined fears that melted away,
Biopsies that were benign,
Malignant ones treated with radiation and faith.
Differences resolved, mistakes corrected, argu-
    ments settled, communication restored.
All this from your loving hand. I respond to your
    love with my love. Thank you, Lord.

For the record, I conducted eleven weddings, twenty-four funerals, and nine baptisms.

Pam celebrated her twenty-sixth birthday this year and began a ministry at Bethanna, while Dave, age twenty-four, continued with Ron and welcomed Pam into his apartment in Warrington, Pennsylvania. Kim transferred from Gordon College to Salem State.

We began the year on a positive note. The annual meeting flowed beautifully. One special event was the motion by the congregation to declare Horace Hylan a deacon for life. He replied, "This is the greatest gift my church could ever give me." Then he went back to the dishwasher!

I spoke briefly sharing my joy and gratitude. "During 1992 we worshiped the Lord Jesus Christ in freedom and joy for another year. We were given opportunity to teach our children. We were blessed financially so that we could end the year in the black. We spent a sizable sum to maintain our beautiful meetinghouse. We broadcast our worship services on cable TV. We launched community dinners. Our Maundy Thursday service took on fresh meaning, with a newly written script. We are looking for an associate pastor and I trust we will find and hire him/her soon. We expanded our confirmation program from ten weeks to eight months. We are getting ready for a very special anniversary year this November. God is good!"

A highlight for me was the passing, by secret ballot, of our largest budget, $265,222.00. Our pledges for the coming year were about $10,000.00 shy of our needs, but the congregation was not discouraged. This was a great encouragement to me. We were beginning to trust God's provision.

After several months of meetings of the special group appointed in the summer of 1990 to discuss and listen to the concerns of the congregation pertaining to the disruption of June 3, 1990, the issue appeared settled in the minds and hearts of the majority. However there remained a few of our church family who refused to let the issue die. Their beliefs led them to misrepresent my opinions about Freemasonry and the serving of Holy Communion.

Because these individuals continued to share their opinions, I was forced to address the diaconate in an effort to clarify where I stood on the issues. I said in part, "I am not opposed to Freemasonry. It is the oldest and largest fraternal organization in the world and has a positive reputation for good works. I am not a member but have never criticized the organization. And I am not opposed to individual masons nor have I ever refused ministry or fellowship with anyone. Just the opposite is true. I enjoy my opportunities to work and discuss with masons on this board, the board of trustees, and those in our Stephen Ministries program. I am not opposed to hiring an associate pastor who may be a member of a lodge and finally I am not opposed to welcoming the lodge to worship at our church in the future."

Along with a mischaracterization of my opinions and actions regarding Masonry, there was a deliberate effort to twist the statement I made back in 1990 about serving the Holy Communion. I told the diaconate back then that I would not conduct a service of Holy Communion when those serving were members of some other organization other than our church. The board understood my statement and we moved on.

However some took my words to mean that I would be selective as to those I would serve. This hurt me, and I would never withhold the sacrament from anyone who wished to confess their sins and express their gratitude to their Savior. Nevertheless there were those in the choir who refused communion. Several in the congregation saw this refusal and were saddened and confused, as was I.

On the first Sunday after our annual meeting, I called forward our newly elected officers, board, and committee members and gave them their symbolic towel. Since they were declaring their desire to serve, I thought it was an appropriate time for me to make a commitment also. So I wrote the following in the next *Church Herald*:

> No one knows what is over the next hill, but just in case you may have had reason to wonder about where my scales tip or just how sold out I am to the work of ministry, let it be known that I'm in for the duration: alone or surrounded by friends, rejected or respected, tired or eager, by myself at the desk or standing in front of you all. God has called me to serve First Parish Congregational Church and that's what I must do. For me, there are no other options. It is a matter of obedience.

I knew that this public statement about my plans for the future was necessary to put everyone's mind at ease, or perhaps let others realize that I was not going away.

In February, I conducted a funeral for a widow who with her husband worshipped regularly at the 9:00 a.m. service. In June, she wrote to the diaconate offering to purchase fifty copies of a new hymnal for the chapel.

Because the choir doesn't sing at the 9:00 a.m. service, the congregation has the opportunity to have a brief hymn sing during the service. *The Pilgrim Hymnal*, which we were using, was published in 1931 and lacked many hymns and songs that the worshippers wanted to sing together.

When the diaconate received the offer, they asked the Music Committee for their support. The committee was strongly opposed and being aware that the UCC was working on a new hymnal due to be published in 1995 said we should wait to see that new UCC effort. "Perhaps the donor would consider redirecting her gift toward that hymnal if we decided to buy it."

I had a suspicion that the reason for their rejection went a little deeper. Music is a vital part of worship, and a new hymnal, especially one that was not produced by the UCC, would reflect a more conservative theological perspective. The thought of a shift to the right was not welcomed by the committee. (This committee would become very problematic in a year or two.)

When her gift was refused, she purchased a flowering pear tree, which grows in the church's front lawn.

I walked for the second time on Good Friday to raise funds for Sharing Inc. There were forty-five members of the church who contributed $648.00 to the cause. As the years went by, there developed a growing sense of pride in my efforts. Contributions grew and so did the number of folks who joined me for a lap or two.

August 1 marked my tenth anniversary as pastor of First Parish, so the diaconate marked the day with a large bouquet of chrysanthemums delivered to our door. The card read, "Ten years—Wow! We appreciate you both. The Diaconate."

Our son David lived with Pat's parents when he first moved to Pennsylvania. After a few months, he got his own apartment in the home of a church member. When Pam moved south, she and Dave rented an apartment together in Warrington, Pennsylvania. A young woman named Sharon Reynolds lived in the apartment next to theirs; she took notice of Dave but assumed that Pam Weisenbach and David Weisenbach were married. She was surprised and pleased to discover that they were brother and sister. This made a big difference!

They started seeing more of each other, and when things began to grow seriously, Dave asked Sharon about her religion. Sharon was surprised initially at his question but shared that she was Catholic.

As time went on, issues of Christian faith would arise in their conversation. She kept asking him questions about his faith forcing Dave to say, "Can I introduce you to my grandfather? I think he can help answer some of your questions?"

They met together with "Poppy," Pat's father, several times, and eventually Sharon confessed her sins and asked Jesus to forgive her. They began worshipping together; she was baptized by immersion, and finally Dave brought Sharon to meet us in Massachusetts. He announced that he had proposed marriage, and she said yes! We were pleased and excited for them.

Their wedding was in Pennsylvania on October 9. I conducted the ceremony, and despite tears, we made it through. A reception was held at the fire hall in Warrington. A wonderful time was had by all.

God had much in store for these young people, and they have worked hard to follow God's direction.

The wedding was in October 9, and in October 14, we began teaching another Stephen Ministries class with nine candidates. We now had twenty ministers and four leaders. I didn't have much trouble matching our ministers with members of the church family who needed some special care.

Then on Sunday, October 24, the Associate Pastor Search Committee recommended to the congregation that Gail Lynn Miller be welcomed as our associate pastor.

Gail was born in Vermont but grew up in a suburb of Milwaukee, Wisconsin. She studied at St. Olaf College and Northwestern Theological Seminary. She came to us from Colonial Church in Edina, Minnesota, where she has been active in youth ministry. Her first Sunday with us was on November 7, 1993.

Over all 1993 was a good year and a busy year. Kim graduated cum laude from Salem State and I conducted twelve weddings (116 over ten years), twenty-four funerals (242 for the ten years), and twenty-one baptisms (188 for the ten years). We also welcomed 312 new members in those ten years, and worship attendance went up from 172 to 218. Income increased from $155,300.00 to $265,000.00. To God be the glory.

It finally arrived, our 350th annual meeting. *Wow!* Here is what I wrote in late January, a week after the annual meeting.

> As I reflect upon this very special occasion, two thoughts come to mind.
>
> First and foremost is just how grateful I am, how grateful we all must be, just to be included in such an event. It is a great privilege, isn't it? To be the beneficiary of such a proud history; to be

an inheritor of the blessings that have come our way because others have gone before us, those who have labored, prayed, tithed, served, centuries ago. What a privilege is ours! They had to be sacrificial in the sharing of their wealth and energy. They had to set themselves for the struggle with discipline and fortitude. And none of them lived to see the fruits that we enjoy today. They just carried out their responsibilities before God and together with their brothers and sisters labored on.

They focused on one thing; they kept their faith alive in their own experience in order to transfer it to the next generation. This thought leads to another; with this gratitude comes a sense of humility.

We know very few of the particulars concerning our earliest brothers and sisters. So much of their lives has faded into the misty past. All we really know for sure is that they were given the opportunity to love, to serve, to pray and give—and many of them took it! They were faithful to God who extended that opportunity...and then they died.

And so it will be with us. We are given that same opportunity—for a short time—then we too will die. All of us play a very small part in the very large purposes of God. It is for us to be faithful in our day as they were in theirs

The committee has been working for years, the time has finally arrived. A booklet containing our history has been written, another pictorial directory planned, a trip to the Museum of Fine Arts to view our ancient communion silver, a gala concert and Interfaith Thanksgiving service are in our future as well. This hopes to be very special!

The committee had also suggested that this special anniversary would be a good time to tackle a few long-standing building maintenance issues. We borrowed $106,000.00 from the Savings Bank and repointed the stones of our entire meetinghouse. We were able to repay most of the debt through a small capital campaign.

Much to my surprise, the church council, on the recommendation of the diaconate, conducted a secret collection to honor my tenth anniversary. "We know that a personal computer is on your wish list, and we want you to use this gift toward that purpose." Enclosed with their card was a check for $1,400.00. This was a great and loving gesture, greatly appreciated.

Our vacation that year was a celebration of thirty years as husband and wife. We were near Moosehead for two weeks, one week at Spencer Pond (Lunkers this time), and the second at Chesuncook Village two hours north of Greenville.

It was quite an experience to preach in the refurbished chapel, once the church and school of the town. Only four people attended the worship service. We had a very relaxing week but would not volunteer to go again.

This was the year that I requested the diaconate to consider the idea of developing a sabbatical policy for the church. I was aiming for February 1–April 30, 1995. Pat and I would travel to Puebla, Mexico. It would be our desire to help nurture the Christian church there. At that time, Pat's brother Jack and family had been missionaries in Puebla for over fifteen years. Jack assured us that I would be able to make a contribution. We could minister to the students in the school, serve the missionary personnel, preach through a translator in a Spanish church, help Jack with some administration, and teach at the seminary in a limited capacity. We enrolled in a Spanish class at the Vocational School in preparation. It looked like we were going to go.

In August 1993, David Renner died; he was thirty-two and the son of Joyce Langone. This tragic event left us all raising the age-old question, why? "Lord help us to trust you, no matter what."

His mother Joyce wanted to do something special to remember David; actually she did two things. She was a faithful attender of the 9:00 a.m. chapel service, so she purchased a brass advent candleholder to be used each Advent season. The following year, she gave a gift large enough to install and maintain two exterior lights to focus on our tower. As one drives up Main Street, the lighted tower guides the way.

Pat planned our annual Christmas open house with a Mexican theme that year. We received this note.

> Dear Pat and Pastor Rich,
> Thank you for yet another "Open House" for which you have become quite famous. The Mexican theme was very appropriate and we all enjoyed the delicious food, lovely decorations, the warmth of your home and fine fellowship. It has helped to put us right in the spirit of Christmas. Thank you for all you did to make it such a happy occasion. My husband would have loved it.
> With love,
> DT

My annual report for 1994 included reflections about that very special anniversary year.

> Special thanks to the Anniversary Committee who planned and facilitated events during the year. We were all treated to dinners, trips, exhibits, worship services, picnics, customs, memorabilia, and community events including a float in the Town's Fourth of July parade. Our Anniversary Worship service in November welcomed former minister Rev. John Robertson, Mass Confer-

ence minister Rev. Benny Whiten, and the Rev. Dr. Paul Sherry, president of the UCC. It was quite a service of celebration.

Sadly our planned sabbatical had to be cancelled. Pat and I decided that the timing wasn't right. I think both of us were a bit nervous about being away for three months. There was still a degree of opposition within the congregation, and we were sure we should be present if any disruption arose.

Our worship attendance grew to an average of 226 that year. And for the record, I conducted ten weddings, twenty-five funerals, and nineteen baptisms.

It is also worth noting that a church member sent me $100.00 every month for the whole year. "You should have gotten a raise," was written in the note from JM.

At our annual meeting in January, I described the past ten years as the end of the beginning. Over those beginning years, many steps had been taken, decisions made, programs launched, and differences resolved. We had laid a new foundation for a new era in the life of First Parish. There were still many issues to be confronted in the years to come, but I sensed that a critical mass of committed believers had been assembled. I felt that I was ready to move forward and that there were many in the congregation who were eager to join me. The time of planting and quiet witness was over. Thank the Lord.

On Sunday, February 5, Pat, Pam, and I sang a trio, "Here I am Lord." Several spoke of their gratitude as they passed through the greeting line. I was very grateful to share the musical gifts God has given to our family.

On Tuesday, February 14, I met with our minister of music who stated that he expects to make all musical decisions and was disappointed that he was not consulted about the trio in the February 5 worship service. He told me that providing special music in the worship service is a privilege reserved for members of the choir. Anyone outside of the music program of First Parish must gain his approval. He saw this as his way of exercising quality control.

I responded that I have musical ideas and contributions and will exercise my options from time to time. Our bylaws and his job description both clearly state that the minister of music and the pastor will plan worship services together and that the pastor has ultimate authority over the contents of the worship service.

Meeting to discuss and pray with the pastor at planning sessions was something that the minister of music thought was unnecessary. He saw his responsibilities as narrowly confined to music and had little desire to communicate with me, and he depended on the Music Committee to do that. This lack of communication between organist and pastor would ultimately have very serious implications within a very short time.

At the February council meeting, the chair of the diaconate read a letter she had received that was very critical of me. The letter was unsigned she said. The council was quick to come to my defense and stated that in the future, anonymous correspondence would not receive any consideration. I was very grateful, while the chair of the diaconate was frustrated and embarrassed.

In March 8, Gail told me that she had been interviewed by a church in Acton and was extended a call to serve at that church. She was actually approached in September 1994 by the pastor and showed some interest in the position. She wanted to leave in May 21. I asked if she would stay through June 4, the end of the confirmation program. She was not open to any changes in her plans.

About a week later, the pastor of the Acton church called me saying, "You don't know me but I owe you an apology." I responded, "You are correct on both counts." It was very unprofessional for him to approach someone who had only been at her position for eleven months. As I reflect back, I'm sure that the stress within the congregation was a serious source of pain and fear leading her to seriously consider the first opportunity to move on.

There were two big family events in May and June. Molly Lynne was born to Dave and Sharon on Tuesday, May 16. We drove to Pennsylvania and saw them on Wednesday evening. Then I drove back to Massachusetts for Gail's last Sunday on the May 21 and then drove back to Pennsylvania till Wednesday, May 24. It was a blessing to welcome our first grandchild. Dave confessed that he cried at the delivery.

While at the hospital, I was very surprised to bump into my childhood friend George Stockberger IV. He and his wife welcomed their first grandchild, George Stockberger VI, same floor, same day.

The second big family event was when Brian Albushies proposed marriage to Kim, and a wedding was planned for July 6 of next year. Thank you, Lord.

In September, we selected another Search Committee to find and hire someone to replace Gail, but as the trustees began to put the budget together for 1996, they realized that if we delayed the search and the hiring of another staff member, we would not be under as much pressure to raise the necessary funds. Fortunately a letter was composed and signed by thirty-six church members urging the church council to find and hire a person to assist me and work with our youth, ASAP. The council agreed and the search was on.

We had a very unique experience that same month. Gen. John R. Galvin, a Wakefield native and former Supreme Allied Commander of NATO, became the dean of the Fletcher School of Law and Diplomacy at Tufts University. In that capacity and in an effort to foster communication between the United States and the Soviet Union, he proposed to give a group of Soviet generals and admirals the opportunity to visit a small town in America.

He brought these leaders to Wakefield, his hometown; our middle school is named after him. He arranged visits to Harts Hardware, a Chevrolet agency, and First Parish Congregational Church. He asked me to speak to them for a brief time and to provide a dinner meal for one or two in our home.

I felt very privileged and arranged to provide a copy of a Bible in Russian for each distinguished visitor. General Galvin repeated this program for at least two more years. (An interesting historical note was mentioned by the general; his grandfather, also a Wakefield native, helped to rebuild our meetinghouse after the fire in 1909.)

God provided an amazing gift that fall. A church member sent a card saying how disappointed she was that we had to cancel our planned sabbatical. She thought that I handled the loss in "a very classy" way. Inside the card was a check for $8,000.00!

Praise God from whom all blessings flow!

Thoughts on Baptism

One of the greatest challenges I faced at First Parish had to do with the service of Christian baptism. The congregational church observes both modes, infant baptism and believer's baptism by sprinkling or immersion.

It was always a challenge when a couple requested baptism for their child but had little or no relationship to our church or any church. I was usually caught between the desire to foster Christian growth within the family if they took this step seriously, and the haunting doubt that there was little chance for growth to occur.

Do I explain the serious promises the couple will be making before God and in front of the congregation on a Sunday morning and then believe the couple understands the implications of these three important promises?

- Do you know the Lord Jesus Christ as your personal savior from sin? (Yes.)
- Is it this faith that leads you to bring your child for Christian baptism? (It is.)
- Are you prepared with God's help to provide a Christian environment, Christian encouragement, and Christian example for your child? (Yes.)

If the parents acceded to the questions I asked, I proceeded with the baptism, but often the families did not fulfill their vows. I always felt used and somewhat complicit in these cases.

The other choice was to tell the couple that I didn't see Christian fruit in their lives and that any verbal statement they might make would be hypocritical and meaningless. That was hard for me to say.

I consoled myself by trusting that perhaps the Holy Spirit might speak to their hearts and they would in time fulfill their intentions.

Besides this, it got even more complicated if the couple had been raised at First Parish but left and never grew in their faith. Now the child they were bringing was the grandchild of a church member who was eager to have the baptism move forward.

There were two or three cases when I had to refuse them, this invariably caused trouble. But this was bound to occur in a church like First Parish where in the past little biblical instruction took place and genuine faith didn't have a chance to grow.

Over time the diaconate did see the necessity of protecting the meaning of Christian baptism by establishing a policy that required at least one member of the family to be a participating member of a church. It is for the church/diaconate to help the pastor and take a stand. I was very grateful when this finally happened, but it took years.

Fortunately there was at least one family that did take their promises seriously, started attending weekly worship services, then joining, and serving. This was so encouraging to me.

For the record, average attendance was 237 for every Sunday of the year. (In the past, average attendance would be calculated for only nine months, eliminating the three months of summer.)

I conducted ten weddings, twenty-eight funerals, and twenty-four baptisms in 1995.

At our annual meetings, I was always asked if I wanted to add anything to my report. I felt that this was my chance to speak informally to the membership. This wasn't a sermon, but just a few minutes to share what was on my heart. Here is a small portion of what I said as we began 1996.

"If a stranger were to ask you, 'What are you building here at your church?' He would probably be given a variety of answers. Let me tell you what I would say in answer to that question. I want you to know my heart. I want you to know my primary goal. It is not more members, a balanced budget, or a new pastoral assistant.

"My goal is be build a community of loving people eager to share that love with the Wakefield community. Jesus said, 'Loving and serving one another is the clearest and most powerful way to let others know you are my followers.' That is my goal. I trust that this is God's goal. Is it your goal? Will you join me in this building project? Will you stand with me as a sign of unity and mutual support?"

The majority of the group stood immediately, while others followed slowly. Several, including Pat, told me that they were grateful for the opportunity to stand and declare their support. I thought it was a good start for the year.

But alongside the positive response at the meeting, there was a simmering conflict within the Music Committee. The minister of music believed that he had complete authority concerning the music chosen and presented at every service of the church. I had unknowingly trespassed that rule when Pat, Pam, and I sang that trio back in February 1995. I brought further disappointment when I had opportunity to speak with our organist telling him that I had complete responsibility for every service of worship and would continue to exercise that authority as long as I was pastor. Sadly, whatever relationship we had deteriorated rapidly during the next twelve months.

On Good Friday, I walked for the fifth year to raise funds for Sharing Inc. I was delighted to receive financial support from ninety-six people, and they gave a total of $1,070.00 that year.

We welcomed David Albert Weisenbach in May 9. The grandchildren are beginning to add up!

In July 6, our daughter Kimberly wed Brian Albushies. The Weisenbachs and the O'Briens gathered for a marvelous family event. Pat mentioned to a friend, "There are three days in your children's lives that are more special than any others—the day they are born, the day they marry, and the day they have a child."

We are, of course, grateful to our loving God for the privilege of parenthood, for the blessings are beyond measure. The gift of a child comes from the Lord's hand, and we have been blessed three times. God's promises to care for them throughout their lives have brought such assurance! (And now that they are older, we are the recipients of their loving presence, prayers, and generosity.)

The service was a delight complete with a trumpeter and tears. We were so fortunate that all four of Kim's grandparents were able to attend—Gram and Gramps and Granny and Poppy.

We had a reception at the Franciscan Center in Andover followed by a breakfast at the Lord Wakefield. Almost everyone stayed throughout the weekend and enjoyed an extended time together. The bride and groom flew to Bermuda for their honeymoon. When they returned, they moved in an apartment in Reading.

At the April council meeting, the chair of the Christian Education Search Committee reported that the search looks promising and that we can expect to have a director of Christian education on board by September 1996 as approved and funded at our January 1996 annual meeting.

In July 16, Sandra Bisson was interviewed and she was hired on August 29, 1996.

Passion Play

In 1990, Horace Hylan journeyed to Germany to attend the *Passion Play* performed by the town of Oberammergau, Germany. The townsfolk present the play every ten years as their expression of thanks to God for preserving them from the Black Plague (1346–1453).

Horace was so impressed by the power of the play that he came home determined to investigate the possibility of having a similar play performed by our congregation. He made such a strong case before the diaconate that they agreed with him. He of course had to write the script, recruit the cast, conduct the rehearsals, build and store the props, and communicate his vision to everyone. He did all of that within a year, and in 1991, First Parish performed its first *Passion Play* on Good Friday.

The popularity of the presentation grew, so in 1996, Horace proposed that it be presented on two nights, Maundy Thursday and Good Friday. Each year he would write more text, build more sets, and expand the cast. When Horace turned ninety, he stepped down as director, and the play continued through 2015 under the direction of Pamela Weisenbach Abkarian. After a few years, she rewrote the script and added music, which greatly enhanced the production.

To see the play was a very moving experience, and I believe that it was used by God to present the gospel message to the community. It ended with Jesus being put into the tomb, which was posted with Roman guards. Communion was offered at the conclusion and an invitation to return on Sunday morning to hear "the rest of the story."

Sunday's worship service began with women walking down the aisle holding small bottles of spices. They encounter an angel with the news, "He is not here. He is risen just as He said." Mary lingers and becomes the first to meet the risen Christ Jesus. She then turns and runs up the aisle shouting, "He is risen! He is risen!" Jesus shouts to Mary, "Don't forget to tell Peter!" At this point, the organ and a five-piece brass ensemble sounds the opening strains of "Christ the Lord Is Risen Today!" I invite the congregation to stand and we sing praise to our risen Savior. As you can imagine, this was always a wonderful opening to our worship service.

Serious Conflict

In preparation for the Christmas Eve service that year, I informed the minister of music that three members of the congregation—a violinist, soloist, and guitarist—will be part of the evening. I received a written response from the Music Committee, not the minister of music. The committee informed me that our minister of music did not want to discuss differences between himself and me but would prefer to have the committee communicate his desires.

Their letter stated,

> As it is the Music Committee which has the responsibility/duty to make decisions regarding music at First Parish, we are concerned to exercise fairness to everyone. At our last meeting, the committee discussed and made its final decisions about the music for the 11:00 p.m. Christmas Eve service. This (your) request now comes at

such a late time that it is impossible for us to give it fair consideration since we do not meet again this month. We are not willing to make an exception to allow for your request. In the future we do expect that anyone requesting to participate in the music at First Parish contact the committee no later than the committee meeting prior to the date of the request so that the matter can be discussed fairly by the committee as a whole.

The Music Committee didn't realize that I was *not* making a request. I was *informing* the minister of music that a violinist, soloist, and guitarist would be sharing their gifts. I was responsible to plan and lead the worship services at First Parish, and I was simply doing my job. The committee, in thinking that they were in charge, were in conflict with me. I was frustrated and saddened by their actions.

It was also a serious disappointment that the minister of music refused to talk to me in person but chose to have the committee communicate his wishes. The committee, it seemed, was more than happy to do his bidding.

Relationships worsened when the violinist, soloist, and guitarist did perform that Christmas Eve. Despite the growing differences between me and the minister of music and his committee, it was a year blessed by God.

My annual report reflected many signs of grace—the *Passion Play*, a growing Stephen Ministries, faithful Sunday school teachers, choir members, ushers and greeters, coffee servers, twenty-six new members and the hiring of Sandra Bisson as minister to youth, a wonderful Hongo concert, a granddaughter's first steps, a new grandson, and a son-in-law added to the family.

This was the year that Pat decided to join DOTS (Dozens of Terrific Stamps). She had been making cards for a few years and buying materials from her sister Kathy. This year she would become part of Kathy's downline and start demonstrating and selling herself. For twenty years, she had house parties, crops at the church, and workshops at Edgewood LifeCare Community and Place of

Promise. Every year she spent twelve hours a day at her booth in the Coolidge Building during the ten days of the Topsfield Fair, and the best part, she traveled to places around the country to attend annual convention!

She is no longer a consultant with the company, now called Close to My Heart (CTMH), but she continues to make cards, saving us money, and filling scrapbooks with pictures and journaling. All the pictures in this book are ones she has taken, cropped, arranged, and preserved.

Most afternoons find her in her workshop—our bedroom—preparing projects. She never sits and watches TV without cutting, coloring, or arranging papers and pictures for an upcoming event. She is a very creative person; before stamping, there was rug braiding, stained glass, crocheting, candlewicking, flower arranging, and taking care of the family.

This was the year that Pam moved back to 27 Curve Street and started studies at Salem State in the theater department. She also began working as a DJ for weddings and other such events.

For the record, I conducted eleven weddings, thirty funerals, and thirty baptisms. Weekly attendance was 241, and we ended the year with over $5,000.00 more than we needed and didn't have to use any reserves again!

At our annual meeting, I had opportunity, as usual, to speak to the congregation, sharing my heart, casting a vision for the future, and seeking to build unity. I was very aware that the opposition was growing within the Music Committee and had no idea how it might be resolved. But I wanted to do something that would strengthen my relationship with the people. So I referred back to the service of installation in the fall of 1983. I passed out copies of the promises I had made at the time and also the response of the congregation to those promises. Then I asked all those who were present at that service of installation fourteen years ago to stand with me. Then I invited everyone else to stand so we could together reaffirm our commitment to one another and to God's will and purpose. I was glad that God gave me that opportunity.

In January, I was invited to attend the regular meeting of the Music Committee to defend the music selections I had made for the Christmas Eve service. The one friendly member of the committee called to tell me, "They plan to skewer you."

I had shared my anxiety with a few leaders who decided to attend the meeting along with me. I was encouraged by their support.

The committee wanted to know why I didn't honor their decision to deny my "request." I stated as clearly as I could that I have always understood that my role as pastor gave me the necessary authority to plan worship services. In my relationships with the two previous ministers of music, my suggestions and requests were always honored.

My relationship with our present minister has been different, and he states that he alone would decide what would be sung or played and who would be allowed to participate musically. I differed strongly with him and said so, and our congregation contains several who are gifted musically yet do not participate in the formal music program of the church, but they should be encouraged to share their gift.

The minister of music finally asked me, "If you and I differ, who has the final say?"

I responded, "I do."

I and the other guests were dismissed and the committee made a motion reinforcing their understanding of where the final authority lay. That statement was included in their minutes and presented to the church council at council's February meeting.

> In response to the meeting with Pastor Weisenbach on January 23, 1997, regarding the role of the Music Committee, a motion was made, seconded, and passed. It is our decision that the Music Committee has the authority to make final decisions regarding any and all music that takes place in Worship Services, congregational meetings, and other functions.

At their February meeting, the council saw this statement as "overstepping…and creating authority they didn't have." The council made two motions, a motion instructing the committee to reconsider their recent claims and a second to establish an ad hoc committee to assist in the task of improving communication between the pastor and the minister of music. The first meeting would be scheduled for April.

In February 9, Rev. Bob Mendelssohn, a member of Jew for Jesus, preached on that Sunday in preparation for the Lenten season.

As in the past, the diaconate served a simple soup supper on Ash Wednesday. We sat at tables in the dining room, I read a brief communion meditation (usually something by Max Lucado), and then we shared communion together. This simple forty-five-minute service began the Lenten season for several years.

This year was my sixth effort to raise funds for the poor in the American South through Sharing Inc. I announced a change in the distribution of the funds raised. Sharing Inc. concluded that local churches were encouraged to withhold one-third of the funds collected to be dispersed among local food banks. So for the first time, a sizable portion of all we raised would be given to the food banks in Wakefield, Melrose, and Saugus.

In the first five years, we had raised $4,368.00 for Sharing Inc. That year 121 members and friends gave an additional $1,380.00.

In May, I announced the formation of a fifth Stephen Ministries training session. At that time, there were eighteen ministers in the program and five leaders/teachers. I believe that this training program added much to the health and ministry of the church. Not only did persons who needed loving care receive it, but also the spiritual health of every minister and leader was deepened. Many received a clearer understanding of the gospel message, along with answers to why and how to share it. An added benefit was the fact that many learned how to pray aloud with their care receiver. This practice was a challenge for some, but all met it and reaped the blessings.

The ad hoc committee met in April to help better the communication between me and the minister of music. Unfortunately, he told the moderator, two days before the meeting date, that he would not be attending. He shared several reasons—he was not clear as to the purpose, he was very busy and feels that this conflict is simply a matter for the Music Committee to resolve, and he felt that the meeting did not concern him. The committee met without him.

A second meeting was called for June 10. All members of the committee were in attendance, but one issue we discussed confused and angered our minister of music greatly. For the sake of confidentiality, the committee decided that we would not publish any notes of our conversations till some actions were decided. The minister of music saw this as an attempt to cloak our actions in secrecy.

A third meeting was called for July 1. Both the minister of music and Music Committee chair left messages with the moderator that they were no longer going to participate in the meetings. The ad hoc committee met without them but were becoming very confused.

In July we joined the Pedersens and the Whitmans for our long anticipated trip to England. We enjoyed a wonderful two-week tour with our friends, and then Pat and I flew to Ireland for another two weeks. Little did we know what was happening back home!

In July 6, the minister of music resigned after nine and a half years. This came as a great shock, especially to the members of the ad hoc committee. There was nothing indicating that such a decision was forthcoming.

In light of the music director's resignation, the moderator called a special meeting of the council for July 14. The purpose of the meeting "was to discuss the resignation of the music director." In an effort to inform council members of what had transpired, a timeline was presented covering the events from November 1996 to July 10, 1997. After prayer and much discussion, the council made two motions.

> The moderator is in receipt of the music director's resignation dated July 6, 1997; that he tried to reach the director via telephone to discuss the letter; that, unable to do so, he is sending this letter asking the director to contact him by Friday, July 28, 1997, so that they can talk.

A second motion instructed Sandra Bisson [remember, Pat and I were in Ireland] to inform the congregation of the director's resignation and that the council is saddened and disturbed and working toward an amicable resolution of the matter.

I was disappointed that I was in Ireland for the month and unable to be a part of those discussions and decisions, but remain very proud and grateful for the careful actions of the church's leadership. I was particularly grateful for the way our moderator, Greg Lanick, handled the situation. He worked tirelessly, and I believe he was God's man for that time.

The council never heard a word from the music director. He was able to gain a position at the Second Congregational Church in Beverly; the chair of our Music Committee resigned as well and joined the music director at the Beverly church.

We were able to call upon church member Ron Martin, already organist at the Wednesday Service and the 9:00 a.m., Sunday service, to play for the 10:30 a.m. service as well. In November, we hired Regina Matthews as our interim organist and choir director.

My brothers Bill and Paul arranged a surprise eightieth birthday party for Dad in September 14. We gathered at a restaurant in Belfast, Maine, for lobster. "It couldn't have happened to a nicer guy," was Dad's response.

In October, the church marked the thirtieth anniversary of my ordination.

Dear Rich,
Congratulations on thirty years! You mean so much to each of us.
Love, First Parish
[Along with a lovely card was a catalogue instructing me to order a new doctoral robe.]

Life in the church seemed to recover in the fall. We began Sunday school classes and dedicated our teaching staff, we marked the tenth anniversary of Stephen Ministries, and our daughter Kim preached a sermon in October 6 marking Pastor Appreciation Month. She did a wonderful job. (I am a little prejudiced though.)

In November, things became disruptive, threatening, and scary. A church member and member of the choir wrote a letter sharing that he had received an anonymous letter calling for my resignation. He agreed with the contents of this letter and sent it to several church members, more than a hundred. This member believed that I had forced our music minister out of his position. I did have serious differences with him, but we had worked together for more than nine years and was prepared to continue as long as our communication would improve, and I thought it could and wanted to work toward that goal. He is a very competent musician.

On November 28, 1997, I wrote in the *Church Herald*,

> My heart is heavy as I write to you all. Heavy with sadness over the division that has surfaced within our congregation.
>
> The division has occurred as a result of the resignation of our organist/choir director. His leaving this past July was greeted with surprise and sadness by everyone. The church council had established a special committee to try to improve relationships; unfortunately it did not accomplish its purpose.
>
> I am happy and grateful to God to see that most of our congregation, although missing our music director, have sought to move on. My heart is heavy because a small percentage of our membership continues to carry their anger.
>
> An anonymous letter has been sent to scores of our members and friends, a letter which seeks to destroy our fellowship. This letter has been a

shock and source of pain to many of us; I know, you have told me. There is even a petition at a downtown candy store inviting church members to register their opinion. Such behavior can never be God's way for First Parish.

Despite these events I want to assure you that Pat and I know the peace of God in our hearts. We (I) sleep well and are seeking to trust the Lord.

The council's actions, under the leadership of our moderator, have been a great source of support and encouragement. Your calls, cards, hugs, and prayers have sustained us greatly. Thank you. Thank you. Thank you.

Your church council has worked overtime to seek and share God's way through this mess. I believe their decisions and plans are the right thing to do and will help us heal. A letter to our entire congregation should be arriving within a week to ten days explaining in full what has been planned.

One final request. The anonymous letter-writer urged people to withhold their financial support in a further attempt to bring harm. I am truly grateful for your response to our stewardship campaign thus far, but I can say that there will be several who will not pledge this year. This will hurt our efforts. We will only meet our goal and its 3.6% increase if you show your support. Please consider a bold commitment, believing that God will help you do your part at this critical time.

Here is a brief summary of the letter the council sent to the congregation.

> The year 1997 has been a difficult year for First Parish. Since the departure of our minister of music, there has been much confusion, conflict, division, and misunderstanding.
>
> Toward an effort to bring about reconciliation, council has hired a team of facilitators to lead the church through a project in which we will hear the concerns of our members, develop a list of recommendations for the church to act upon, and learn the communication and conflict management skills we will need to deal with our disagreements more effectively in the future. This project will last approximately six months and will cost $6,000.00.
>
> At our upcoming annual meeting, council will present fifteen names of church members willing to serve on the Core Group.
>
> Council believes that this project represents the best opportunity for our church to face its troubles, deal with them effectively and move forward as a unified body that honors our God and Savior. Please pray for First Parish.
>
> Your moderator for the Council

During these stressful months, my prayer was for assurance that remaining at First Parish was the best for God and His people. There were times during the year that the thought of moving on seemed a possible choice. But then I would recall the miraculous way in which God brought us back to New England. It was very clear to me that God wanted us to stay at First Parish, so we decided that we would remain till the time became clear that we should begin seeking another place to minister.

For the record, I conducted twenty-one weddings, twenty-three funerals, and twenty-five baptisms. By God's grace, we ended the year with a $19,158.45 surplus and enough pledges to cover next year's proposed budget of $220,770.00.

Both Dave and Sharon and Kim and Brian were able to move into new homes that year.

The family again gathered at Ladore, the Salvation Army camp in the Poconos, for our annual reunion, this time marking the year when both our parents would celebrate their eightieth birthdays. Dad had sustained an operation on his acoustic nerve, and all went well. Kim began teaching third-grade boys as a reading specialist at a Jewish school, and Dave was hired by Crompton and Sykes, a construction company, building and refurbishing gas stations.

On Friday, December 5, we had to put our dog Sydney to sleep. He was about eight years old, typical for dogs of his breed. He couldn't walk or eliminate and probably had cancer. Pam, Kim, Brian, and Pat took him to the vet. I dug a grave and made a cross. We buried him in the rain, shared memories, and prayed.

The church member who had distributed the anonymous letter back in November decided to write one of his own on January 21, 1998. Here is a portion of his letter.

> A petition calling for a special meeting of all members of the First Parish Congregational Church of Wakefield has been signed by fifty-four of your fellow members.
>
> Our church has come to a defining moment in its wonderful 353-year history. On Sunday, February 1, 1998, at noon following the Worship Service we will help to decide our future as a Congregational Church. We will be asked to vote by *secret ballot* on which direction we want to see our beloved church go: as a fundamentalist church with Rev. Richard A. Weisenbach as its leader or to continue in the tradition of main-

stream Protestant Christianity, open to a diverse community of believers.

We need a new minister! And remember, even if you are an "inactive member," you still hold the right to vote. This is a difficult time for all of us. Please remember, Jesus also battled the religious establishment of His day in the name of tolerance and acceptance. We are not alone when we walk with Him.

Sincerely,

J—— A——

Our moderator instructed the clerk to post a notice of the special meeting to be held on February 1, 1998. This announcement of the meeting called a strong reaction from many in the congregation. A group of sixty-four members and friends signed a letter and distributed it throughout the fellowship.

To members of First Parish Congregational Church,

Two very important dates to remember, both dates concern the possible dismissal of our pastor, January 28, the annual meeting and February 1, the special meeting. To retain our pastor it is absolutely imperative that you attend both meetings to exercise your right and privilege to vote.

Enclosed you will find a blue ribbon that we ask you to wear proudly in support of our beloved pastor. Please wear it when at church until this crisis has been resolved!

I wrote my "RAW Material" article in January 23. In it, I referenced two historic documents of First Parish—our 1644 covenant and the questions and answers that I and the congregation spoke during my installation on November 27, 1983. Both statements stand clearly upon the Bible, the foundation of Christian faith and life. I was trying to remind my brothers and sisters that what I had been preaching for the last fourteen years was in line with the original covenant of the church and the words of installation. I firmly believed that I stood on solid ground. Of course, there were others who believed that things change over time and the church must change with the times.

On Sunday, January 25, I dedicated the fifteen members of the church who had been appointed to serve as a core group. This is what I said,

> God in grace has brought us to 1998 with all its joys and challenges. You have accepted the heavy responsibility of working with God's Holy Spirit, our professional facilitators, and one another to help our congregation make important steps into our future. Thank you for your willingness to serve.
>
> As you begin your work, be assured of our gratitude and prayer. You all know the importance of listening, you will discover how necessary and difficult that task truly is, and you will need God's help. Let us pray together.
>
> Almighty God, you have been faithful to us through the centuries. You have promised never to leave us or forsake us. We would take steps together in 1998 only because we are depending upon your promises. Oh God, the task of these brothers and sisters is great: to hear each other, to listen in love, to speak kindly, to exercise patience, to withhold judgment, to act with courage, to pray earnestly for your mind, to build unity around your truth. Father God, make your truth clear to all. This is indeed our only hope of oneness.

You have made us with our differences, help us respect what you have created, and seek our common ground in your gospel of grace and new life. Create a new thing within our congregation. Plant your seeds within these hearts that they will truly respond to your direction. Grant joy and hope to these. May they know your presence in their hearts and in their midst.

Strengthen their facilitators and remind us all to hold them daily before your throne of grace in prayer. Hear our prayer through our Savior and our leader, Jesus Christ. Amen.

The next week, February 1, we dedicated our newly elected officers and board and committee members. As usual, I gave each a shop towel symbolizing the main task of leadership—service.

I failed to record the text and title of my sermon for the morning, but it was a Sunday to remember our Savior at His table, so it seemed appropriate to read this note before sharing Holy Communion.

Today we all face a major challenge to the life of our congregation. I will not be with you as you speak and listen, discuss, and decide. [Our bylaws prohibit the minister from attending meetings when his/her tenure, salary, or behavior is discussed.] So at this timely moment let me say, I am truly sorry for the damage I have done to the body of Christ during my time among you. I sincerely ask for your forgiveness. I pledge myself and my energy to our upcoming process of facilitation to speak and listen to all in love, and regardless of the outcome of today's vote, I love you all.

Now let us all come to the Table confessing our own sins to our Savior.

I stood in the receiving line, greeted many folks, and then went home to await the results of the meeting. Pat, of course, remained to attend the meeting.

I was surprised and delighted to welcome Dean and Jane Peterson and Ed and Sandy Whitman to our home that afternoon. They drove to our house in Wakefield to be with me while I waited. Such dear friends! (A check of my records shows that I conducted four funerals in January and four in February. It was a busy month.)

The minutes of that special meeting stated that there was a motion brought to the floor stating, "The facilitation process should be completed before any meeting to dismiss the minister." This was the belief of both the diaconate and council, but the motion failed.

As you can imagine, there was much discussion, even before the motion to dismiss. In addition to the issue of postponement, there was the issue of a secret ballot that was voted down, 171 voted against while 137 in favor. I'm sure this was a great disappointment to many who had hoped that their vote would be kept confidential, as JA's letter had promised.

Finally the question was called to vote on the motion to dismiss. By God's grace, it was defeated 214 against and eighty in favor.

It should also be noted that a request from thirty-four regular attenders was sent to the diaconate requesting to join the church before the meeting, allowing them to vote against the motion. Council felt that this was inappropriate. It was nice however to realize that there were others in the congregation who stood with me. They were welcomed into membership in February 15.

The following week, I wrote to thank everyone for their support and added a special note regarding the blue ribbons that had been distributed by my supporters.

These ribbons came from a group who met without me. I had nothing to do with them but certainly appreciated their efforts, though the ribbons appeared divisive to many. So I encouraged all to do what I had done, put the date, February 1, 1998, on it and use it as a bookmark at Colossians 3:13 that reads, "Bear with each other and forgive whatever grievances you may have against one another. Forgive as the Lord forgave you."

Later that month, Pat and I took advantage of a kind invitation from Ed and Charlane Chapman to go skiing at Mount Abram in Bethel, Maine, staying at one of their two slope-side condos. Sadly I broke my left radius bone!

I have already mentioned the Oberammergau *Passion Play* that had inspired Horace Hylan. In May, I wondered if anyone would be interested in going to Germany for the 2000 presentation. I had received an invitation from a travel agency encouraging me to do a little recruiting for them. If I could bring a certain number—can't remember how many—of paying passengers, then that would reduce the cost for Pat and me. We were able to sign up enough and began planning for the trip.

I was surprised to hear from the cochair of the diaconate. He believed that the trip appeared selfish on my part and it would hurt the church and me, so he encouraged me strongly to cancel it. I don't recall hearing from anyone else who felt the same. We went and had a wonderful time.

The following month, God provided another organist/minister of music, Mark Peterson. He started on Sunday, March 8. He and I got along famously. We met every week to plan the music for the service. He introduced me to new music, and I was able to introduce him to material he hadn't discovered. We developed a very rewarding relationship. We even went to a couple of Red Sox games together. His wife Eunja was a gifted soprano soloist who participated in the choir and sang solos periodically.

The Music Committee provided a thank-you event for Ron Martin and Regina Mathews for filling in during our time of need.

In May, Dad had his heart attack. We all gathered at Grandview Hospital, Sellersville, Pennsylvania. He was able to recover from a seven-hour operation. Praise the Lord!

In June, we were able to install a new organ for the Covell Chapel, an Allen digital instrument costing $13,620.00. We had received $10,000.00 in donations and the balance came from trust funds. It was a real blessing and remains there today.

In July, we were able to join members of Pat's high school class of 1958 for their fortieth reunion. After a dinner together, several of us boarded a cruise ship in New York City and made our way up our eastern coast and then into Canada. We had a very relaxing time and then off to Maine for a vacation at the Phoenix Center in Blue Hills. We were part of a group of ministerial couples for a week of kayaking and spiritual retreat facilitated by George and Gary Ensworth.

Unfortunately we broke down on our trip. I pulled into the rest area just inside Maine and called a repair shop in Eliot. The transmission of our overloaded Ford Taurus gave out. We were very fortunate to be helped by a mechanic who took us to his shop and provided us with a rental car. (Total cost was $1,775.00.) We arrived in Blue Hills about three hours late, but it didn't seem to be a problem.

After the retreat, we drove back to Eliot, shifted all our gear into our repaired Taurus, and drove up to Moosehead Lake, Lily Bay State Park this time. We were pleased that Brian and Kim joined us to help us celebrate our thirty-fourth wedding anniversary. Kim had prepared a delicious dinner and announced that a new grill would be coming, a gift from all three children. Kim also whispered to Pat that Brian feels ready to become a parent!

Unfortunately while packing up our camping equipment, I smashed the pointer finger on my right hand. I had to keep it pointing up as I drove home.

We learned that Vern Davis had died that year. He was the owner of Beaver Cove Camps and the one who welcomed us to our honeymoon cottage thirty-four years ago.

The core group met all summer, and they had four goals—improve communication and conflict management skills, engage as many members as possible, voice and address current issues, and create momentum and positive energy for the future. They presented their final report in October 20. Here is a summary of their work and recommendations.

> Many current issues have been voiced and addressed; one, the Masonic affair, we believe, has been resolved except to those who are liv-

ing in their own constructions of reality. While there are still differences concerning it, most are resolved to move ahead now and leave it behind them.

The group's most pressing concern is that Pastor Rich understand the impact some of his behavior has had, and is having, on members of the congregation. The subgroup has been very direct with him about their concerns, and Pastor Rich has been very responsive in their meetings with him.

The group has learned how to deal with each other's differences with respect and understanding. They have been able to separate "the issues from the person." This has led to a strong sense of group cohesion. The best way the facilitators can describe it is to say that "the middle has expanded, and the extremes have diminished." The group has come to be able to handle its own internal conflicts in a constructive way—not resolve them but to manage them.

The group met seventeen times, February 11 to December 6. A subgroup met with me ten times, while the whole group met three times with the entire congregation and once with the church council. They offered several recommendations.

Three bylaw changes: adopt the "Covenant for Working and Worshipping Together," create a Parish Relations Committee and reestablish the Personnel Committee. They also required the pastor to attend and complete a course on managing people and building successful relationships with others, as part of his continuing development and training and finally, hire an associate pastor. [That sounded pretty good to me!]

Sadly, after the final report was given and the core group was thanked and dissolved, five members of the group left the church. They had certainly labored long and hard but believed that the church had taken a direction that they could not agree with.

After the facilitation was complete, I received some correspondence from the lead facilitator, Dr. M. B. "Jerry" Handspicker.

> Rich, I sense a great spiritual opportunity for you and for the congregation at this point. You can combine the rigor of evangelicalism and the openness of the UCC by showing they can not only co-exist but do so in creative interaction. You are one of the few I know who could pull this off. And right now with the people in the group who are working with you, you have the resources for self-development which few pastors are offered. They find it takes a lot of energy to engage in their work; it is not easy to be as open and specific as they have been with you. You have already begun to respond, and they have sensed it. Together you can be a rush of wind through the life of First Parish, the wind that is the Holy Spirit.
>
> Be assured that our prayers are with you all. We have come to love and respect you all, to groan with you, to rejoice with you, and to hope for you in the Lord.
>
> Yours in the Triune Name,
> Jerry (M. B. Handspicker)

I believe that the work of the core group and especially the skill of the three facilitators helped First Parish turn another corner. God used the conflict, the special meeting(s), the group, and several faithful leaders to enable the church to move through a very difficult experience and emerge better prepared to move into the twenty-first century. I wrote in my diary, "I feel that I have been courting FP for the past sixteen years. About a year ago, I proposed marriage and after the special meeting(s) they said yes." After I shared this with Pat, she reminded that the other girl feels jilted! She was right of course

Actually the other girl wasted no time in rallying the opposition. They called for a second petition and a second special meeting, convinced that they lost the vote the first time because they were not allowed to vote by secret ballot.

I walked for Sharing Inc. for the sixth time and have been able to raise $7,083.00 so far. I conducted fourteen weddings, sixteen funerals, and twenty-three baptisms that year.

Our annual meeting for 1999 fell in January 27. I again took the opportunity to speak to the congregation. Here is what I said.

> It was back in December that Pat and I first heard about the possibility of a second petition and second special congregational meeting. We were heartbroken and filled with sorrow and fear. As those days of Advent passed, we prayed for God's peace and direction.
>
> In January 3, I was informed by our moderator that a petition calling for my dismissal was indeed delivered to the church. We were sad and angry, confused, and embarrassed. We seriously considered resigning, just so the pain would stop—ours and yours.
>
> The next morning Pat and I walked the lake, as we usually did, and took the time to share what we might do. By the time we arrived home our path was clear. We concluded confidently that since the congregation invited us to be pastor back in 1983, it should be the congregation who should decide whether we should remain or leave. It meant that we could lose in public but we didn't believe that it was right that a small group

of people should determine such an important decision for the majority.

Since making the decision to remain at our place of ministry, we have enjoyed the peace of God. We will rest and rejoice in God's will expressed through you on Sunday, January 31. We are eager and available to serve God and you here at First Parish and recommit ourselves to that task.

In January 19, Sandra Bisson, our director of Christian education, wrote and sent a letter to the congregation. It was a call to join her in a concert of prayer. She encouraged everyone to pray, wherever they were at 6:00 p.m. on Tuesday, January 26.

She requested prayer for me and the family, healing for everyone. God's will to be done at the annual meeting and special meeting and for revival at First Parish. This call was a great encouragement to many, especially me.

The church members who promoted a second petition and meeting were much better prepared this second time than the year before. They had met at Golden Rule Lodge to plan their strategy. I discovered proof of this as I cleaned up the sanctuary before a funeral to be held in February 1. In one of the hymnal racks, I found a list of sixteen church members who were prepared to speak for dismissal and the order in which they would be called upon by the moderator. The clerk's minutes of the meeting revealed that those who spoke matched the predetermined list I had found. Fortunately, Robert's Rules of Order require that speakers for and against the motion must alternate. This did produce some balance to the argument.

The main reason a second meeting was called was the belief that if a secret ballot had been allowed the year before, I would have been dismissed. So the first order of business was a call for a secret ballot. It took three tries. The first lost, 141-145. A recount was requested. The second won, 145-144. After this vote, one of the tellers informed the moderator that some people had voted both yes and no! The moderator called for a third and final vote. The vote for a paper ballot passed, 146-145. (It should be noted that Pat voted for a secret ballot. She wisely realized that a secret ballot would remove any doubt as to the direction the congregation desired to go in the future.)

Finally the motion to terminate the pastor was defeated with 293 cast—117 yes and 176 no. After the meeting was over, our area minister, Rev. Chuck Harper who had attended the meeting, came to the house with the news.

A week after the vote, a church member gave me a check for $10,000.00. "You have helped me so much, Pastor." I was over-whelmed and grateful.

After the vote, twelve folks wanted to join the church. Just like a year ago, attenders realized that membership is important if you want to help build a congregation. Again I was very encouraged. I wrote the following prayer in my journal:

> Lord God give me a heart for my people as you have given me for my physical children. May I love and encourage the men as I do my son and the women as I do my daughters. Help me finish well throughout the coming years. Give me your goals and make clear why you have kept me here. Amen.

In February 24, we welcomed Nathan Andrew to the fam-ily—Dave and Sharon's third child. He came quickly, being born on the gurney in the hallway, which was better than the back seat of their car.

It was the first week of June that we received a call from Sharon telling us that Dave was using his table saw in his garage and acci-dentally cut off the ends of both his thumbs! One was more serious that the other but both required care and time to heal. Sharon, being a nurse, provided excellent care. (He has recovered but has difficulty picking his nose.)

In June 20, we held a service of reconciliation. It took six months to prepare and received input from over thirty members. It included special music for the occasion, the participation of Chuck Harper, spontaneous prayers from the congregation, Holy Communion, and a covenant of unity. We concluded with this prayer.

> Dear Lord Jesus, as members of the body Christ, teach us to unite with one another beyond our differences. Teach us not to gossip. Teach us to listen with love and respect. Teach us to be servants to our brothers and sisters in Christ. Teach us how to say "Forgive me" and "I'm sorry."
>
> We go forward, Lord, in tiny steps, we *all* want to move toward you. We recognize our need for you and without you we are empty. So fill us, renew us, unite us. Lord, guide us and help us along life's journey to be a house of worship that would make us pleasing in your sight. We ask for forgiveness when we stray and seek your direction to bring us back to you and your Word. Accept us now, we pray. We commit ourselves to you here at First Parish Congregational Church from this day forward. Amen.

As I read the prayer we prayed together during that service of reconciliation, I was again so grateful to God for developing such excellent spiritual qualities within the congregation. This is a wonderful prayer written by someone from the core group.

In July, Pat and I took advantage of two invitations from church members who summered in Canada. We drove to Fredericton, New Brunswick, and then all the way up along the Miramichi River to the summer home of Ida Montgomery. Then we drove down to Cape Sable Island, Nova Scotia, to visit John and Bonnie (Smith) Young at Clark's Harbor.

In August, we had an O'Brien family reunion at the Carson/Simpson farm. Dad O'Brien had worked for months to include everyone. It was quite a time, especially for Kim who began false labor pains and had to spend the weekend at Abington Hospital. The next day, there was a second OB family gathering at the "Buckingham Palace," home of Pearl and Ron Geho.

We got to Lily Bay that year but it was very windy. I put up a tarp hoping to break the wind, but we finally did something we never did before—we left a day early!

In September, I spent two days at the Center for Career Development and Ministry. It was a recommendation of the core group that I undergo a series of psychological tests to affirm and strengthen my pastoral skills. At the end of the month, I reported back to the diaconate.

> After interviews with two psychologists, I was admitted into the center's program.
>
> I spent more than twenty-five hours taking eleven psychological inventories. I had a physical exam, submitted four references, and you—the Diaconate—paid $1,345.00.
>
> I was at the center on Thursday from 9:00 to 4:00. On Friday, Pat joined me for the day at the center.
>
> I have come to a clearer understanding of the Core Group's recommendations. Realizing that my personality has strengths and weaknesses and that my weaknesses can hurt people, hardly my intention, but, sorry to say, it happens. To be specific, my personality exudes confidence. This can be an asset—most of the time. But as pointed out by the Career Center, I often overlook/discount those who don't see things as I see them. In my confidence, I unwittingly give some the impression that I don't need them or their contributions. This is a serious flaw. I am seeking to heed the Holy Spirit's prompting in this area.
>
> Sadly I learned that I have lost the support of many. I am committed to seek to regain that support wherever possible and try to be a bet-

ter listener. I am praying for the gift of humility, which is always a good place to begin.

Finally my ministry among you must be a mutual ministry. I need you to pray for me, forgive me, speak the truth in love to me all to God's greater glory.

After giving my report to the diaconate and church council and then summarizing my goals in the *Church Herald*, I believe the great majority of the congregation was very grateful and better prepared to move into the future with me as pastor.

Kim went to Melrose-Wakefield Hospital on Saturday, October 9, and at 12:30 a.m., Sunday, delivered Tyler O'Brien Albushies. There were issues requiring a fast ride to New England Medical Center. Brian and Kim were on an emotional roller-coaster for several days, along with us and Granny and Poppy who drove up from Pennsylvania.

Baby Tyler arrived home in October 16. We were all so grateful. As a child, he was slow to speak and suffered several operations on his ankles. He also lives with several allergies but has adapted and is making progress by the grace of God and the loving support of this parents.

He enrolled in the Clark School in Rowley Massachusetts and graduated in 2017. Kim and Brian extended themselves to ensure that Ty got the support he needed. Brian drove him to school most mornings, while Pat and I took our turn picking him up.

He became an intern for the town of Wakefield over the spring of 2019 and was hired by the town as a summer worker. He is now enrolled at Bunker Hill Community College and has a standing invitation to work for the town whenever he can. Good for you, Ty!

As you can imagine, the two special meetings that called for my dismissal added additional pressure on the congregation, especially in the area of stewardship. In November, I introduced the concept of faith promise giving. I wrote this in our newsletter,

I want to issue a challenge to you to give more. I say this because I know that every one of you wants to give more, but… Well, here is the challenge. When your pledge card arrives this month, will you pray this prayer to God before you put down any numbers?

Dear Lord,

I love you very much. I love First Parish too. I want to give more than I have in the past, but I don't know how I can ever afford it. The amount I want to put on this card is more than I can presently afford. I don't know where the money will come from, but if you provide it, I'll give it. So this is *a promise filled with faith*. Please help me to trust you and please provide so I can keep my promise to you and First Parish. Amen.

I have no way of knowing who or how many actually made a faith promise, but God did provide for our needs in 2000 and we were able to hire an associate minister in 2002.

At Thanksgiving, we enjoyed another Weisenbach family reunion at Camp Ladore. Pat set up a table at the Topsfield Fair, our son Dave began thinking about moving to Maine and building a log cabin, and Pam graduated from Salem State receiving several awards from the theater department.

And for the record, I conducted thirteen weddings, sixteen funerals, and nine baptisms.

Before I leave this year, I must state that the support of so many encouraged us during those two plus years. Here are portions of just a few cards/letters we received.

Dear Rich and Pat,

I just finished my Bible reading for the morning and I'm in Philippians. This verse stuck out loud and clear. "Do not be anxious about anything, but in everything, by prayer and petition, with thanksgiving, present your requests to

God, and the peace of God which transcends all understanding, will guard your hearts and your minds in Christ Jesus" (Philippians 4:6–7).

I do not need to add anything else except our love and prayers for we know it is in His hands.

Dad and Mom

Dear Dad,

"Blessed are you when they revile you and persecute you, and say all kinds of evil against you falsely for My sake. Rejoice and be exceedingly glad, for great is your reward on heaven, for so they persecuted the prophets who were before you" (Matthew 5:11–12). We always admired how you have had the guts to get up and go to work every day. You are doing a *great* job. Thank you for all your hard work, clear instruction, listening ear, and love. We love you.

Kim, and Brian.
Happy Clergy Appreciation Day!

Dear Pastor Rich,

I'll bet there was a ton of prayers offered up for you and God heard every one of them! I am so grateful to Him for what happened on Sunday. I love you.

From a lost sheep that you brought into the fold way back in 1984. Thank you,

Love, E. T.

Dear Pastor Rich

It was with a growing dismay that I watched events unfold at the church. I believed that everything would blow over and all would go back to what it was before. I realize now that it was wishful thinking on my part. Unfortunately we are not members of the church. I always thought it was not important to join. I realize now how wrong I was. Believing in the power of prayer, you will have mine, for the fortitude to get through this and for the outcome to be in your favor.

J. L.

Dear Pastor Rich,

A number of things about the membership at First Parish confuse me right now, but I am confident that you have steadfastly preached the gospel and that all of your interactions with me have been supportive, loving and understanding, and motivated by a desire to help me grow spiritually. My prayers are with you and your family.

A. L.

Dear Rich and Pat,

You are on our minds much of the time these days and we're praying that God is sustaining you in this onslaught against you. We are praying that you may have friends to confide in and that your convictions will lead you down the right way. Our friendship and love to you all.

S. H.

Hi Rich,

I just wanted to tell you how much I admire what you do, how you do it and what you stand for... I pray that you never change and never give up. You should also be aware that many people like myself admire your calm, good-natured grace and hope we would be like you if confronted by similar circumstances.

M. P.

Rich,

I wanted to write and express my relief and joy that you and Pat will be continuing your ministry at First Parish. I admire you and Pat for your strength in the Lord... I will be forever grateful that God called you to First Parish. Hearing you preach the gospel has changed my life completely. You both are an inspiration.

PS. I don't think that evangelicals are a bunch of kooks anymore. I think I was the kook all along.

J. B.

Pastor's Prayer Group

I must mention one other source of encouragement that played a pivotal role in my life and ministry during those dark times.

Every Thursday morning, I would gather with three or four other ministers in our town for prayer and supportive conversation. This group's membership changed over the years of course, but their value was vital and consistent.

I think a minister needs a group of peers to share his/her joys and frustrations, questions, and failures. I don't think it is wise to share these issues with members of the congregation, since they may get the wrong impression. When I'm frustrated at someone's actions or remarks, I need someone to listen and respond who has had those exact same feelings and knows they are only temporary. I think that my venting before a church member might send the wrong message.

Others may have a different take on this issue, but for me, that Thursday group was part of God's salvation. I remain forever grateful for the input these men afforded me and would credit their love and prayers as a major reason I remained at my post.

For the record, those men were Rev. Burt Lebo (Greenwood Union Church), Rev. Peter Brown (First Baptist, Wakefield), Rev. John French (First Baptist, Stoneham), Rev. John Stoeckle (Hope Alliance Church), and Rev. Mike Carl (Christ the King).

The annual meeting of 2000 only took an hour and the bulk of the time was receiving a report from the diaconate concerning progress made by the core group's recommendations. We voted to adopt the "covenant for working and worshiping together," to establish a Parish Relations Committee and reestablish our Personnel Committee. I reported that I attended the Center for Career Development and Ministry in September and was enrolled in a four-day conference titled "Conflict Management in Congregational Life" taught by Speed B. Leas to be held in June in Cornwall, Connecticut. A plan was also developed to hire an associate pastor. The congregation was pleased with this report. Praise the Lord.

We got off to Moosehead for Valentine's Day and stayed at the Greenville Inn. We got snowed in with eleven inches and had to stay an extra day (so sad, guess we made up for the day we lost last year to the wind). We visited the Greenville Log Home factory and the Corner Store. (Dave would eventually buy his log home from this company.)

Pat led a women's Bible study on Thursday mornings for many years. While sitting at my desk one morning, I overheard them singing a praise chorus, "In my church Lord, be glorified." I got up and went into the Fireside Room where they were meeting and told them through tears of gratitude how much their presence and faithfulness meant to me. That group continues today and is a source of great blessing to the congregation.

In March, Pat's mother had a heart attack. For a while, we feared she might be taken from us, but the Lord was gracious and Granny lasted seven more years but sadly suffered for Alzheimer's disease. Those years proved to be very trying for Pat. Mother had forgotten so much, including who Pat was. Visits often ended in tears and broken hearts.

In April, I received a final letter from the Center for Career Development and Ministry. Here is a few lines from that letter.

> It seems that good and productive work is being done and that church leaders have used the outside input as a roadmap for going forward. You

and the congregational leaders are doing a fine job in this regard. Congratulations!

Working through the situation has been a great challenge for everyone and it appears to have been handled very well. Such hurtful experiences, dealt with honestly and faithfully, can lay the groundwork for health in the church for many years to come.

Grace and peace,
Rev. Jean Wright, DMin

I read this letter to the diaconate and all heard a very positive description of our church and the way we all have handled the difficulties. I was surprised when there wasn't a single word of reaction. It is amazing how such a major issue of the past is so quietly resolved. The matter of my behavior, character, qualifications, and ignorance, once hotly debated, fell over like a dead man. I thought of Revelation 5:3, "No one could open the scroll or even look inside it." The struggles of the past had been sealed.

I walked around the lake for the ninth time on Good Friday and was able to add almost $2,400.00 to the running total.

Mother and Dad flew up for the *Passion Play* and Easter worship, but their flight was delayed. Pat picked them up at the airport and was forced to deal with several challenges including a dead battery. They never did see the play. That was a shame, since I know it would have given a boost to their faith.

A special congregational meeting was called to hear a report from the diaconate concerning progress on the core group's recommended bylaw changes. They made the following three motions:

1. Only active members shall be able to vote at church meetings.
2. Only active members may serve on boards and committees and be officers of the church.
3. A two-thirds vote is required to dismiss the pastor.

All three changes were passed.

These were long overdue changes brought about by the two special congregational meetings of February 1998 and January 1999.

The board also shared that they are working on our membership lists trying to define "Active" and "Inactive." They corresponded with all members, called many, and prayed for all. They later established membership categories, which was a critical step toward membership integrity.

In May 31, Dave and Sharon sold their house in Warrington, Pennsylvania. By God's grace, they made a $36,000.00 profit and headed north to Maine. They pulled their thirty-seven-foot mobile home to Walnut Grove Campground in Alfred. He was able to buy a building permit ($3,098.00) and soon after staked out the foundation.

The day after Father's Day, we drove up to North Waterboro and with Dave began to clear the land. It took thirty years, but the land we purchased back in 1970 would finally be made useful. We were all very grateful and excited.

Poppy arranged for another family reunion in July marking their sixtieth wedding anniversary and their eightieth birthdays. We gathered at the Memorial Chapel at Valley Forge. It was an appropriate place since Poppy's grandfather carved much of the oak ornamentation in the sanctuary including the organ screens and pew ends. We attended the worship service, had a picnic on the grounds, and climbed up the tower to observe a man playing the carillon.

We arrived home and had just enough time to pack for our European Alpine vacation, including the *Passion Play* in Oberammergau, Germany (July 13–26). We were able to enlist eight others to join us for this amazing experience.

I took a video of the trip and tried to capture the beauty of Frankfurt am Main, the Rhine River, Heidelberg, Lausanne, Liechtenstein, the Black Forrest, Innsbruck, Salzburg, Vienna, the Neuschwanstein Castle, Rothenburg ob der Tauber, Mannheim, and Munich. It was quite a trip!

When we returned, I had an opportunity to repair some bridges. The father of one of the families who were critical of my ministry died suddenly. There were four daughters and a son in the family. Three of the daughters were very active in the church and disappointed with the direction I was pursuing. Things were awkward when I visited their home, but fortunately, two of the children were not part of the church and were able to speak openly, providing me with good memories of their father. I was glad that the family allowed me conduct the service. It provided an opportunity to serve them and seek to bring comfort from God's word. All three daughters wrote me thank-you notes.

By the middle of July, Dave had made great progress. Their mobile home was on the site, the septic system was functioning, and a steel girder was in place. Then electric, phone, and water were connected, and interior basement walls were up. The first load of logs arrived from Greenville in August 17.

Pat and I would get up at 4:30 a.m., drive to 10 Highpoint Circle, and help unload the logs. We even laid the first course. We were traveling to Maine almost every Sunday afternoon through Tuesday, and we had a great time together. Granny and Poppy came and helped, so did Ed and Charlane Chapman. A thirty-year dream was coming true.

Sharon's Christmas letter at year's end gave this exciting progress report.

> We spent the best summer ever living in a 32 x 8 foot trailer. We started off at a campground and in July we graduated to the property on Lake Arrowhead. David worked diligently day after day clearing the land, pouring concrete and all the other jobs needed to erect a masterpiece... Anytime we hit a bump God brought us back to the beauty and reassured us of His faithfulness to carry us through... The memories we have made we will cherish for a lifetime.

After the affirmation we received from the congregation, things moved along more easily, but as you might imagine, there were some members who were disappointed and frustrated. These folks looked for any occasion to point out my faults, mistakes, errors, etc. Of course that wasn't very hard to do. After one such mistake, the diaconate received a letter from an angry member. The issue was thoroughly discussed, and at the conclusion of the meeting, every member prayed for me and healing for the wounded member. I was so grateful for the loving support I received that evening.

In November 6–13, we took advantage of the very generous offer of the Billy Graham School of Evangelism providing an all-expense paid seminar in one of three locations. We flew to Alberta, Canada, and spent a week at a hotel built by the Canadian Railway beside Lake Louise. The association provided wonderful accommodations and informative workshops. It was a grand experience. We rented a car and were able to visit Banff and Calgary. I bought my Tilley Hat on that trip and lost it nineteen years later.

We again spent our Weisenbach reunion during Thanksgiving at Camp Ladore in Waymart, Pennsylvania. This was the year that we visited a coal mine.

And for the record, I conducted eleven weddings, twenty-six funerals, and twenty baptisms.

At the 2001 annual meeting, I had very little to say. "The only thing I want to do tonight is to say thank you. Thank you, Mr. Moderator. Thank you members of the Parish Relations Committee and Personnel Committee. You have laid a great foundation. Thank you, Ruth and Roy. Your love, prayers, and support have sustained me. Thank you, Pat. And thank you members of First Parish for the privilege you have given me to serve here."

March 17 was Sharon's thirtieth birthday, so Pat and I got up early enough on March 19 to help Dave clear out their storage unit and move everything into their new house. It was a long day but we got the job done!

At our June council, we discussed and voted on three resolutions recently voted upon at the Annual Meeting of the Massachusetts Conference of the UCC.

The conference encouraged the churches to support gay marriage, but our council voted (17-3) to reject that action. The conference voted to encourage the churches to advocate for abortion. Our council disagreed (16-4). The conference encouraged the churches to begin a dialogue with the Unitarian Universalist Society. Our council was against this as well (20-0). It was becoming clear that First Parish and the Massachusetts Conference of the UCC were moving in opposite directions.

I was always aware of those in our congregation who held different opinions, especially about abortion and gay marriage. I tried to give room for both views within the church believing that there is often more than one Christian answer to issues. I didn't want folks to separate from us over these questions. The person and work of Jesus Christ is the basis of our common faith. We ought to give space to our brothers and sisters when it comes to debatable questions.

In July 30, Gordon College hosted a two-day Alpha Conference. Twenty-one members from FPCC attended and benefited greatly from the fellowship, worship seminars, and talks by Nicki Gumbel. Over fifty First Parish friends and members have tasted Alpha so far. We planned a third course for September.

In July, our organist and minister of music Mark Peterson announced his departure. Bradford College, the school where Mark taught, was closing forcing him to seek employment elsewhere. He became the conductor of the Barton-Wilson Symphony Orchestra and the Barton College Choirs, Wilson, North Carolina. When he left, he wrote a note to the church.

> This has been much more than a "church job" for me. It has been a place where we have always felt warmly welcomed and I have had the opportunity to make music in a magnificent surrounding.
>
> The choir has been a constant joy to work with and I have always felt a true respect and

partnership with these wonderful people. My relationship with Pastor Rich has been unique in my experience. He has been the perfect colleague, whose musical insight, instincts, and vision have helped me to become a better musician and worship leader. He has shown me the beauty, inspiration, and truth of the Gospel of Jesus Christ. For this, I will always be grateful.

Mark's last Sunday with us was August 12, and the choir planned a special farewell song and special coffee hour after worship. We immediately formed a search committee to find and hire a new minister of music.

I was dumbfounded one morning while sitting in my office. When the door opened, in walked Angus MacFeeley and his wife and daughter along with his brother Bill. The MacFeeley family was a faithful part of Union Congregational Church when we served it in the 1960s. All five MacFeeley children were a part of our youth group. Angus and Setsuko live in Hawaii and attend Good Shepherd Lutheran Church where Rev. Dan Baron serves as pastor.

The family was gathering at Sister Janet's home in Magnolia, and we were invited. It was a great joy to hear how these young people had grown and especially to hear of Angus's maturing faith in Christ. I learned later that Bill and his wife are very active in their church as well.

By September, we were back in the swing of things. Here is the lineup of activities.

The *Church Herald* listed the coming events for September:

- Stephen Ministries Annual Homecoming Dinner: September 6
- Rally Day: September 9
- Adult Choir Rehearsal: September 12
- Alpha Celebration Supper: September 19
- Membership Seminar: September 22

The special congregational meetings during the dark times of 1998 and 1999 produced many results. Obviously there was much pain, confusion, anger, expense, misunderstanding, and sadly the departure of several families from the fellowship. The votes also made clear the need for a serious look at how the church dealt with conflict. This required the formation of the core group, which made—with the help of professional facilitators—over a dozen recommendations, a few involving me directly, a two-day visit to the Center of Career Development and Ministry and a weeklong seminar on "Conflict Management in Congregational Life" held in Cornwall, Connecticut.

And of course the votes determined the direction the church would take into the future. The diaconate and church council were largely responsible for policymaking, especially in the areas of membership and bylaw changes. This also necessitated a careful look at how the pastor and the board are to relate to each other. One of the criticisms launched in my direction was that I was too authoritative. It is here that I wrote to the diaconate in an attempt to put forth my thoughts concerning this important relationship.

> The relationship between the minister and the Diaconate is clearly a partnership; neither party is superior to the other. The minister is not the boss of the Diaconate nor is the Diaconate the boss of the minister. Our bylaws call for the "Minister to seek and cherish the advice and assistance of the Diaconate." This balance, though difficult to manage, is necessary. Giving the Diaconate authority over the minister hampers his/her everyday functioning. Giving the minister authority over the Diaconate reduces lay involvement, the hallmark of congregational polity.
>
> The Diaconate has traditionally yielded to the Minister for three reasons: his/her education, his/her experience, and the continuity he/she offers to the church.

Although seeking and maintaining this balance is a great challenge—one that must be renegotiated each year because of the change in Diaconate membership—it is the only way to function. The minister should be careful not to express authority indiscriminately and the Diaconate should not expect to mandate ministerial behavior.

I consider the decisions and actions of the Diaconate—which speak directly to the specifics of my function—to be loving, respectful suggestions and guidelines not mandated policy. And I respectfully request that the Board allow me to function freely without judgment of my experience, training and personal integrity.

Over the remaining years of our ministry together, the diaconate and I labored in a fruitful and enjoyable manner.

911

Everyone remembers what happened on September 11, 2001. Here is something I found on the Internet and shared with the congregation through the *Church Herald*.

Putting Our Lives in Perspective
On Monday there were people fighting against praying in the schools.
On Tuesday you would have been hard pressed to find a school where someone was not praying.
On Monday there were people trying to separate each other by race, sex, or creed.
On Tuesday they were all holding hands.
On Monday we thought we were secure.
On Tuesday we learned better.

On Monday we were talking about heroes as being athletes.

On Tuesday we relearned what "hero" meant.

On Monday people were fighting the 10 Commandments on government land.

On Tuesday the same people all said, "Thou shalt not kill."

On Monday people argued with their kids about picking up their rooms.

On Tuesday the same people could not get home fast enough to hug their kids.

On Monday people were upset that their dry cleaning wasn't ready.

On Tuesday they were lining up to give blood.

On Monday politicians argued about budget surpluses.

On Tuesday grief-stricken they sang "God Bless America."

It is sadly ironic how it takes horrific events to place things into perspective, but it has. The lessons learned this week, the things we have taken for granted, the things that have been forgotten or overlooked, hopefully will never be forgotten. (Chuck Swindoll)

The diaconate concluded the year with an after-worship dinner in November 18. They named it "Pasta for the Pastor." A very generous member of the board paid all the expenses. It was an occasion for the congregation to show their appreciation for Pat and me. During dessert, time was given for anyone to share their personal words of love and gratitude. It was a very special dinner!

We journeyed to Moosehead twice this year, the Lakeside House in February where the husband snored and in August as usual. We stopped on our way to greet Samuel John Weisenbach, the fifth grandchild.

We also made a trip to the Pittston Farm and enjoyed a sumptuous dinner, scores of flowers, and humming birds. We also learned the sad news of the passing of dear Georg Ensworth.

For the record, I conducted eleven weddings, twenty-six funerals, and fourteen baptisms.

In the January 11 *Church Herald*, I wrote about how much I benefited from the monthly meetings I had with Roy Evans and Ruth Ross. These two served as cochairs of the diaconate for three years. I would mark my calendar R+R (for rest and refreshment) to indicate another meeting with them. Their love and loyalty provided the strong base on which I felt I could continue as pastor. I honestly believe that without their presence, I would have probably left First Parish. I suppose God could have provided others, for there certainly were those who could have filled the position, but they were just what I needed on so many occasions. Thank you, Roy, and thank you, Ruthie.

In February, God led a friend of our church to give $10,000.00 to our Outreach Committee. The committee voted to use $2,000.00 to purchase five hundred copies of the Jesus video. The committee had a plan; every person who attended that year's *Passion Play* (March 28 and 29) would receive a free copy of the video. I encouraged the congregation to invite a friend or family member to the play. This was a great opportunity to share God's love. We gave away 450 videos on those two nights.

The new *Passion Play* was outstanding, as I mentioned earlier. Pam rewrote the script and added music, and the attendance was 644.

The Outreach Committee decided to divide the remaining $8,000.00 between World Relief (WR) and the Boston Rescue Mission (BRM). Eric Hanson (WR) and John Samaan (BRM) were both able to preach and bring their personal thanks on two succeeding Sundays.

After moving into their home at 10 Highpoint Circle, Dave landed a job with a local construction company, Allied Cook, but within a year he decided to start his own business, Integrity Builders and Contractors, "We do it right even when nobody is looking."

I can remember hearing Dr. Glenn Jamison tell me that Dave is the kind of person who will be self-employed; he didn't say so, but I think that Dave would find it very hard working under a boss. I enjoyed driving to Maine to work alongside him. I was able to assist on five separate occasions that first year.

To celebrate Valentine's Day, we again traveled to Northern Pride Lodge in Kokadjo, Maine. We started this habit in 1985. You drive up Lily Bay Road till the paving ends, and then you are there. The sign says, "Population... A Few."

The lodge was originally a hunting camp built by the Oakes family in 1896. Present owners, Wayne and Barbara Plumber, both Maine Guides, care for the site sitting on five acres and boasting 550 feet of frontage on First Roach Pond. There are three ponds in that area who got their name from Father laRoach who first evangelized that part of the Maine woods. We have visited them for several years and usually drop by in August to mark our wedding anniversary.

February was also the month that the diaconate voted to redesign the order of worship. We moved the announcements to the very beginning of the service, followed by an opportunity to greet one another. Having any announcements in the middle of the service appeared to be an interruption. We moved the offering to follow the sermon as our response to God's word. All saw the reasons for the change and we transitioned easily.

On Sunday, March 3, Mrs. Kay Doherty came to our service of worship. She came to preach and tell her story of how the Holy Spirit moved her to try and offer some practical help to poor children in Mississippi. She began walking on Good Friday in 1972 and Sharing Inc. was born. Over the years, more than $2,000,000.00 has been distributed to meet serious needs over those thirty years.

Kay came for another reason, and 2002 marked the tenth anniversary of my decision to walk around Lake Quannapowitt on Good Friday. Over those years, I had walked 200 miles, sixty laps around the lake. The congregation had contributed $13,927.00. In March 29, I walked for the eleventh time. A total of ninety-four families/individuals contributed to the cause.

The Sunday of Kay's visit was Don Hodgkins's first Sunday as our new minister of music/organist. He has continued to minister from that position until today.

Over the years, several Rotarians had asked me to consider joining their club, but I never saw the need and felt busy enough without adding another weekly activity. But when Eric Sidmore, DC, asked me, I had a change of heart. I joined in April 22, and it was the right decision. The club brought me into contact with community leaders and gave me opportunity to fellowship with those outside the church.

Weekly meetings began with a lunch followed by a speaker. They always said grace before the meal, and before long, I was asked to pray on a regular basis. As time went on, it wasn't unusual for a member to ask me to include a person or circumstance in my prayer for the morning. I even conducted three funerals for members who passed away. I was in Rotary for ten years and developed a deep respect for this worldwide organization.

Rotary is a service organization ready to take on projects in the community and around the world. In fact, it is Rotary International along with the Bill and Melinda Gates Foundation that have eradicated polio except in two or three countries. This is an amazing accomplishment. I also began to ask for their support for my Good Friday walks for Sharing Inc., and many members responded.

I should have joined Rotary much earlier, but the ten years I did belong was very fulfilling. When I retired, the club honored me with the gift of my second Paul Harris pin, Paul being the Chicago attorney who founded Rotary on February, 23, 1905.

As I have already mentioned, the Stephen Ministries program was launched in 1987. By May 2002, we marked our fifteenth anniversary, and we had trained forty-four individuals by then. Each Stephen Minister made a two-year commitment to serve their needy brothers or sisters. In May 19, we commissioned five more. I am happy to see that the program is still functioning after thirty-two years, and the recent training and commissioning of Pastor Dale will help ensure continued ministry.

We hired Sandra Bisson in August 1996. She ministered to our youth while attending Gordon-Conwell Theological Seminary. In May 12, we conducted an ordination service for her, and June 9 was her last Sunday with us. She moved to Second Presbyterian Church, Newport News, Virginia, to begin a ministry to youth and start a doctoral program. Here are a few sentences taken from a longer piece that I wrote for the June *Church Herald.*

> You have been with us for almost six years. On the one hand, it is hard to believe it has been that long. On the other, it is almost impossible for many of our young people to believe that you weren't always here. Every youth gathering has been a time and place where our children enjoyed themselves in safety and heard about Jesus and his love.
>
> On a more personal note, you have filled the pulpit when I was away and every report was positive.
>
> Thank you, Sandra. Goodbye and God bless.

ALPHA

In April, we announced the forming of a fifth Alpha program. It began with a dinner that Pat provided and later coordinated with the help of others. The program always began with a joke from yours truly and then a forty-five-minute video talk by Rev. Nicky Gumbel.

Alpha is "an opportunity to explore life and the Christian faith in a friendly, open and informal environment." Nicky was the associate rector of Holy Trinity Brampton, United Kingdom. He wrote the course in 1990, and it has now been translated into 112 languages and shared in 169 countries.

God has used the Alpha program, introduced to us by Dave and Irene Whitehead, along with Stephen Ministries to help transform

First Parish from a struggling congregation in the 1960s and 1970s to the vital and growing church it is becoming today.

In May 28, I received the news that my brother Dave's youngest child, Brie, died of complications from epilepsy. She was twenty-three. Our family drove down to Lansdale, Pennsylvania, to the home of Mother and Dad. The service was held in the chapel of Dock Acres, the Mennonite complex where Mom and Dad lived. I led the service and my brother Bill preached. We also gave opportunity for others to share memories. I remember that our daughter Kim gave some very touching remarks. We returned to David's house in Telford and sought to support one another. I cannot imagine the grief that my parents had to endure, and of course the devastation upon my brother Dave and wife Dorothy was life changing.

September always feels like the beginning of a new church year. The worship hour changes—the 9:00 a.m. chapel service begins again, Sunday school starts, and boards and committees take up their responsibilities. In addition we introduced a big change in the music in Sunday worship. We welcomed a praise band into the service, guitars and drums. They called themselves CornerStone. The new sound was most appreciated, but this wasn't everyone's cup of tea.

In an effort to help with the transition, I shared a letter in the *Church Herald.*

> Dear Pastor,
> Was it the organist's idea or yours that our peaceful worship service was shattered by that new hymn last Sunday? The music was sacrilegious, something one would expect to hear in a den of iniquity, *not* a church. Don't even expect me to sing it the next time.

This was written in 1847 and was critical of "I Love to tell the Story." I guess new music and new instruments have always been a challenge.

In September 29, we introduced a new church hymnal. This was a change I had been praying for. We presented the *Celebration*

Hymnal to the congregation and gave everyone the opportunity to purchase a copy or two in memory or in honor of a special person. It didn't take very long to fill the hymnal racks. Others purchased one of four specially bound copies for the pulpit area, and another bought a ringed binder copy for the organist. After the Bible, the hymnal is the next important worship aid to any congregation. I was so grateful for this addition to the church.

In September 11, our sanctuary became the gathering place for the entire town to remember the tragedy of a year ago. All the congregations were invited to participate in the service of music and prayer. Both Fire Chief David Parr and Police Chief Steve Doherty were in attendance and each had a part.

Sandra Bisson's primary ministry was with our youth, and the core group suggested that when she left, the church might consider a new position of associate minister for Christian education. This new staff person should be ordained or soon to be and focus more energy toward a pastoral role. Youth ministry would also be his/her responsibility but should develop a team to assist in the running of the youth program. The search was on for another person.

Pat and I had always prayed that our children would marry mature Christians as their life partners, you know, like we did. As I reflect on the choices that they made, it seems that they all married pre-Christians. I mean individuals who had a good heart and were open to that part of the gospel that they saw in our kids. I'm sure the faith of Pam, Dave, and Kim was noticed by Gadar, Sharon, and Brian. These three were not put off by Christian words, Christian habits, and Christians beliefs; they were attracted to them. And as time passed, I believe each pre-Christian partner grew in their understanding and commitment.

This transition was particularly evident in Pam's relationship to Gadar. We observed a long and serious struggle between the two of them, each speaking lovingly—most of the time—as to their lifestyle and expectations for their future. Pam held back her lifetime commitment till she saw signs of God's Holy Spirit working within Gadar. They did come and Pam made mention of the necessity of unity in her short speech during their wedding ceremony.

Spiritual growth has been slow and steady in all three in-laws, and Pat and I are so very grateful to God and the loving faithfulness of our children to their mates.

Pam and Gadar married in October 12. It was a wonderful service, carefully planned by Pam. The music was very special, especially the processional. I well up with gratitude every time I hear that bagpipe begin to play "An Irish Cathedral."

Added to the excitement and blessing of Pam and Gadar's special day was the expectation of the matron of honor's pregnancy. We had a stool hidden away just in case Kim needed to rest during the ceremony. But not only did she and Brian participate in the wedding, but also they danced at the reception. Then their second son John (Jack) Richard Albushies arrived four days later on Wednesday, October 16.

The reception was held in the Brooksby Barn, Peabody. Almost all the Weisenbach/O'Brien families were in attendance along with friends from both families and First Parish. Sadly the weather was uncooperative, canceling the planned hayride.

Probably one of the greatest challenges parents face is to trust their children's choices for a life partner. Pat and I praise God for the three families we have been given and pray for them all—all twenty-two of them.

In November 20, we hired Rev. Daniel Ledwith. He had attended First Parish along with his family for several years. We began 2002 with renewed joy and expectations.

We did get to Moosehead in August where we went on a moose safari with Wayne Plumber, had fun at the Kiwanis Auction, and dined well at Blair Hill.

The church received a $400,000.00 legacy from Ruth and Louise Boardman and I conducted nine weddings, twenty-three funerals, and seventeen baptisms.

The big question facing the 2003 annual meeting revolved around the budget—what's new? Because we hired Dan Ledwith, the budget had to go up. The council approved a budget of $398,093.00, but this required the use of our reserves and a small portion of the recently received gift from the Boardmans. There were those who had difficulty with this decision, but I wrote a piece for the *Church Herald* urging support. By God's grace and the faith of the congregation, the budget and the way to achieve it passed.

In March 26, Scott Mitchell began to demolish our kitchen and upstairs bathroom. We were pleased that the church voted to take on this project. It also included new combination windows throughout the house and a new bay window in the kitchen and a dishwasher! Several men of the congregation pitched in their time and energy.

The project was finished in May, a long slog but well worth the resulting improvements. It was nice to hear Pat exclaim, "I love my new kitchen," several times in the succeeding weeks.

Pam and Gadar moved into Kim's room temporarily and then in November 11 to a cute house in Concord, Massachusetts. We, along with lots of help from others, moved them in. As usual, Pam was able to decorate her new place, making it warm and inviting.

It was around this time that I began to mark Mother's Day and Father's Day by selecting short articles about moms and dads and assigning them to members of the congregation to read in place of the sermon. Involving the people is usually a good idea and having them read something humorous, uplifting, spiritually healthy, and touching emotionally worked well for several years. It was a great idea.

I was sitting at my computer at home when I received the following e-mail: "Are you able to come to KUC to help us celebrate our ninetieth anniversary? All expenses paid!" It took me fifteen seconds to shout to Pat, "Want to go to Hawaii in September?"

The congregation decided to celebrate its ninetieth anniversary because their favorite pastor Rev. Bill Steeper would probably die before the 100th.

We were met by Stan Shota on Friday, September 4. It had been twenty years since we left in 1983, and upon our arrival, it was as if we had never left. Peter Kamakawiwoole was the pastor now, and he and Rhonda were wonderful hosts. They opened their home to us, and on one of our evenings, they invited several church members for food and an informal concert by Gay and Randy. It was very special, and we were touched by the love and good memories of our years together. We arrived home in September 10 to the news that Benjamin Edward Weisenbach had been born in September 8.

When I arrived in 1983, the custom on All Saints Day was to read the necrology. After a year or two, I suggested that we might instead remember our forebears on Memorial Day, and we called it Rememeber Sunday.

I would invite the families who had lost a loved one during the year to write a brief love letter to be read during the worship service. This might also boost the attendance on that Sunday. The idea caught on. We received touching letters, read each one during the service, and rang a bell to mark each person. Oftentimes families would worship together on that day.

Since the church was gathered on November 4, 1644, we began to concentrate on the anniversary of the congregation on All Saints Day when we would read our ancient covenant. The shift in timing worked well for many years.

August 1 marked our twentieth anniversary at First Parish. I figured that no one remembered. (We were at Moosehead till August 17, and it was Wilson Pond that year.)

Then on Thanksgiving Sunday, during the coffee hour, Chris Hurren and Jen Black, cochairs of the diaconate, called for everyone's attention and announced that there was one more thing to be done. "We must honor Pastor Rich and Pat for twenty years of service here at First Parish." We were very surprised. The diaconate had invited the congregation to contribute to a gift; they gave us $900.00 and two tickets to the Stoneham Theater. In addition to this, the board reserved two nights at the Rabbit Hill Inn, Lower Waterford, Vermont (more about that in 2004).

Along with these gifts were several cards and loving notes. Here are a few samples:

> Thank you for preaching the gospel every week.
> Thank you for bringing us closer to God.
> Thank you for your obvious undying love for the
> written Word of God.

Your teachings and guidance have helped to
reopen our eyes, ears, and hearts to the Lord.
We see the Bible with new eyes and it seems we
can't get enough of it!
We are a stronger family today because we have
been listening and learning.
Thank you for introducing me to Jesus Christ.

Again my parents invited all of us to Camp Ladore to our annual Thanksgiving reunion. We were all able to get there except for Brian who had to work. He did send Kim with a short video he had edited describing our reunion of a year ago and those of us who got sick with the Norwalk virus. The video was like a newscast with Channel 7 personalities talking about our family. It was quite a hit! As usual we had a wonderful time but I noticed that Dad was showing signs of fatigue, memory lapses, and stiffness in his joints. As it turned out, the next year would be our last.

Dave bought twenty acres in Parsonsfield, Maine. He had plans to build a new place there, but it didn't work out. He still owns the land. He also took the necessary time to build a second floor onto Brian and Kim's home on Gould Street, Stoneham.

For the record, I conducted six weddings, twenty-one funerals, and thirteen baptisms.

The Rabbit Hill Inn's brochure said, "Is a finely detailed two-hundred-year-old inn—elegant, thoughtful, and at all times comfortable. Every detail is tended to graciously and meticulously. Experience life at a pace designed to pamper and soothe, at a place where all your senses will be indulged. Let us play host to a memorable stay."

The diaconate arranged for us to enjoy the best room in the house, $385.00/night. We relaxed in the Jonathan Cummings Suite, third floor of the main house. "Fire placed bedroom with queen canopy bed; fire placed dressing room bath with a forty-four-jet whirlpool. Screened and furnished mountain facing porch." Need I say more?

There were two more surprises—Jen Black's parents sent a bottle of wine to our dinner table and Tom and Lisa Roderick arranged for a horse-drawn sleigh ride. Bruce Brink hooked up his team, Duke and Bob, and we headed off into the woods. It started to snow and Pat and I began singing, "Winter Wonderland." Perfect!

On Wednesday, February 4, tragedy struck our family again. My brother Bill called to say that his only son Matthew died while asleep in his dorm room. At age eighteen, he had just started college.

Our whole family drove to Katonah, New York, where Bill was serving as pastor of the First Presbyterian Church. The greeting line at the funeral home was endless. Cynthia and Bill stood expressionless at the foot of Matt's casket and greeted all who attended. It was a very sad event.

The funeral was at First Presbyterian on Monday, February 9. The family gathered in the church library and Bill asked me to pray before entering the sanctuary. The service was a testimony to God's care in times of confusion, anger, and deep grief.

> One lasting memory was the words of the last hymn we sang,
> Come, ye disconsolate, where'er ye languish,
> Come to the mercy seat, fervently kneel
> Here bring your wounded hearts,
> Here tell your anguish;
> Earth has no sorrows
> That heav'n cannot heal. (Thomas Moore)

The death of a child often breaks a marriage. I'm sure Bill and Cynthia had their struggles, but they have weathered the storm.

A portion of Matt's ashes are interred under the weeping cherry tree in the front yard of their summer home in Bayside, Maine. It is also the final resting place for a portion of Mother's and Dad's ashes as well Mother's sisters, Clara and Ida.

Later that month, I met Pastor Hyung Lak Choi, the pastor of a small Korean congregation who had been meeting in Boston and was looking for new worship space in or around Wakefield. We chatted in the Fireside Room, and I discovered that he is an evangelical brother.

I wrote to the board of trustees encouraging them to talk with Pastor Choi about renting the chapel. The board agreed, and in April 1 a very positive relationship was begun.

We joined together in worship every Christmas and Easter. Their choir sang one year, and on another they shared a Korean dance in customs. Then during the coffee hour, they presented delicious goodies.

They worshipped at 1:00 p.m. followed by a meal in the Fellowship Room. We were always invited. It truly was a match made in heaven. He sent this note,

> Dear Rev. Weisenbach,
> Thank you so much for the warm welcoming our church! You are the best pastor ever I met. God bless you and your family and your church.
> Boston Korean Love Church,
> Pastor Choi

Community Dinners/Clothing Closet

In April, the youth group, with the help of Dan and Mandi Ledwith, decided to offer an Easter dinner for the poor, elderly, and lonely in the Wakefield, Reading, and Stoneham areas. They received considerable help from Jill Sullivan and Darcy Hildreth. This first dinner grew into a twice a year tradition and community dinners every Easter and Thanksgiving.

In addition, Bonnie Mercurio launched "the Clothing Closet," free clothes every month. After a while, the closet was opened in conjunction with the dinners, and these ministries together attracted scores of visitors.

Donations flowed into the building, and within a few years, the Women's Thursday Morning Bible Study would spend hours sorting and arranging in preparation for the next open closet. I think Pat was the driving force behind this effort. Both the community dinners and the Clothing Closet are ministering today.

Resurrection Sunday was again an opportunity to share the gospel through the *Passion Play*. A fund-raising pasta dinner raised $800.00, and offerings after the two performances added $1,200.00 more. The diaconate voted to give Pam $1,000.00 plus expenses. We were also able to serve the gospel through the community dinner, Clothing Closet, and Good Friday walk. That year ninety members and friends including twenty-one Rotarians contributed $2,130.00.

Dan Ledwith's Ecclesiastical Council was conducted by the CCCC in April 21, and his ordination was celebrated at First Parish in May 23.

We were busy throughout the summer. Pat went to convention in Dallas, Texas, and we celebrated Mother and Dad's sixty-fifth wedding anniversary and got to Moosehead Lake with a stop to see Dave, Sharon, and the family; they gave us two new canoe paddles as an anniversary present.

The church entered a float that year in the town's Fourth of July parade. We took first prize, $600.00!

Then on Saturday, September 25, we launched our "Homecoming." It was an open house to introduce the church and community to a program developed by Rev. Rick Warren, pastor of Saddleback Church, Lake Forrest, California.

The kickoff to this a six-week series was Pastor Rick preaching on the topic "What on Earth Am I Here For?" Thousands of churches tuned into the simulcast. We erected a huge screen in the sanctuary and projected his talk. He introduced "Forty Days of Purpose," a program for the local church based on his book, *the Purpose-Driven Life*. Pastor Rick ended his talk with an invitation to come back to church on Sunday.

I was prepared to preach a series of six sermons based on the five purposes of life—worship, fellowship, discipleship, ministry, and evangelism.

An important part of the program was the introduction of small group Bible studies. As the program got underway, we had 150 people meeting together every week in one of twenty groups.

After the forty days passed, I preached in November 14, and the sermon was entitled "How to Safely Land after a Spiritual High." Here is how I began my sermon.

> During my thirty-eight years of ordained ministry, I have encountered various programs for the local church. Most produced results which were temporary. However, there were three that have brought lasting benefit.
>
> *Stephen Ministries* comes to mind. This program came to First Parish on 1987. We have trained forty-nine members so far to minister Christ's care to brothers and sisters. Another twenty-session class is scheduled to begin on January 13, 2005. Several have signed up. I challenge you to consider this opportunity.
>
> *Alpha* is another program with lasting results. We began the program in the fall of 2000. We have repeated it eight times. A ninth round is scheduled for January 12, 2005. Over 150 of you have participated in this eleven-week program including a dinner, video, and small group discussion.
>
> A third program is the one we have just completed, *Forty Days of Purpose*. What an exciting time we have had together! I have to tell you, Pat and I are on a spiritual high!
>
> You have bought over three hundred copies of the book, *the Purpose-Driven Life*. And scores of you are benefitting from your participation in your small group.
>
> These three programs are slowly transforming our church. Praise God!

Our attendance is up by 15%. Our giving will follow I'm certain. And I am sure that our community involvement will multiply too.

These are all signs of God's blessings resulting from members and friends seeking to fulfill their purpose: to *worship God*, to *fellowship* together, to become a Christian *disciple*, to *minister* to each other and to *evangelize*, to share the gospel with someone else.

I believe that Forty Days has had lasting results. This program was followed by two others, "Forty Days of Community" (2006) and "Forty Days in the Word" (2012). I am so thankful to God for Rick Warren; First Parish grew as a result of his ministry to us.

That year was our first Pie Social. We took advantage of the town's annual lighting of the common. Hundreds would gather to hear a few carols and meet Santa. We figured if so many townsfolk are at our front door, why not give them an invitation to come into the meetinghouse to get warm, have a piece of pie, and listen to Don Hodgkins play some favorite Christmas music on the organ? We also invited the children of the community to take turns ringing our bell. Great fun! The custom continues through the present.

This was the year that the State of Massachusetts legalized same-sex marriage. Every UCC congregation received a letter from our conference minister, Rev. Nancy S. Taylor. She saw this as "a harbinger of the freedom, equality, dignity and justice God intends for all who inhabit God's creation. Many will reach out to support the commitment and celebration of these weddings."

This support for the state's position by the conference made it more challenging for our congregation to continue our partnership. Of course there were members of First Parish who saw same-sex marriage as only fair but they were in the minority. This declaration by our conference minister only further distanced us from the UCC.

I tried to give those who believed differently the respect and support I felt they deserved.

We again gathered for what was to become our last Thanksgiving family reunion at Ladore.

We launched Marriage Alpha that year and marked the church's 360th anniversary in November. In December, a group of us traveled to Worcester to hear a Bill Gaither concert in the DCU center. And for the record, I conducted six weddings, twenty funerals, and sixteen baptisms.

Our annual meeting went very well in 2005. We enjoyed a delicious dinner, honored our fifty-year members—Brenda Applin, Ida Mae MacLeod, Pearl MacLeod, and Janet Sharpe—and thanked sixty board and committee members who completed their terms.

The business went well too. We elected members to replace those retiring and passed a budget of $405,568.00 giving the staff a 3 percent raise. The average pledge that year was $26.85 per week.

During last year's Kiwanis auction, we purchased reservations at the Greenville Inn (February 20–22) and decided to give them to Dave and Sharon. I'm sure they enjoyed themselves.

Dad began to fail in January and passed away in March 14. Throughout this entire ordeal, Mother's faith in God's promises sustained her. I remember coming into her living room and seeing her clutching her Bible to her chest and mouthing a prayer, undoubtedly praising God of His dependable provision and for her sons and daughters-in-law. I was deeply touched by her love, faithfulness, and inner peace midst the storm.

In May 14, the Christian Education Board sponsored a High Tea for the community. Kim, who was on the board, wrote a paragraph of welcome.

> Thank you for coming. We believe you are not here by chance, but that Jesus has a plan for your life. If you are searching for a place to learn and grow, come see if we are the place for you. We'd love to have you in our family. Our prayer for you today is that you are filled with Peace that overcomes any problem you face, Joy that over-

flows from realizing how blessed you are simply because the love of your life—Jesus Christ—smiles when he looks at you. We pray we are able to serve you with joy today, and through us, may you get a glimpse of who it is that loves you so much.

Again, thanks for coming.
Kim Albushies
For the Christian Education Board

I remember chatting with Kim in the church kitchen the morning of the High Tea. She seemed a little nervous, which was certainly understandable. She saw this as her first real effort to evangelize others through hospitality. She was moved by the song "I'm divin' in, I'm goin' deep." She did both that day. I was proud and grateful.

People did come, over forty. "This is just what I needed," one guest was heard to say. The board was encouraged to plan another such activity.

We did vacation at Beaver Cove, visiting Moosehead Lake for the thirty-fifth time. The whole family joined us.

Dave moved his mobile home to Ashby, Massachusetts, and Pam and Gadar lived in it till October 15. He pulled it back to Maine the next day. Then they moved to our home for a month and then to their apartment on Water Street, Wakefield. In October 17, Gadar was offered a management position at Blockbuster Video, and he took it.

In October 15, the church began to install a French door between the living room and the porch. It was a nice improvement.

On Sunday, October 16, we dedicated the memorial garden. This was the vision of Horace Hylan. He believed that a garden filled with blooming plants, trees, and shrubs all nestled next to our massive granite meetinghouse would be the perfect place to memorialize loved ones.

We began to receive the cremains of those who passed away, and the office kept a careful record of where each was located. In addition to a physical place in the garden, each memorialized person's name was carved on one of sixteen granite slabs arranged under a pergola. A portion of Mother's and Dad's ashes were interred in 2009.

Back in May, the congregation took a serious step. It voted to pursue dual affiliation with the CCCC. I saw this as a positive decision, hoping to appeal to the majority of the congregation yet remaining in the UCC, which was important to a minority.

In November 13, Rev. Steve Gammon, conference minister of the CCCC, preached from our pulpit. A meeting of the congregation followed. We voted to join the CCCC, but remain in the UCC for the present. Ninety members were present, there was very little discussion, and the motion to join passed. The meeting took three minutes!

In light of Dad's passing, we decided to gather at Bill and Cynthia's for our annual Thanksgiving reunion. We had a grand time together, with great food, a hike, Mother doing some funnies, and all of us marching around the house to the marches of John Phillip Sousa.

As September arrived, I began sensing among the leadership a different attitude toward the dark days of 1990–1999. Those difficult struggles provoked by the Masonic order, the resignation of our minister of music, and the theological shift that I introduced called the church to deal with a very challenging question, "Just what kind of church is First Parish?" (Of course I had been praying from the first day of our arrival that we would ask this question. It did not occur to me then that it would take over twenty years and three serious conflicts to precipitate that discussion.)

After hearing a biblical message over those years, these new ideas and the addition of new members forced the church to face this important question head-on.

The clear and important differences that grew year by year were at first rarely recognized or discussed in the open. They were growing but we were all fearful of bringing those differences to the surface so they might be talked about and resolved. I always felt that it wasn't the right time. I think that we really didn't know how to talk to one another about such serious differences. They were kept to the parking lot and the telephone lines. We covered up our differences for years. I knew they were there, and I knew they were inevitable. The Gospel of Jesus Christ will always bring conflict, but if we didn't have to talk about our differences, we could more easily convince ourselves that everything was fine. After all, who wants to provoke an argument?

The resignation of our organist and the anonymous letter of 1997 took things out of our hands by shining a searchlight upon the serious divisions within the membership. If we wanted to move forward as a church, we had to try and understand one another.

I suppose I could have resigned my position like many were calling me to do. It was what I was preaching that was causing all the trouble. "Just leave. Find another church and leave us alone."

But I could not deny that it was God's miracle that brought us from Hawaii to Massachusetts. I was convinced that I was called by God's Holy Spirit and Word to reintroduce the message of the gospel to these people who hadn't heard it for at least forty years. After all, the church's founding covenant that I had discovered while reading the congregation's history made it clear that the message of the Bible is the only foundation upon which to build a Christian church.

As I have already said, we began reading that covenant every November on All Saints Day. I was simply trying to remind the church of their roots; sadly, not everyone wanted to hear about their roots.

Their reluctance to listen was understandable. With the absence of biblical truth, the members of the congregation were left to work out their own course. This usually results in a person striving on their own to please God through self-conscious effort. It boils down to this—salvation through striving and human effort or salvation through humble confession of sin and dependence on God's grace.

E. Stanley Jones speaks of those who seek God and salvation as those who try climbing up a tall ladder of self-achievement or those humbly receiving love and forgiveness from the God who meets us at the bottom rung.

Of course, meeting God at the bottom rung is admitting that climbing is a futile effort. And then there is the question, How high do I have to climb? Will I ever feel assured of success? Plus the fact that asking forgiveness for one's sins attacks one's pride. This admission is a giant hurdle and many stumble over it.

But after the trauma, the blue ribbons, the special meetings, the core group, the service of reconciliation, and my visits to the Center for Career Development and Ministry, the congregation began to see those dark times as teaching moments brought by God's Holy Spirit. They came at just the right time—God's time. By God's grace, we identified the conflict, faced it, dealt with it, were open to learn from it, and have become stronger because of it. The church had become more confident about their direction, more unified, and more open to new ways and ministries. There would be more lessons, more opportunities, and more challenges in the coming years but we were becoming dependent upon God's Spirit and Word to move ahead. I believed that First Parish had turned a major corner in her 361 years. We were again seeking to be a place where God's truth and love were freely and confidently shared. Praise God!

This was the year that I suggested to our minister of music that a Messiah Sing-Along might be a good community outreach. He took my suggestion and extended an invitation to the churches of Wakefield to come to our sanctuary on Friday, December 16. This was the first of what is now a tradition.

In December 13, we welcomed Abagail Joy to the Weisenbach family. She is the sixth child and last child given to Dave and Sharon.

And for the record, I conducted ten weddings, fifteen funerals, and eight baptisms that year.

By this time, we had participated in Stephen Ministries for nineteen years, training almost fifty church members. In January, we started another class with seven enrolled. As I have said, this program enriched our congregation in at least two ways. Obviously we increased the breadth and depth of pastoral care provided to our membership. Secondly, the training was a boost to the spiritual understanding of each prospective new minister. Every one of them grew in biblical knowledge and Christian practice.

Starting last year, our associate pastor was beginning to raise questions in the minds of a few parents.

He continued to do an acceptable job when asked to preach, but sometimes fell short in other areas. He did well in areas he enjoyed but often failed to serve when things didn't suit him.

This year was the fifteenth performance of the *Passion Play*. It seemed to improve every year. The cast was more experienced and confident, and the congregation saw it as an opportunity to invite family and friends. This year I was Caiaphas. I even grew a beard! I wrote in the *Church Herald* that my part in the play gave me a new perspective.

> On Good Friday night, as I reflected on this event, it occurred to me that the play is a wonderful example of how the contributions of many come together to produce a powerful whole.
>
> Everyone's gift is vital. Some people had a large part, some small. Some made customs, others operated a spotlight, some moved pews, others lugged scenery, some served communion, others prepared it. See what I mean? Every part fit together to produce a magnificent result.
>
> So thank you, each one who contributed so much to the play and let us continue to pray that God will nourish all the seeds planted within the hearts of our community.

In June, thirteen of us attended a Promise Keepers rally in Albany, New York. This is a ministry directed toward men, encouraging them to become better husbands, fathers, and friends. We had a great time together. On the following Sunday, Al Ward and Mark Hathaway shared their reactions, while Dom Mercurio shared at the Wednesday service.

In July, I attended my first CCCC's annual meeting with the encouragement of Ed Whitman. It was held in St. Cloud, Minnesota. Our church had been welcomed by the Credentials Committee and received the approval of the board of directors. (I'm sure my friend Ed Whitman pulled a few strings to make this happen so quickly.)

I made a brief speech describing First Parish and our recent decision to pursue dual affiliation, after which I requested formal acceptance as a sister church in the CCCC. The members of the annual meeting voted to welcome us as members.

A year after I retired, First Parish voted to leave the UCC. I anticipated this decision but was sad to hear that as a result of this decision, a few faithful members left the fellowship.

Poppy had a stroke on Sunday, September 3. Scott Markloff found him lying on the living room floor. We suspected that he had been there for a few hours. We got a call at 12:30 a.m., so Pat drove through the night to be with her family.

After therapy, he recovered enough to live back at the house, but Granny was becoming a challenge. She was suffering from memory loss and became very protective of Poppy. She didn't appreciate so many "strange" women attending to her husband. Her behavior became a heavy burden for Pat to bear. Not being recognized by her mother was a devastating loss.

Toward the end of the month, her booth at the Topsfield Fair provided a positive activity.

We had a very enjoyable family time at Emily and Mike's wedding in October 8. I took a video of the service, and Bill and Cynthia helped Emily plan the reception, which was stunning. Mother looked elegant, as she said grace in a dress Cynthia helped her pick out. All of us danced the night away.

In August of last year, Hurricane Katrina made landfall in Florida, Mississippi, and Louisiana. It caused $125 billion in damages and took 1,836 lives. It is considered the worst natural disaster in American history.

On Sunday, September 17, we launched Forty Days of Community. This program was very similar to the program we initiated back in 2004. Again the key element was small groups and an eight-week preaching series. There were thirteen groups, and each was challenged to act together and develop two projects, one to serve someone in the church and a second a project to serve the community.

This program stimulated several church members who wanted to do something to help those rebuilding after Katrina. Steve Gates contacted churches in Bay St. Louis, Mississippi, and then organized the first group of men and women who traveled to the area to help with the cleanup. We sent off each group with our prayers, best wishes, and some desperately needed items. They returned after a week or ten days with heartwarming stories.

Some members of the group collected pine cones, unique to the area, made Christmas tree ornaments, and sold them to the congregation to raise funds for the next trip. A second group of five went South in December 2. Three more trips were planned for 2007.

These visits were generated from one Forty Day group, another group reached out to Place of Promise in Lowell, and another started a shawl ministry.

In December 22, I received the following invitation:

> Dear Pastor Rich,
> We would like to cordially invite you and your loved ones to a luncheon to celebrate your commitment to First Parish. Our church is blessed to have your dedication and we would like to share this time with you to show our appreciation for everything you do.
>
> With Love,
> The Monday 40 Days Community Group

This invitation was extended to all the members of the staff. Sadly, the two secretaries had other things to do and did not attend. I was so disappointed that they chose to reject the love of others.

This decision did not come as a surprise; however, the office staff was not supportive of me or the direction the church had taken. Over the years, I had received many reports from those who visited the office telling me of having overheard strong criticism of the pastor. This situation was a heavy burden on me for most of my thirty years at First Parish.

We scheduled a celebration Sunday in November 5, our 362nd anniversary, to share what had been accomplished by the groups. It was a very special day!

My sixty-fifth birthday fell on a Tuesday that year, the night the church council met. Much to my surprise, they had planned to serve coffee and cake to mark the day. These events came as a great encouragement to me, such a change of attitude from six years back.

The church fair was the weekend of November 17. Hundreds of items were displayed and priced, and crowds filled the dining room and vestry. By Saturday night, everything had to be removed and prepared for the Saturday night AA meeting and then rearranged again for the community dinner and Clothing Closet. It was a whirlwind of activity. After things quieted down, I wrote for the *Church Herald*,

> After all the activity over this past weekend, I got to thinking about how active our congregation has become. As one of you said to me as you passed through the greeting line, "This church is cookin'!"

I found this description of a living church in a periodical and included it in my remarks.

> Living churches always have parking problems; dead churches don't.
>
> Living churches run out of refrigerator space in their kitchen; dead churches have plenty of space.
>
> Living churches have lots of noisy youth; dead churches are fairly quiet.
>
> Living churches' expenses frequently exceed their income; dead churches sock away any excess.
>
> Living churches grow so fast that you forget peoples' names; in dead churches everybody had known everybody else for years.
>
> Living churches focus on people; dead churches focus on problems.

Living churches are filled with loving, generous hearts; dead churches are filled with nervous contributors.

Living churches move out in faith; dead churches operate totally by human sight.

I'm so very grateful for First Parish; a living church.

One morning, I arrived at the office to discover that someone had broken in and stolen money that was intended for the poor. I shared this sad news with the Stephen Ministries meeting that night.

The next morning I found a check under the door with this note,

I am sorry that some yellow-bellied varmint came into our pastor's office and stole some money. Hope this will cover your loss.

Love and peace,

Jan

It's just another example of loving, generous hearts. On Christmas Day, I received the following note:

Dear Rev. Weisenbach,

As a member of the Boy Scouts community these past seven years, I have come to appreciate the kindness and generosity of your church towards our troop. But even more, as a resident of the Wakefield community, I have seen all the great contributions your parish has provided to our community. The church is always a hubbub of multiple activities that benefit so many around us.

I have enclosed a monetary donation that I hope will help to continue all these activities. I only ask that the contribution be listed as anonymous for

I do not wish any recognition for this in any form. I feel the warmth of your giving to the community each time I visit and see all your good work.

Sincerely,

———

A check for $3,000.00 was enclosed. What a blessed Christmas present!

Other events of the year included major decisions by Brian and Kim; they sold their Gould Street, Stoneham, home and bought 18 Brewster Road, Wakefield.

In November, Dave came from Maine to add a second floor to their new home.

We did get to visit Moosehead Lake and Northern Pride that year, and Dave bought a pontoon boat for Lake Arrowhead. He brought it up to Beaver Cove that year.

For the record, I conducted six weddings, twenty-two funerals, and eleven baptisms.

The church council decided to reschedule our 2007 annual meeting from the last Wednesday in January to the last Sunday in hopes of having more in attendance, and more members did attend.

I took the opportunity to share some statistics.

7: First Parish members who traveled to Mississippi to help with Katrina relief

9: Number of small group ministries[1]

11: Number of Alpha courses conducted since the fall of 2000

12: Small group Bible studies held every week

14: Percent of increase in Sunday worship attendance in 2006 over 2005

15: Number of active Stephen ministers

———

[1] Stephen Ministries, Project Hope (Mississippi trips), Saturday Breakfast team, Clothing Closet team, Community Dinner Ministry, LIFE Luncheons (a luncheon program for senior citizens organized by Roy Evans. Several women helped prepare the meal.), Shawl Ministry, Sound team, and Place of Promise team.

15: Number of years Pastor Rich has walked on Good Friday for Sharing Inc.

60: Percent of membership who attend worship services regularly

200: Average attendance in 2006 (fifty-two weeks)

335: Total membership of First Parish Congregational Church

$2,482.00: Money First Parish members contributed to the Good Friday walk in 2006

$25,161.00: Total given to Sharing Inc. since 1992.

$31,630.00: Amount of money given toward the cost of rebuilding our chimes

$227,260.00: Pledge total in January 2006

$243,630.00: Pledges received at the end of 2006.

$441,479.00: Total of all gifts to First Parish in 2006

I turned sixty-five in 2006, so Pat and I began thinking about where we might live when I finally retired. After looking at four places in Wakefield, including two family houses and then four condos in Gloucester, we finally settled on a place in Magnolia. It is very interesting that God saved a place for us in the small town where we spent our first six years together. Our condo had been sold to someone else but the deal fell through. When we visited the place and saw the ocean view, and we were sold immediately. I heard the Spirit whisper in my ear, "You ain't seen nothin' yet."

It is small but very adequate for us and comes with a near perfect view of the Atlantic Ocean. We closed in May 21. At that time, my 403(b) retirement account contained $313,123.75. I took out $65,000.00 for a down payment ($49,000.00) after taxes and our trip to Japan ($16,000.00). Thank you, Lord! (It is certainly interesting to note that all us boys own property on the ocean. Bill and Paul in Bayside, Maine, and Dave in Ormond Beach, Florida.)

As usual, Easter weekend was filled with several opportunities to witness to God's power over physical death. The *Passion Play* was a wonderfully blessed time with two performances on Maundy Thursday and Good Friday. That year, Gadar filled the role of Jesus, I was Pilate, Kim was Mary, Pat was in the crowd assembled before Pilate,

Brian worked the video, and Pam wrote, directed, and arranged for sound and music.

On Friday, I walked for Sharing Inc., but due to plantar fasciitis I could only complete three laps. Rich Bardet, Bonnie Mercurio, and Pat walked the remaining three. We collected $2,400.00 that year. I conducted our annual Easter sunrise service by the lake, followed by our worship service in which we were again joined by the Korean Love Church.

I think those Easter celebrations were some of my favorite memories.

Sad news arrived with a phone call from Charlane Chapman. Dear Ed died in April 11 of a heart attack. She found him lying in their driveway. We were able to attend his service at their church in Maine in April 15. Ed was a dear friend and brother in Christ, and we have continued to maintain a loving relationship with Charlane.

In June, we received the following letter of appreciation from First Baptist Church, Bay St. Louis, Mississippi:

> Dear Brothers and Sisters in Christ,
>
> Thank you so much for your love, your prayers, and your ministry to us. God has blessed us through you—through your regular prayers which continue to strengthen us, through your gifts and blessings that you have sent to us, and through those of you who have come down to help us with the physical labor.
>
> We thought Katrina might destroy us, but all that it has done is provide an avenue where we get to see God's blessings first-hand. Our faith in God has been strengthen because of you. Thank you for being God's hands and feet.
>
> With warm regards,
> First Baptist, Congregation and Staff

We celebrated Mother's ninetieth birthday in June 8. We gathered at Bill and Cynthia's house in Katonah, New York. We were all there and were able to take a picture of Mother sitting on the porch steps with her boys and another with her surrounded by her grandchildren and their spouses.

Granny was failing, so Pat drove to Pennsylvania to help her sister Kathy who was bearing the greatest burden.

During that time, I played host to Bill Pugh who was hired to rebuild our chimes. He had come to First Parish from Kansas about a year earlier to take down and rebuild all the electric hammers used to strike a series of long metal tubes. The chimes operated by inserting paper rolls, like a player piano.

Horace Hylan had maintained and repaired those chimes for years, but due to his age, he felt he could no longer climb the stairs and ladders to gain access to the mechanisms. When Bill completed his work, they rang out hymn tunes at noon and 6:00 p.m.

Bill told me that we had one of only a handful of chimes in the United Sates that still functioned. Joe D'Agostino has been able to carry on this ministry for the last several years.

Kelli O'Brien moved into our house in August 26, and we hope to help her get on her feet. Pat is sacrificing her yearly ten days at the fair to better attend to Kelli's needs. Over the months, she showed little progress.

On Saturday, September 1, Granny passed away. We journeyed to Pennsylvania for a memorial service at Davisville Church on Friday, September 7. The two grandsons named Dave (Weisenbach and O'Brien) each spoke and claimed to be Granny's favorite!

On Saturday, we gathered at Sunset Memorial Park for a final farewell. The entire family gathered except for Tim and Michelle who were serving as missionaries in Mexico.

September is always a busy time of the year—Wednesday programs started up, the basement began (a program for youth on Wednesdays from two to five thirty), and a membership seminar was scheduled and a service to rededicate our chimes.

But not everything brought joy. We found it difficult to motivate Kelli, and my pastoral associate continued to be a challenge—we have such different styles. Our moderator was preoccupied with caring for his lady friend, and we had to cancel Alpha because four of the six enrolled failed to return after the introductory session.

The Advent season was again a wonderful time of worship, service, and outreach. Besides our annual open house at the parsonage, the Messiah Sing-Along, two Christmas Eve services, and the Pie social, we added the living nativity.

Trefina Fox had experience organizing a living nativity at a former church, so she approached me with the idea of presenting one on the common. This would be with live animals and a brief drama of the Annunciation and Incarnation. It became quite popular and the church saw the value of this outreach possibility. Dave and Trefina had funded this themselves for the first few years, and then the church decided to fund it for future years.

Mother could no longer drive, so I bought her Toyota Corolla from my brothers. Nephew Pete, who was selling Toyotas at the time, said it was worth about $12,000.00, so I gave each brother $3,000. When I went to trade it in for a 2004 Rav4, the dealer offered me just $5,000.00. I was a rookie at negotiating with used car dealers. I should have left that dealership and gone elsewhere. I have regretted the deal ever since.

For the record, I conducted four weddings, nine funerals, and nine baptisms.

Madison Lynne (9 lb and 1 oz) joined the Albushies family in January 27, 2008. We were all grateful that Kim and Brian had a girl to add to their two boys.

Later that month, Pat told me that her hopes for Kelli were not coming to pass. We decided that she will have to join her mother Kay in Seattle, Washington. She left us in May 3. We were trying to help, but our efforts showed little benefit.

We were able to take her to a Ken Medema concert in Newburyport; he is a blind pianist. She did get to greet him, which gave her great joy.

Kim and the children visited us at the condo in April 20. While holding Maddie, Pat noticed something irregular in Maddie's body movements, rhythmiclike spasms. "Kim, come look," Pat called. "I think she is having a seizure." At twelve thirty the next morning, Maddie was admitted into the Floating Hospital at New England Medical Center in Boston. "This is an emergency," the doctor said. "We need to act quickly." They performed several tests and concluded that she was suffering from infantile spasms, a condition that occurs in one out of five thousand children. I went on line to learn more information about this condition and discovered that mental retardation could result. I was fearful and prayed fervently.

She began treatments with adrenocorticotropic hormone (ACTH) to spur the adrenal gland to send correct messages to the brain. She will need thirty doses, $50,000.00. At first their insurance company refused to pay for this medication. "This drug is too expensive, not on our list." Fortunately the doctor wrote a letter explaining that Maddie's case required this medication. The company changed its mind. We thanked the Lord and the doctor.

In April 24, the doctor sent this letter, "I have never seen a child at this early stage. Your mother saved your daughter's life when she picked up on her movements."

Kim remained with Maddie, never leaving her side, and was encouraged by a wonderful group of her friends.

Maddie came home in April 29. Kim and Brian were apprehensive, of course, and her medication made her irritable, but it would soon be reduced. We were so grateful for the doctors and for God's grace.

Over the years, Maddie has experienced intermittent recurrences, and we all remain trusting the Lord for her future. Her doctor said, "I'm planning to go to this girl's graduation."

We enjoyed the usual Easter season activities—community dinner and Clothing Closet, *Passion Play*, Good Friday walk for Sharing Inc., early morning sunrise service, and combined worship service with the Korean Love Church. Around 115 folks including twenty-seven Rotarians, Fire Chief Mike Sullivan, and Police Chief Richard Smith contributed $3,212.00 to the walk.

In May 16, my retirement account had climbed to $319,254.86, but the next week, it dropped $71,146.06. By October 9, another

$118,567.39 was shed. We were down to $139,541.41 in just five months. Scripture certainly speaks of how fragile material possessions are. I was very disappointed of course but have sought to trust in God's provision. He is faithful!

Our associate told me in May that he and his family would be moving. He hoped to take up ministry in a neighboring church.

Dan and Mandi were a good team and contributed much to the ministry of our church during the six years they were with us including the establishment of 'Mothers' of Pre-schoolers' (MOPS) the 'Basement" our afternoon ministry to youth and our Community Dinners.

Pat and I went hiking in Ravenswood Park in May and left the trail to eat our lunch by a lake. Much to my surprise, I could not find the trail to get back to the car; we were lost!

I am very good at directions, but this time I became frightened. We prayed and walked in the direction I thought was best. Fortunately we came upon a plastics factory, so I went in and asked for help. Vice President Jonathan Lawrence overheard my plea and came out of his office and said, "Come with me. I'll take you to your car." I gave him twenty bucks!

In my prayer for help, I failed to ask God for a vice president to drive us in his car to our car. "Oh ye of little faith."

We joined members of Pat's William Tennent Class of 1958 for their fiftieth reunion. We enjoyed a dinner at Mill Spring in Ivyland, Pennsylvania, and then a pig roast picnic on the twenty-first.

Then a smaller group of us went on a cruise out of New Your City. We toured the coast of the Atlantic Ocean (June 23–27)—St. John's, New Brunswick, and Halifax, Nova Scotia. We really liked cruising and thought we might go on another sometime.

I cochaired our Muhlenberg forty-fifth college reunion committee. Being a minister, I prayed a few times and read the class necrology. I do give $100.00 every year to the college. This school contributed much to my development and I am very grateful.

I got a call from Mother in July 11; my cousin Arlene, who lived close to Mother and Dad, died in July 7. Mother appreciated Arlene's visits and hoped that I might drive to Pennsylvania to conduct her funeral. I drove in July 11, and we had the service on Saturday, July 12. About seventy people gathered in the backyard of Karen and Bill Miller's home. Karen was Arlene's youngest sister. I was happy to serve and witness to God's provision to the grieving and the forgiveness of sins and promise of eternal life.

> Dear Rich,
> Thank you so very much for your beautiful memorial service for Arlene. We all loved the service and we thank you so much for taking the time to come and help us through this difficult time.
>
> Love,
> Jean, Lynda, and Karen and family

Pat's CTMH convention (July 29–August 5) was at the Gaylord Palms, Kissimmee, Florida. The Palms is a fantastic garden resort completely covered by a glass dome. Thousands of plants and several waterfalls and ponds, complete with alligators, filled the circle of rooms, each with its own balcony overlooking the gardens.

During the convention, I spent time with John Wallace, friends from Kwaj, now living on Merritt Island. He picked me up and we spent the day at the Kennedy Space Center.

I stayed with them till August 3 when I received a call from Brian telling me that Peter Verdone died in an accident and asked if I could do the funeral.

His wife Tanya Verdone, née Gerrior, arranged for a viewing at First Parish on Thursday and a graveside service Friday morning followed by a memorial service at eleven o'clock.

We were planning to leave for Moosehead that week, so Pat, Kim, and the children went without me. Brian and I drove up together after the funeral.

Back in May, Pat and I took a lunch to Ocean Lawn, a beautiful sixty-acre spot on the shoreline of Manchester-by-the-Sea and maintained by the Trustees of Reservations.

While there, we met a young couple and their infant child. He wore a T-shirt with "Wheaton" on it. I asked him which Wheaton was he from (there are two, Norwood, Massachusetts, and Wheaton, Illinois). He said he attended the one in Illinois and was in New England looking at the possibility of attending Gordon-Conwell.

I happened to have my wallet with me (I usually wouldn't have had it on a picnic) and gave him my card. I told him that I was a local pastor and our associate for Christian education was leaving and that if he came to Gordon and if he was interested in that position, he could call me for more information. Little did we know what was to come of that "chance" encounter.

While at the Gaylord Palms, I received an e-mail from that student we had met back in May. He wondered if that position at the church was still available. I quickly let him know that it was and that our church had scheduled a meeting in November to decide what to do since there was a vacancy in our staff.

Abram Kielsmeir-Jones

At that meeting, we decided to fill the position with a part-time youth pastor and that I should contact that student, Abram Kielsmeier-Jones, ASAP! I was hoping that he would be hired immediately, but we waited for the new fiscal year. Abram started on January 18, 2009.

That fall, Pat and I were told by the diaconate to make an appointment with a professional photographer. The board was preparing to hang a picture of both of us in the Fireside Room. There are other pastors so honored in that room, but we were the first husband-and-wife team to be given that special honor. Pat was always my partner in ministry, and the congregation recognized and celebrated that fact.

Along with this, the board organized a Pastor Appreciation Day in honor of our twenty-fifth anniversary as pastor. Quite an honor!

Around this time, the leadership felt we ought to sit down together and try to develop a five-year plan. My fast-approaching retirement was on some minds, and there were substantial building repairs that would need attention; perhaps a capital campaign would be in order.

We moved ahead with plans for a capital campaign and even selected a firm to help us, but that was the year of the financial crisis in the banking and housing sectors. Our small planning group decided that we must postpone the effort.

Then, in God's timing, the church received gifts from the final wills of two longtime members. Neither came with strings, that is, the total amount of the gift could be used in any way the church felt was proper. So without a plea for funds from the people, we installed a new heating system, repaired the roof, completely resurfaced the parking lot, and did some improvements on the parsonage. Thank you, Lord!

In my annual report for the year, I made clear that loving God and neighbor must be our top priority. I then went on to lift up the many places in our congregational life where I saw love and service most evident.

At committee meetings, we speak to each other with respect. When someone is hurting, scores of you rush to help and comfort. When someone does something special, many are right there to thank them and encourage them. I love to see that!

And, quite naturally, that love reaches out to our community, far and wide. Teams are sent to Mississippi to help rebuild, food is cooked and served to our community, clothing is shared, canned goods are distributed, meals are delivered to Rosie's in Boston, a *Passion Play* is performed, a living nativity is acted out, pie is served, and our beautiful building accommodates at least ten community groups. They all use our facilities and enjoy them at a cost far below their worth. All this happens, week in and week out, because you give, our trustees coordinate, and Ken keeps the place clean.

I'm trusting that God will continue to guide this church, and as we love Him and our neighbors we will continue to receive His blessing.

Pastor Rich

Of course with all these blessings, activities, programs, gifts, and projects, opposition will oftentimes raise its ugly head; we have to expect it.

Even though it was eight years after those two votes to sustain me and affirm the direction of the church, there still remained those who would criticize, act selfishly, and sow discord wherever they could. These members rarely worshipped, but they were on the sidelines looking for opportunities to disrupt what they felt was harmful.

One such opportunity arose around a funeral. The sister of a member died, and the member wanted to have her sister's funeral at First Parish but did not want me to officiate. This plan is highly inappropriate to say the least. Services conducted in a pastor's church are led by the pastor of that church.

They approached Peter Brown of First Baptist for assistance but he refused. They then went looking for another minister. Our office cooperated with the member's request informing me of what was planned.

Fortunately the minister they finally found wanted to talk with me before granting the member's request. We did discuss the affair, and I explained that although I was hurt and the request (demand) was against long-standing practice, I would yield to the wishes of the member. The service proceeded and the guest minister admired my decision and told me so.

I suppose I could have refused the member's request, but I felt that adding to a grieving family's sadness was not the thing to do.

I began thinking and praying harder for those members who were so unhappy. I wrote in my journal, "They do not understand how love behaves. They don't recognize love because they have not seen it. Help me, Lord, to love them." God always brought peace when I kept this in mind.

We did escape to Northern Pride Lodge that February, Pat returned to the Topsfield Fair in October, and the church replaced the air-conditioning unit in the Covell Chapel. YEA!

And for the record, I conducted six weddings, eighteen funerals, and fifteen baptisms.

During the year, we were all very aware of the far-reaching effects of the financial crisis. I tried to write a short piece about the dangers of spending, motivated by emotion rather than genuine need.

> One thing is clear; our culture has experienced an epidemic of overindulgence. According to the Center for American Progress, household debt averaged 133.7% of disposable income in late 2007—a record. For every $100.00 a family earned, they spent $133.70. Millions are using credit cards to pay for essentials such as medical bills, car repairs, and rent.
>
> There is nothing wrong with enjoying the resources we've been blessed with as long as we're debt free, tithing to God's work, and acting generously toward those who are less fortunate. But falling prey to emotional spending will get us into trouble every time.
>
> When emotions like boredom, depression, stress, inadequacy, and guilt or even positive feelings like "I deserve to celebrate," take control, we are headed down a dangerous road. I'm sure we are all familiar with the scenario. We wind up using spending as an ineffective Band-Aid. The benefits are so temporary and we provide our children with a terrible example to follow.
>
> I believe during this particular time, God has given Christians a special opportunity to display financial discipline. I trust we are up for the challenge.

The annual celebration of the crucifixion and resurrection of our Savior was again the highlight of the year. There were many opportunities to rejoice together, serve our neighbors, and witness God's power over physical death. God blessed us tremendously!

After the celebrations of Easter, it is always a good time to emphasize the natural desire to spread the Word through words and actions. So on the last Sunday of May, twelve members of the congregation took two minutes each to describe the one particular ministry opportunity to which they were committed. After the service, all twelve speakers took their places behind display tables in the vestry answering questions and "plugging in" interested folks.

The following is the list of the projects and speakers who shared that morning:

1. Food Pantry, Becky Fosnock
2. Place of Promise, Tim Hildreth
3. Prayer Shawls, Linda O'Neil
4. Project Hope (trips to Mississippi to rebuild), Steve Gates
5. Rosie's Place, Barbara Parish
6. Stephen Ministries, Pastor Rich
7. The Basement, Maurine Doyle
8. Monthly Birthday Cakes, Linda D'Agostino
9. Clothing Closet, Angela Faylor
10. Community Breakfast, Earl Sheaff
11. Community Dinners, Jill Sullivan and Darcy Hildreth
12. Compassion International, Ernie Chandler

By God's grace, people became more and more aware of the opportunity and privilege of ministry in Christ's name.

One Sunday, Ken asked me for a food voucher for a needy person who was waiting down in our kitchen. I had none at the moment, so we agreed that he would give the person $20.00 out of his own pocket and I would reimburse him with church funds.

A church member overheard our conversation, came to me, and pressed $100.00 into my hand. "Please, let this cover it," she said.

This is just another example of the many I could cite expressing the love and sensitivity of so many in the congregation.

In the fall, the church council voted to ask the congregation to participate in a survey designed to assess our spiritual health. The survey, entitled Church Health Assessment Tool (CHAT), was developed by Leadership Transformations, Inc. (LTI), to ask our members and friends to respond to seventy questions about ten specific areas of church life. The council interviewed Dr. Steve Macchia, founder of LTI, and believed this tool would help us, especially as we face the challenges and opportunities of the next few years.

On Saturday, November 21, Pam called to report that Gadar complained of chest pains, sweating, and tingles in his left arm. An ambulance took him to Melrose-Wakefield Hospital for a heart catheterization. On Monday, we knew his condition was serious and he was transferred to Massachusetts General. He was scheduled for open-heart surgery to repair six blockages. The operation took twelve hours, after which the doctor called Pam. "All went well. He should have a bright future."

By God's grace, Gadar had a wake-up call, not a come home call. He returned home in December 1. He made slow and steady progress with the strong and loving support of his wife Pam. She was a rock of trust and confidence as she gave her husband into God's care.

Pam's call on the Saturday of Gadar's attack brought a dual message from Pam; of course he needed medical attention immediately and she would be with him. The second was a request, "Dad, can you fill in for me in tomorrow's Thanksgiving drama?"

Pam had written and rehearsed an original drama for Thanksgiving Sunday. She played the part of an on-the-street interviewer, and the personalities she interviewed were representatives of God's creation, animals, flowers, etc., each answering the question, "Why are you thankful?" Each animal and flower listed several of their characteristics, "My beauty...my many uses...my strength...my speed."

Finally the interviewer (Pam and now me) asked a human being (Gadar), "And what do *you* thank God for?" He isn't prepared or equipped to answer her question, which prompts her to turn to the people in the congregation, "How about you? Anyone thankful to God this morning?"

We had prepared a few to be ready with their gratitude, and after hearing their testimonies, another dozen chimed in with their thanks. It was a blessed time.

I was a weak substitute for Pam's role, and I cannot remember who filled in for Gadar. All went well but we missed Pam and Gadar and held them our prayers that morning.

We did enjoy Northern Pride Lodge in February and Beaver Cove in August.

Jayna LaVerde began taking pictures of the members of the congregation for a new pictorial directory.

And for the record, I conducted seven weddings, twenty-five funerals, and six baptisms.

On Saturday, February 27, 2010, twenty-two helpers from church gathered to move Pam and Gadar to their new home in Methuen, Massachusetts. After church, Kim and Dave joined Pat and me to help get them settled in. It was a great house with a lot of character located at the end of a dead-end street. Pam took to it immediately and decorated it inside and out. I remember the double front door, the hall and stairs, and especially the kitchen with its own bathroom snuck behind a door that once was a stairway. The garage was stuffed full with Pam's craft supplies and on the second floor antique farm implements. The family gathered several times for the holidays.

During that year's Super Bowl, Focus on the Family paid for an advertisement describing the decision of Tim Tebow's mother not to abort her child, feared to be abnormal. Tim was born whole and healthy and later developed into a football player who eventually won the Heisman Trophy in 2007.

I first heard about the commercial from the weekly e-mail I received from our denominational headquarters. I was surprised, and then embarrassed, to discover that our leaders in Cleveland, Ohio, were against the ad and very angry at CBS for airing it.

I was surprised because the UCC advocates inclusiveness. "We exercise an extravagant welcome to all" is the denomination's self-description. Their reaction to the opinions of Focus on the Family was harsh and judgmental, hardly welcoming. I don't expect that our leaders and sister churches would agree with Focus on the Family's position on abortion, but rejecting it so strongly and then demanding that CBS refuse to air it is wrong. People can think for themselves on such matters. I'm sure that there are differences of opinion at First Parish on the question, but mutual respect is the goal, not rejection.

This unreasonable reaction from our denominational leadership only added more reason to rethink our relationship with the UCC.

In April, my "RAW Material" column in the *Church Herald* was a listing of 129 church members and friends, including twenty-two members of the Wakefield Rotary Club who had sponsored me on my nineteenth walk for Sharing Inc. Over those years, we have raised $37,000.00.

In April 30, Jayna LaVerde announced that the pictures she had taken for the church directory were available for delivery. She along with Pam Abkarian and JoLynn Foster made this possible. Her photos were great!

"Dad, this is the worst thing I have ever had to deal with," our son Dave confessed to me over the phone that he had inadvertently started a fire in his recently completed addition to the home of Keith and Cheryl Stackhouse.

He put a final coat of urethane on the floor and tossed the rags into a bucket, but they combusted spontaneously after he left the job site. He was devastated.

He told the whole story to Keith and Cheryl and the Buxton, Maine, fire marshal. All three were very understanding and Dave's relationship with the Stackhouse family actually improved. Their insurance supplied enough resources to rebuild completely.

In July, I again piggybacked on Pat's CTMH Annual Convention, this time in Washington DC. Pat had pain in her knee, so that curtailed her participation with me but she still enjoyed the convention.

I spent my time visiting some of the sites in our nation's capital. I walked everywhere, the Smithsonian Institute, the Library of Congress, Ford's Theatre, the Supreme Court, the Vietnam Memorial Wall, the memorials of Jefferson, Lincoln and Franklin Roosevelt, the National Gallery of Art, the National Museum of American History, and the Air and Space Museum. I did purchase a tour of the National Cemetery at Arlington, which included the changing of the guard at the Tomb of the Unknown and the eternal flame at President Kennedy's grave. All contributed to a lasting memory and a heart filled with gratitude.

One funny memory occurred as I walked across the mall. I overheard a mother explain to her teenage daughter, "No, dear. There are no stores. This is a different kind of mall."

The highlight was a concert in the National Cathedral in July 4. It was very special.

I discovered during my years of ministry that one of my main functions as pastor is to encourage the members in whatever they were doing or planning. That was very easy to do at First Parish, especially on the third Friday of the month.

On those Fridays, I just wandered around the meetinghouse encountering the small group preparing a meal for Rosie's—nine volunteers preparing chicken, rice, and carrots for about eighty hungry souls in a women's shelter in Boston. Then just as many generous hearts pulled out all the clothes that had accumulated in the closet during the month, sorting, folding, and arranging them on tables in order to be ready for the scores who come the next morning. Many folks started coming early because another group of members started offering breakfast before the Closet opened.

What a blessing I received, and every pastor I know would be grateful to experience a similar chance to see the church functioning so graciously.

When I recall the dark times (1990–1999), I marvel at the transformation God's love, mercy, and grace wrought in the hearts of so many. The change took many years but His faithfulness surrounded us at every turn.

I have referred to the Chat survey that we conducted at the end of last year. My annual report for 2010 was a summary of the results. About a third of the congregation took the online test. The overall goal was to discover how healthy we were as a church.

The following are the areas of church life that the Chat tried to access:

1. A healthy church seeks the direction of the Holy Spirit.
2. A healthy church worships God in ways that engage the heart, mind, and strength.
3. A healthy church provides training and resources for all ages.
4. A healthy church encourages believers to work with God and one another.
5. A healthy church is intentional in its efforts to build loving relationships.
6. A healthy church identifies and equips individuals to become servant-leaders.
7. A healthy church demonstrates the love of God outside of their building.
8. A healthy church reaches out to other churches for learning and celebration.
9. A healthy church utilizes facilities to provide maximum support.
10. A healthy church teaches that all are stewards of God's resources.

The survey asked each person to identify three areas (out of the ten) as the strongest sources within First Parish. Both congregation and leadership, whose results were kept separate, agreed that number one (God's empowering presence) and number two (God exalting worship) are two of First Parish's strongest areas. This indicates that as we gather together, we experience worship as refreshing, renewing, uplifting, and meaningful. Praise the Lord!

The leadership chose number five (building loving relationships) as their third source of strength. The congregation chose number ten (we are all stewards) as number three. I saw these results as very encouraging. Praise God!

In August, we gathered in Pennsylvania to celebrate Poppy's ninetieth birthday. We all gathered at 875 Rozel Avenue before traveling to a local park for lunch.

At about midmorning, two men delivered a tractor to the parking lot across the street. There they unloaded the John Deere tractor that Poppy had sold them, hoping they could restore it, a project Poppy never quite got around to completing. As the tractor crossed the street and entered the driveway, Poppy's eyes lit up as he recognized the familiar "putt-putt." I'll never forget the smile on his face as he hurried to the porch to greet his old friend and the two men who finished the job. It was all arranged by his son Jim. Great job, Brother!

Pat went back to the Topsfield Fair, filling her booth from 10:00 a.m. to 10:00 p.m. for ten straight days.

And for the record I conducted eight weddings, twenty funerals, and five baptisms.

At about 10:00 a.m. on Saturday, January 8, 2011, Gabrielle Dee Giffords drove to the Safeway supermarket in Casas Adobes, a suburb of Tucson, Arizona. She was planning to give a political speech when suddenly a gunman shot into the crowd killing six and wounding thirteen, including Giffords.

Once again our nation was forced to confront a senseless shooting, again our president Barack Obama would speak at the funeral, and again the tragedy of a gun in the hands of the wrong person created horrific sorrow. And again this event proved that the serious problem of gun violence is beyond our ability to solve.

We live in a broken world and only the healing and restoration of the human heart by the spirit of God can bring about the peace we all seek. I believe that only the prayers of confession and supplication by God's church can bring peace and healing to our weary world.

On Tuesday, I went to Rotary and knew I had to include this tragedy in my opening prayer.

> Almighty God, You made our world and your power holds it together, so it is to you that we naturally turn when the world begins to crumble. We are all saddened, angered, confused, and threatened by the recent tragedy in Tucson, Arizona. We cannot explain such events. All we can do is bring our troubled world to you for correction.
>
> Please bring healing and restoration to the thirteen wounded including Congresswoman Gabrielle Giffords and your hope and peace to the six families who grieve, wisdom to our leaders, and common sense to our troubled society. We are wandering in a wilderness. Have mercy on us, your wayward children, and give us wisdom to change our ways and follow your truth. Your teaching, your warning, your power within us is our only hope. Amen.

In January 23, Tom Masaki, the chair of the Pastoral Search Committee that called me to KUC in Honolulu, Hawaii, went to be with the Lord. He was ninety-four. I wrote in my journal that he was used by God to teach me some very important lessons, most of which I would never have chosen, but needed to learn.

To be specific, I began to learn the value of suffering, patience, humility, and trust in God's plans. I believe that the lessons of KUC prepared me to pastor First Parish. God knew I had a lot to learn if I would be effective in a new location.

Our relationship with the UCC has had its ups and downs. Back in 1984, the congregation voted to redirect our mission giving away from the denomination's projects. In 2005, we felt we needed to look at our relationship more closely, so we invited executives from the UCC and the CCCC for some meetings. After seven months of discussion and prayer, we decided to keep our relationship with the UCC, but broaden our perspective by joining the CCCC.

In 2008, some of our members were very disappointed by the decisions of the UCC and asked the church council to again take a closer look. In 2010, our Chat survey indicated that 48 percent of those responding believed that an informational meeting on the subject would be helpful.

We announced two upcoming meetings in the month of March. We gathered to listen and learn. We wanted to hear from these two groups and perhaps make a decision sometime in the future.

I was surprised to see Sharing Inc.'s founder, Kay Doherty, walk down our aisle a couple of weeks before Good Friday to thank me and all of First Parish for twenty years (four hundred miles) of walking and support. I walked again and received the support of over one hundred members, friends, and fellow Rotarians.

We were able to present the *Passion Play* again. Pam Abkarian's skill and commitment made this annual event possible.

One major lesson learned after the experience of two special meetings calling for the removal of the pastor (1998 and 1999) was the need to clarify the accuracy of the membership rolls. The diaconate proposed an amendment to our bylaws requiring all who wished to be counted as active would reaffirm their desire every three years.

Recommitment to Membership Covenant

As an expression of my Christian life, I (we) reaffirm my (our) membership at First Parish Congregational Church and recommit myself (ourselves) to the following statements:

A. Regular attendance at public worship
B. Systematic and proportionate financial support of the program of the congregation

C. A commitment to love and support my brothers and sisters

D. A desire to share my faith in Christ with others

E. A willingness to assume positions of service as my time and ability allows

Signed: _____

Date: _____

Please place this in the offering plate or mail to the church office.

After a few weeks, I wrote a liturgy of membership reaffirmation that we included in the worship service for May 22.

Ever since we purchased our condo, we wanted to remodel the kitchen. In May, we spoke with Home Depot, but when our son David heard about our plans, he strongly suggested that we contact his friend Kent Whitten. Kent looked at the job and gave us a bid equal to that of Home Depot but providing completely new cherry cabinets rather than simply refacing them as Home Depot had suggested.

I withdrew $25,000.00 from my 403(b) retirement plan; after taxes were taken out, that $25K became $18,750.00. We bought a Bosch dishwasher, a microwave oven, and refrigerator from Doyon's in Gloucester for a total of $1,800.00.

We went to Jordon's to look at living room furniture and settled on a sofa bed and recliner for $2,400.00. (At the time my 403(b) went from $193,000 to 161,000.)

I took out another $15,000 ($11,300.00) to finish the job—install a tile backsplash and carpet and hire an electrician. We spent a total of $42,204.00 on the project. By June 16, we were finished and very pleased with the result and so grateful that we had the resources to do it.

In July, our staff took a big hit; our office administrator, Linda Hunzelman, required cancer surgery. She returned to the office in early 2012, and she worked for about a year and a half and then had to resign. She was a faithful and capable worker who served the church with integrity. Sadly, she died on January 20, 2015.

Then Abram KJ, our youth minister, announced his resignation, effective August 21. Here is a portion of his letter.

> I am writing to tell you that I have been offered a full-time position at Gordon College: Director of Christian Life and Worship.
>
> I have loved my time of ministry at First Parish. This church has been a wonderful place for us. Pastor Rich is an outstanding minister and friend, the Christian Education Committee has been unwavering in its support of my ministry, the adult volunteer leadership team is one that any minister would envy, and the youth and families have been a joy.
>
> May God bless us all as we seek to follow His ongoing call.
>
> Abram Kielsmeier-Jones

I was disappointed to hear that Abram would be leaving at the end of August. Since February 2009, he displayed an outstanding performance of his responsibilities. He loved our youth, worked well with his youth team, is extremely well organized, preaches with clarity and fervor, and is an excellent ministry partner. I missed him very much.

We were blessed by another visit of Gay and Randy Hongo in July 30–31. The Outreach Committee arranged for permission to use the lower common for a concert. The Hongos sang and danced hula for over two hours. We hoped to attract the attention of Saturday walkers and joggers and give them a lei, some fruit, and a glass of Hawaiian punch (what else?). As we look back now, we asked much of these artists—two hours straight without a piano, just ukulele and their voices.

In the late afternoon, Pat and I took them up to Magnolia for dinner. They took complete responsibility for the Sunday service the next day and did a fantastic job, as usual.

After the service, we took them to the parsonage for lunch with Kim and Pam. In the afternoon, we visited Izzie Harris, a friend from Union Congregational Church, Magnolia, who was dying of cancer. She had a piano and Gay and Randy sang a few duets for her. Izzie and her daughter Robin were so very grateful.

After our time with the Harris family, I drove them to a church in Boston where they ministered again. These two are truly servants of God to the church and the world.

In December, we heard that Randy was seriously ill with kidney issues and multiple myeloma. We were so saddened by this news and admired Gay and Randy as they together adjusted to his condition. They continued their ministry till he died on December 16, 2017. It was our privilege to know them and be counted among their friends.

We did enjoy Moosehead again and celebrated our forty-seventh wedding anniversary with dinner at West Branch Camps, followed by our annual stop in Bayside to visit with my brothers.

On Wednesday, September 21, we announced the beginning of two small groups. Nicki McLennan led a class focusing on personalities in the Bible and Nicki Gumbel, founder of the Alpha course, introduced a follow-up class entitled "the Jesus Lifestyle," an eighteen-part course based on Jesus's Sermon on the Mount. As always, those who invested the time were richly rewarded.

During the coffee hour on Sunday, October 23, I was surprised to hear the coffee drinkers pause and sing happy birthday to me. The next day, I turned seventy!

My pastor's report for 2011 was a summary of the events of the year including Abram's leaving, the retirement of six Stephen ministers, the passing of seven beloved members, the brief return of Linda Hunzelman to the office, and the fact that we again ended our year with a financial surplus. Praise the Lord!

Pat returned to the fair, we put shelves in the closets of our condo, and we celebrated Maine Maple Sunday with the family and received the gift of an electric fireplace from our children.

And for the record, I conducted one wedding, eighteen funerals, and seven baptisms.

The annual meeting flowed easily through the warrant and then dealt with the pleasant task of accepting a legacy gift of $141,687.00 from Phyllis Skyrme. We voted to restore the drainage system beneath the rear parking lot and then resurface and reline it. After that vote, on a motion by JoLynn Foster, we decided to tithe this gift by designating $14,169.00 to the Outreach Committee. The committee sent $10,000.00 to the Boston Rescue Mission and the remainder to His Mansion. I was very grateful to observe this decision on the part of the congregation. Praise God!

In January, we launched a third Forty Days event, "Forty Days in the Word." The congregation rallied support remembering how helpful these programs had been; sixty signed up on the first day forming ten small groups, and eventually, half of the congregation was in a small group.

In March, Gadar took advantage of an offer to buy a 7/11 convenience store in Cranston, Rhode Island. The store had been under-performing and was about to close. The move was very difficult for Pam, leaving family, church, job, and house but she supported her husband and trusted in God's provision. It was a challenge for all of us. Pam and Gadar's contributions and fellowship were missed greatly.

We celebrated the resurrection of Jesus Christ with a very uplifting worship service, again with the Korean Love Church joining us.

Pam did direct the *Passion Play* for the last time; however she wrote an entirely new script.

We had been performing a drama beginning with the woman caught in adultery through the placing of Jesus's dead body in the tomb. This second production was easier to produce and required just thirteen actors. This version was set on the Saturday after the death and burial of Jesus.

Each character held a candle and reflected on the life and death of Jesus—some were brokenhearted, some happy with Jesus's removal, some angry, and a few were hopeful. Again Pam was used by God to bring to life the questions, hopes, and hasty conclusions of those involved in those historic events.

I did walk around the lake six more times and conducted an early sunrise service in the playground behind the meetinghouse.

The Whitmans and the Pedersens arrived in our driveway on Friday, June 8. All six of us piled into a huge black limousine and headed to Boston where we boarded the Norwegian Dawn headed to Bermuda.

We were at sea Friday and Saturday and arrived at King's Wharf on Sunday, June 10. We docked there till late afternoon on Tuesday.

The brochure said, "Take an incredible scenic tour encompassing the entire island of Bermuda. See the Somerset Bridge, Gibbs Hill Lighthouse, pink sand beaches, and explore the town of St. Georges."

Jerry was our very capable and talkative driver/guide. Ed took a dip off the pink beach while the rest of us ate lunch. We shopped in Hamilton and enjoyed the Bermuda Underwater Environmental Institute (BUEI).

We set sail on Tuesday arriving back in Boston on Friday morning. This was a great way to celebrate our seventieth birthdays with dear Four Seasons friends.

At the June council meeting, I read this announcement.

Retirement

Ever since 2006, when I marked my sixty-fifth birthday, I have been thinking and praying about the question of retirement. I know some of you have been wondering as well. I know that when that time finally comes I will *not* look forward to doing nothing! I want to be able to have enough energy to make a contribution to the kingdom of God, wherever I am. After prayer and many long conversations with Pat and several of my colleagues, I believe that it is time to make an announcement.

I plan to announce my retirement to the congregation this Sunday, July 1, to be effective on Sunday, June 30, 2013... When that Sunday in June arrives, it will be just one month shy of thirty years that I have been able to serve this wonderful congregation.

Interim Ministry Training

After my decision to retire, the diaconate graciously provided the time and funding for me to attend a three-part training session provided by the Interim Ministry Network. These sessions were held in Devon, Pennsylvania, and held for one week in April and another in September. The third session was conducted over the phone and Internet.

The hope was that this course would help prepare me and the congregation for the future.

In the annual report for 2012, the following was included in the report of the diaconate:

> We received the news of Pastor Weisenbach announcing his retirement after thirty years of faithful service. It is a little bitter and a little sweet. Even though we knew this day would come, we understand that this is surely a process to move through and adjust to. There will be changes, along with emotions, that we all will have to experience. There will be sadness for our loss, but also a joy for the new journey which allows Pastor Rich and Pat to discover and explore the future our Lord has planned for them. Pastor Rich and Pat will be greatly missed. Their love, support, spiritual guidance, and direction will live on through each and every one of us as they pass the torch to shine brightly for the next one God places in this position. We pray for a

smooth transition for all. Thank you seems so inadequate for the gift of leadership Pastor Rich and Pat have given over the past thirty years, but it is with grateful hearts, we offer our love to both Pastor Rich and Pat for all the blessings the future holds for them.

In August, Pat and I traveled to Lansdale, Pennsylvania, to attend the annual Strohmetz reunion held at my cousin Karen Miller's house. After that we dropped by to see Poppy. As it turned out, that was my last visit with this loving, generous, Godly man.

We went off to Moosehead and took a ride to Smyrna Mills, an Amish settlement. We also enjoyed a dinner at West Branch Camps, guests of the Goodwins.

Sadly we learned that Poppy's condition had worsened. He developed pneumonia leading to congestive heart failure.

Pat and all seven of her siblings gathered at 875 Rozel Avenue from September 1 to 10. Poppy died on Monday, September 10. A burial service was conducted on Saturday, September 15, at Sunset Memorial Park.

His casket, fashioned by monks, was a simple pine box. At the family visiting hours, everyone was invited to take a permanent marker and sign their name and number on the casket. (It had become the family tradition to assign every person a number when born or upon marriage into the family. Pat is number one, and I am number ten.)

At the grave, his pills, M&M's actually, were strewn across the signatures before it was lowered into the ground. On Sunday, there was a two-hour service of memory, celebration, singing, and thanksgiving to God. The family used 1 Peter 1:3–4, 8–9 (KJV) to summarize his testimony.

> Blessed be the God and Father of our Lord Jesus Christ, which according to his abundant mercy hath begotten us again unto a lively hope by the resurrection of Jesus Christ from the dead,

to an inheritance incorruptible, and undefiled, and that fadeth not away, reserved in heaven for you... Whom having not seen, ye love; in whom, though now ye see him not, yet believing, ye rejoice with joy unspeakable and full of glory; receiving the end of your faith, even the salvation of your souls.

In October, the council announced the names of an Interim Minister Search Committee. It was an excellent committee, Jolynn Foster, Ron Martin, Lou Prosperi, John Arena, Tom Gordon, Jen Black, and Mark Hathaway. They were originally told to find both an interim minister and a settled minister, but that task was too great. A second committee was formed later to search for a settled pastor.

Hurricane Sandy hit the East Coast from October 22 to November 2 causing $68.7 billion in damage. Jen and Andy Black asked, "Can't we do something to help?" The congregation responded by packing two trailer loads of clothing, toiletries, cleaning supplies, furniture, and $1,400.00 worth of gift cards. Jen and Andy trucked these materials to a friend of Linell Nestor's who worked on Staten Island as a social worker.

October is always a busy month for the family; we remember two weddings and four birthdays. This year we added another event. We all gathered at the church's memorial garden to bury a portion of Mother's and Dad's ashes, and the remainder joined those of Matt Stuen, Aunt Clara, and Aunt Ida under the cherry tree in Bayside, Maine.

The family enjoyed the Christmas activities including our last open house for the congregation. We had Christmas dinner together, then Pat encouraged the children to choose the furniture they would prefer since we were downsizing. She gave each daughter a pack of different-colored Post-its and told them to put down their first, second, and third choices. There was some negotiating. In the coming years, we were happy to see our things bringing joy and beauty to another home.

I must write a few lines about our home for thirty years; it was just right for our family, we loved the place.

We had a garage for the car and tools and a basement for the laundry and workbenches for Pat and me. The attic was available for storage of off-season clothes and Christmas decorations and a great place for the grandchildren to look for treasures. Everyone had their own bedroom, but Dave did have a little trouble keeping his neat and clean. The wood stove in the living room was such a treat on cold mornings, and as they say, "Wood for the stove warms you three times."

Every Christmas, Pat sent me to the attic to bring down the decorations. She spent days placing our beautiful collection of ornaments, willow tree figures, and various other holiday-themed items in just the right place along with live greens from the yard. She began on the Monday after the first Sunday of Advent. We enjoyed the beauty and memories and shared it all with the congregation on our annual open house. I was in charge of the lights in the windows and the lights outside around the front and back porches.

Then there was the annual Easter candy hunt. We "hid" candy all over the house and allowed the children and grandchildren to find as much as they could all to the playing of Rossini's "William Tell Overture." Great fun!

The place received three major repairs while we were there—the front porch was rebuilt, the door to the porch off the living room was widened, and the kitchen and bath were completely rebuilt along with new windows throughout. And to Pat's joy and surprise, a bow window was installed over the sink in the kitchen.

We were especially happy to work in the yard. Our vegetable garden contained string beans, zucchini, tomatoes, chard, lettuce, and flowers. Dave helped us install a pond and fountain, which became a serious hangout for the birds. The kids gave me about two dozen paving tiles to build a patio and later a wrought iron bench. Many breakfasts were enjoyed in that spot.

We planted two trees, a Japanese red maple that attracted grandchildren who wanted to climb and our favorite, the peach tree. Each September, it yielded an abundant crop of fruit that dressed up our breakfast cereal for weeks. It was also the perfect place to hang a bird and squirrel feeder. The crop was so heavy that I had to prop up the limbs. It blew down after we left, and our neighbor Dick Jennings made us a pizza cutter with a handle spun from a piece of the trunk.

We did travel to Pennsylvania for our annual post-Christmas dinner and Yankee swap with the O'Brien family. But as you can imagine, our time together was quite subdued given the absence of Poppy.

I wrote my last annual report citing the high level of cooperation and mutual love and support I observed among the membership. I took the opportunity to read my report at our annual meeting.

> When I stop and observe our functioning together as a team: joining hands and hearts in prayer after a committee meeting, working out a difficult decision or policy, cooking for Rosie's, singing a hymn, teaching a child, serving a community meal, rehearsing an anthem, setting a goal, tackling a challenge, organizing the Clothing Closet, bearing a Christian witness, reaching out to a new face, memorizing lines for the *Passion Play*, whatever it be, my heart rejoices. Truly, your love for one another is the most powerful Christian advertisement to our town.
>
> It has been observed that people may visit a church because of a preacher who talks about God's love, but they will stay in that church because of people who demonstrate God's love. By God's grace you are a congregation who seeks to demonstrate God's love, revealed through your determination to live out our Covenant of Working and Worshipping Together.
>
> A part of me wishes I was just arriving at First Parish rather than leaving after thirty years, but I'm reminded of Paul's words to the church

in Corinth. "I planted the seed, Apollos watered it, but God made it grow" (1 Corinthians 3:6–7).

Pat and I, with our bag of seed and watering can, will be moving on; God remains faithful to His garden, and as you remain faithful, you will "bear much fruit" (verse 5).

So thank you for the privilege of laboring with you these many years and may you continue to follow the Savior, all to His glory.

With Joy and gratitude,
Pastor Rich Weisenbach

When I finished, I received a standing ovation and the budget passed unanimously. The meeting was over in forty minutes.

We did travel to Northern Pride Lodge that Valentine's Day and Beaver Cove in August. Pat set up shop at the Topsfield Fair for the fourteenth time.

And for the record, I conducted five weddings, nineteen funerals, and six baptisms.

After more than thirty years, the office administrator Jane Wilkins retired. She made the announcement in January 10, effective in January 24. This was also the year that she marked fifty years as a member of the congregation.

In February 23, I got a call from Abram Kielsmeier-Jones telling me that he would be leaving Gordon College to become the pastor of Union Congregational Church in Magnolia. I could never have imagined how God would intertwine our lives together since our meeting at Ocean Lawn in May 2008.

In March, Gadar was leaving the store and headed to the bank to make a deposit of $27,000.00. As he approached his car, two men met him, and they had a gun and demanded the bag he was carrying. Corporate headquarters covered a percentage of the loss, and Pam and Gadar had to make up the rest.

In February 13, we got an invitation from KUC to join them for a celebration of one hundred years as a Christian congregation. The event would be in August and airplane flight, hotel, and car would be made available. It was a memorable time. We were put up in a hotel in Waikiki and provided with a car. There were many activities planned and meaningful worship services.

Upon our arrival at the airport, we were greeted by Jim and Janet Ohta with an invitation to attend a free breakfast at the Hawaiian Monarch. After the meal, we were presented with a number of possible activities and encouraged to choose one. We decided to go to Kualoa Ranch on the windward side. This was a very interesting place with opportunities to visit an ancient fish pond, a glass-bottomed boat ride to catch a glimpse of sea turtles, relax in a hammock, or take a ride up a mountain. There was another opportunity to tour the many venues used for Hollywood films. In the evening, we were treated to a very authentic meal and hula.

The next day, we enjoyed a meal at the home of Vernon and Marion Von along with Peter Galuteria, Tak and Elva Yoshihara, Gay and Randy Hongo, and Peter and Rhonda Kamakawiwoole. It was a very healing time together.

Saturday was a time for fellowship, games, and food under tents arranged in the open green space on the church campus. Sunday's worship service gave opportunity for the previous ministers to share a memory or two. I spoke briefly and then invited Gay and Randy to join Pat and me in singing "Great Is Thy Faithfulness."

We also enjoyed a visit with Helen Murata and Betty Nakano and daughter Lisa and then meals with Ayako Kageyama and the Chinan family. It was a very memorable time, our fourth and probably our last visit to the islands.

When we arrived home I wrote a thank-you letter and Christmas greeting to the congregation.

Dear Members and Friends of KUC,
When Pat and I think of those who have touched us with love and grace, we think of you.

Your generosity over the anniversary week has settled deeply in our hearts.

When we arrived home I was contacted by a local church whose pastor left them in June. I began a ministry there in November. We would value your prayer support as we take on this new opportunity. The congregation is small and struggling and needs to receive the good news of Christ's coming in a fresh way. So it is with joy that God has given us another congregation to love and serve.

Wishing you all will experience the joy of Christ's presence through His Holy Spirit. Mele Kalikimaka!

Pastor and Pat

Abram KJ called to tell me that in March 17, the congregation in Magnolia will be voting to call him as pastor. He will leave Gordon College and begin his ministry in June 1.

What a gift to be back in Magnolia and to have Abram as our pastor; Pat and I will be looking forward to the times we will be together again.

In May, the Women's Bible Study Group organized a Tea for Pat. All the ladies of the congregation were invited along with Sharon, Molly, Abby, Pam, Kim, and Maddie. It was a beautiful and loving tribute. Pat looked wonderful and was overflowing with gratitude. She had organized that group when we first arrived and led it every Thursday for most of the time we were at the church. Yes, the women were encouraged to wear hats, and many did.

When a pastor leaves a congregation, it is important that two tasks be performed—write a boundary letter and conduct an exit interview.

The letter makes clear that the pastor's duties and privileges within this particular congregation are ending. There should be no competition between the retiring pastor and the new one. Of course there will be exceptions, but the congregation must learn to transfer their support to new leadership. This letter was composed using the guidelines I had received from the interim network class I had taken.

Council conducted a brief exit interview asking me eight questions, but I'm not sure how helpful this was. I responded but had the feeling that we were all doing this because it was suggested by the network.

The Search Committee announced that they had a candidate for interim minister, Rev. Dr. Ron Cousineau. He is very capable and experienced in the field, and everyone was pleased and excited. He would begin in July 1.

We had our last diaconate meeting in June 6. We had little business to discuss, so I took the time to share a strength that I had observed in each and every one of the members. They responded by giving me an iPad and keyboard. (I used that iPad to write this memoir.) We concluded with a prayer circle, and every deacon participated. God gave us a wonderful time together.

Heather Hulse and Sharon Covell volunteered to plan a retirement party for Pat and me to be celebrated in June 9. The church council appropriated $5,000.00 for the event. The only question they had for me was, "To whom should we send invitations?" I gave them a list and kept adding to it as time passed.

The party began with the showing of a beautiful DVD that Pam had composed. Throughout the years, Pam had produced many DVDs celebrating various family events. She has a very special ability of putting her pictures together with the music she chooses. These have become treasures.

I was so pleased to have Dean and Jane Pedersen and Ed and Sandra Whitman attend. Dean and Ed both spoke along with my brother Bill. Other speakers included the town manager Steve Maio, Fire Chief Mike Sullivan, Rev. Peter Brown, Rev. John French, and Horace Hylan.

We were delighted to see Barb and John Wallace from Florida, Ron and Betty Kent's daughter Brownwen from Vermont, and long-time friends Dick and Beth Cairns, all the way from Essex.

A highlight for me was a hula performed by Pam and Kim to the Randy Hongo song "River of Peace." To add a Hawaiian flavor, the Hongos and the Vons sent leis for the family.

Pat and I were joined by all three children in the singing of "Great Is Thy Faithfulness." I had a few closing remarks, and Abram KJ pronounced the benediction. (Fortunately there is a DVD of the event, but it stopped before all the speakers had finished.)

The 2013 Annual Report of the Diaconate included the following:

> A retirement party was held for Pastor Rich and Pat to mark a milestone in the life of our church and also in their lives as well—both of which are so closely intertwined. It was a time of celebration with the telling of stories with words, dancing, and pictures. The afternoon was filled with songs and laughter, hugs, and speeches. The dining room overflowed with love.

In June, Tom Gordon told me that if I offered to baptize anyone by immersion, there would be several who would respond. As it turned out, six adults were baptized by sprinkling in the two services on Sunday, June 23, and ten more went to First Baptist to be baptized by immersion. Each gave a testimony and shared a favorite Bible verse. Among this number was a teenager, Chip Black, and a man aged ninety, Richard Pratt. I was greatly encouraged by this display of faith and obedience.

Our final worship service was in June 30, and what a glorious time we had together. Much to my surprise, the prelude was a Bach violin solo performed by Jamie Buswell. He played "Preludio" from *Partita for solo violin*. What a start for the morning!

There were over twenty-five in the choir, and they sang two pieces. I came down from the dais and called for the children's message. The children gathered, and much to my surprise, about twenty adults scrambled forward. Over the years, people had remarked about how much they learned from those stories. I guess these adults didn't want to miss a word.

Peter Rearick dressed in his armor helped me, and then I completed my preaching series in Ephesians, "Armor for the Future" (Ephesians 6:10–24).

The congregation had assembled a scrapbook and a gift of $7,750.00, which they gave to us. We had a parting liturgy and a men's chorus sang "Till We Meet Again" and then concluded with the entire congregation encircling the sanctuary.

And for the record, I conducted five weddings, fourteen funerals, and sixteen baptisms (ten by immersion at First Baptist, Wakefield).

The congregation sent us off with a scrapbook of pictures, memories, and letters written by over thirty members. Here is a sampling that I trust will lift up God's power and grace in the lives of those who trust Him.

> Pastor Rich, you were my leader, someone I could trust as a pastor and friend in Christ. I am grateful for your devotion and commitment to Alpha that set a path for me to follow. It was the beginning for me. You allowed and encouraged all to think, and then choose. You set the table for us and then let us eat. And I did!
>
> BM

> During our years at FPCC, you challenged me in my faith and really set me on my way. I was treasurer back then and we were not able to balance the budget. You spoke about trusting in the Lord for the balance. It was my first time drawing on the power of Scripture... I love the Lord and

trust Him and I know my relationship with Jesus would not be what it is without your influence.

SD

Thank you for showing love and care to me as a child and *thank you* for ministering to my mom and dad so that they would know Jesus as Savior. That changed everything! I have hope to see them both again, as Jesus is my savior too!

JC

I knew something had happened, there was a change, something special occurred in me. I recalled again, Pastor Rich's words in his prayer of exchange, "My fears for His peace." God did it! He answered the prayer of Pastor Rich on my behalf and I was never the same person again.

RR

Some Observations

Sacrificial Calling, Know the Congregation, A Healthy Marriage,
Gospel Preaching, Patience and Persistence, Comfortable
with Conflict, Develop Leaders, Community Involvement

As I have already mentioned, one of the reasons I have embarked
on this project is to share with the congregations I've served a
slice of their history. I have included Union Congregational Church
of Magnolia, West Congregational in Peabody, KUC in Honolulu,
and First Congregational Church in Woburn as interim. But the
congregation in Wakefield was where I learned the most and where
the greatest transformation occurred. To some extent, I believe that
throughout my years of ministry, God had been preparing me to
serve First Parish. (After all I served this congregation for more years
than the other four combined.)

When I arrived in Wakefield, I had already realized that this
church, once the most influential congregation in the community,
had been, along with most mainline denominational churches,
declining in both membership and finances for about forty years.

The chair of the Search Committee realized this too. He admitted to me that if his church family was going to survive, some major
changes had to take place. I think that he saw in me a leader, he figured, who could provide the possibility of a reversal to the downward
trend the church had been experiencing. I don't think either of us
really understood what this needed transition would mean or how
long it would take, though each of us had some idea of course, but I
know our ideas were not the same.

I was certain that the key to growth of any church was to provide a clear understanding of the Gospel of Jesus Christ. Everything else—attendance, membership, community service, fellowship, foreign missions, Christian education, and finances—would grow out of such soil.

The founding documents of First Parish Congregational Church proclaimed an orthodox statement of the purpose of the Christian church, and it is a wonderful statement, one that is read on the first Sunday of November every year.

Sadly, over the centuries, the truth of that covenant was lost and then rediscovered and lost again and rediscovered again. I was determined to remind the congregation of their roots. The message I proclaimed from the pulpit may have sounded new to many, but in reality it wasn't new at all, only set aside for a time.

I think that reintroducing the gospel to a congregation who had mislaid it and become theologically compromised requires special graces provided only by God's Holy Spirit. There are certain qualities a pastor must possess in order to move a church fellowship from a place of slow deterioration to a place of slow growth and fruitfulness. I have thought about this list of requirements and would suggest that without such spiritual gifts, spiritual renewal is close to impossible.

While at First Parish, I was invited to participate in roundtable brainstorming sessions with other pastors who were in similar local church settings. We were called together by Rev. Dr. Jim Harrell, founder of Overseed, "Recruiting, Equipping, and Supporting Pastors in Mainline Churches" (36 West Ox Pasture Lane, Rowley, Massachusetts). After several gatherings, Jim synthesized the learnings and suggestions from us pastors and then produced an outline for his organization. Many of the qualities that I list below came from those sessions.

Before continuing with my effort to recall my experiences of pastoral ministry, I would pause to list the characteristics and tactics necessary to move a congregation through a spiritual transition. Listed below, in no particular order, are what I would suggest are required for the task.

Sacrificial Calling

When I began to investigate First Parish Congregational Church, Wakefield, Massachusetts, I soon realized that this mainline congregation was typical of those I had known while pastoring in New England for eleven years. I had drawn some conclusions from my frequent interactions with both UCC members and ministers about the culture of these sister churches—their values, goals, beliefs, and practices. So when I decided to respond positively to the call from First Parish, I knew there would be some major challenges. I didn't expect to discover too many members who would share my theological perspective, but I naively thought that all I needed to do was to present the gospel message and members would accept it.

I must admit that I was somewhat desperate at this point to find a position, since I was being forced out of KUC, so agreeing to move to Wakefield wasn't very sacrificial at that particular moment in my career. It was a miraculous answer to our prayers, but I did realize that this call to this particular UCC congregation was going to be difficult, even painful. The sacrifices were to come in God's time.

When I say sacrificial, I mean that one must expect opposition, strong opposition. One's suggestions will often be misunderstood, preaching will be rejected, salary will be minimal, pastoral care will be refused by some, and long hours in committee meetings will become routine.

So I would say that if God calls a pastor to serve in a similar situation, sacrifice will be an ever present companion, not that much different from that of a missionary serving and loving among lost people.

Know the Congregation

It was another sign of God's timing that years before coming to First Parish, I began studies at Fuller Theological Seminary toward a DMin degree. My final dissertation centered upon the upcoming 350th anniversary of the congregation. This required me to read about the church's history. It was during my research that I discovered their wonderful original covenant. This church was founded by forty-four men and women who believed the gospel!

I also read a few of my predecessor's sermons, newsletter articles, and annual reports. He had served for seventeen years, and these readings gave me a pretty clear idea of what the congregation had been hearing and learning before my arrival.

Because of my investigation, I gained an understanding of who this congregation was and where they were coming from. This knowledge proved invaluable. My preaching sounded new to many ears, but I was simply presenting the theological foundation of their church. I knew the congregation's history, the gospel was an integral piece of their history, and it was my responsibility and joy to remind them of that fact.

A Healthy Marriage

When Pat and I arrived in Wakefield, we were about to mark our nineteenth wedding anniversary. We had been in ministry together for all those years in three different congregations. We had experienced the highs and lows of church work, and our relationship had been strong enough to endure the pressures that come with the calling. I had always seen Pat as my partner right from the beginning of our relationship—first as possible servants on the foreign field and then in the parish.

We were both the product of a Christian family, she the oldest of eight and I the oldest of four. I cannot overstate the value of such a Godly heritage. The prayers and example of our parents were gifts beyond measure.

Because we were both aware of how important a healthy marriage was to successful ministry, we nurtured ours in many ways.

We join hands and pray together every day, more than once. We read devotional and secular material after breakfast, we attended two Marriage Encounter programs, and I always took Mondays off in order to be together for a meal out, a day trip, or just working in the garden. We tried to get away together at least once a year for an overnight. We always kissed whenever we separated and when we came together. We kissed every morning and every night after affirming our love. We share the household chores, and cards and gifts are always exchanged on special occasions. Yearly visits to Moosehead Lake, our honeymoon spot, has become a tradition. We walk together each morning and take the opportunity to discuss what was happening in our family and church. And we developed friendships with other healthy marriages.

Because of our common commitment to God's will and purpose for our lives, we have been able to minister together in five congregations. We count it a privilege. Without the support of Pat, I would not have continued in my position. Her affirmation of my preaching and ministry style have freed me to serve our Lord for fifty-five years. Her steadfastness during the dark times pulled us through.

Gospel Preaching

It goes without saying that the key to the success of any transitional ministry is the clear and consistent preaching and demonstrating of the Gospel of Jesus Christ, not only from the pulpit Sunday after Sunday but also in the conducting of weddings, funerals, baptisms, and membership classes as well as small groups and personal conversations.

The gospel message impacts the believer's understanding of service, stewardship, prayer, personal relationships, and behavior. Once the gospel's message and power are understood and obeyed, change occurs. Without gospel truth, the hope of any transition is impossible.

Patience and Persistence

I have mentioned earlier that I saw myself as the tortoise rather than the hare. Every pastor is an invited guest of the local church and must respect the condition of the congregation when he/she arrives. I remember Dr. Barker telling me, "Rich, you can't die on every hill." There may be many situations that need changing, but consistent preaching and witness over time will bring about change, a change that will be more readily acceptable to the people than a my-way-or-the-highway approach. Once one launches a battle, there is always the possibility of defeat. Too many of those losses add up, and an early departure could be in the future.

Of course there will be members in the congregation who want to see change as soon as possible and if they believe that change is not happening fast enough may leave the church and accuse the minister of serious compromise. But the patient pastor will be wise enough to move slowly, seeking to bring along as many members and friends as possible. I've always believed that direction is more important than speed. Persistence is key. Don't expect change overnight. Just keep a clear view of the goal and do the next thing.

And let me add that living out what one preaches is crucial. If one preaches the necessity of confession one better be ready to confess when necessary; that goes for forgiveness as well. If a minister encourages the congregation to tithe, he/she ought to practice tithing. In other words, the fruit of the Spirit listed in Galatians 5, must not only be taught but must be brought before the eyes and ears of the congregation on a consistent basis.

Comfortable with Conflict

The pastor must be willing to live in the tension that exists within a congregation that is biblically confused, ignorant of the work of the Holy Spirit, and unaware of sin's presence, power, and remedy. Jesus told us to expect opposition, pain, frustration, and hatred (Matthew 5:11–12).

Many see conflict as something to be feared, denied, and hidden. But conflict is usually an opportunity for change. One must be willing to sit down and discuss difference, able to listen to others, and prepared to compromise. One must be able to hear criticism and change if necessary, for no pastor will be able to solve every issue, problem, or situation. It will be necessary to live with those who differ and seek to be loving regardless of rejection.

Develop Leaders

Every pastor will eventually retire, take another call, or be fired. So discovering and nurturing leaders is critical. Upon arrival, the pastor must honor and work with the leaders who are in place. They have labored and given much of themselves to the church before the pastor arrived.

All church members seek some degree of commendation for our contribution, and if it is withheld, they will notice. The minister must receive the men and women of the congregation as a gift and seek to labor alongside them. Everyone eventually finishes their term and moves on, some to new responsibilities while others to a time of rest.

Over the years, new members will join the congregation, members who are more aligned with the pastor's teaching, and some of these will possess leadership gifts and be given the opportunity to serve.

I have never served on a nominating committee, so working with persons elected by the congregation is a requirement. Being patient and welcoming with everyone is basic, even when differences emerge. But as time passes and God sends new members, the complexion of the committee or board will slowly change.

I always sought to meet with the chair of a committee before the actual meeting. This usually meant that I drove to the chair's work or home for lunch. The goal was to establish an agenda, one that the two of us were able to agree upon. We always ended our meetings with prayer. Most leaders appreciated our time together; unfortunately some felt intimidated by what they saw as my attempt to push my wishes on them. This was not my intention, and sadly meetings with these leaders became fewer and fewer.

Of course, praying that God would send and raise up leaders is absolutely necessary. Seeking to live humbly and consistently before those chosen to lead in the church will certainly nurture a similar lifestyle in others.

Finally, initiating programs designed to develop discipleship is critical. Leaders will emerge as people are exposed to new opportunities and given responsibilities.

Community Involvement

Every minister should be involved in the community to which he/she has been called. I think that the congregation expects their pastor to be considered a community leader.

Meeting the clergy in town is a good place to start. Of course there will be differences, big differences sometimes, but meeting and respecting the other members of the clergy is a step in the right direction. Building a relationship, even if that relationship is only on a professional level, is the smart thing to do especially when the minister is the new guy in town. Other clergy will help bring you up to speed.

Introducing oneself to the town manager, fire chief, chief of police, and school superintendent is another important connection. Joining a community organization like Rotary is a great way to meet the leaders of a town.

All these relationships help to deepen communication between the minister and the town. As the years pass, those relationships can become invaluable. They also raise the profile of the local church in the eyes of the town and her officials.

I'm sure there are other important characteristics and tactics that I have overlooked, but I trust that these eight will be helpful to any pastor who is called to such a congregation. When one thinks about it, it is a very great privilege and opportunity in which to labor for the Lord.

In July 1, I used Jo Lynn Foster's pickup truck to move my books and papers to Union Congregational Church in Magnolia where I found Abram KJ extending a warm welcome. He gave me two keys, one for the building and the other for his office. What an amazing turn of events to be back where we started forty-nine years ago and with Abram and Sarah KJ whom we met on Ocean Lawn back in 2008. Thank you, Lord, for such leading and provision.

I suppose it is only normal to ask, "Okay, now what?" During the month of July, Abram asked me to preach on the twenty-eighth. Bob Sullivan asked me to conduct his wedding in October, and Ruth Spofford, our Wakefield neighbor, asked me to conduct her husband's funeral. Then on the fifteenth, I received a call from Beverly Nugent, from First Congregational Church in Woburn, wondering if I was available to fill their pulpit for a Sunday in September. I guess the Lord was bringing opportunities my way.

We enjoyed Moosehead in August, while there we were able to conduct a service of committal for Clarice Andrews. She was born in Greenville and was to be buried next to her husband Joe. I had conducted her funeral in Wakefield back in April.

We enjoyed the shooting stars at night. Pat said, "I can't lie down on the dock just now. I'm still drinking!" Then on Sunday, Pat said, "We won't be able to go to church because we have to go to the auction." We all remember these comments from Pat because they are not the kind of thing Pat would ever say; they will always bring a chuckle. We concluded our stay using the gift certificate the kids gave us for Blair Hill, a very fancy bed and breakfast set high on a hill overlooking the lake. We arrived home on the seventeenth and prepared for nine days in Hawaii, joining them for their hundred-year birthday.

First Congregational Church in Woburn (2013-2018)

Repair The Steeple, St. Mark's Rents Our Meeting House, Become A Legacy Church?, Global Evangelical Church (Ugandan) Rents Out Meetinghouse, 375th Anniversary, Leaving FCCW, Pastor Emeritus of First Parish

As I mentioned, I was invited to fill the pulpit at First Congregational Church in Woburn in September and again in October. Our first visits were very depressing to say the least. Their meetinghouse that ached for a paint job was built to hold 1,500 worshippers. The two mornings I preached, the attendance wasn't more than twenty, and they were sprinkled throughout the huge sanctuary.

During this time, I was invited to join a community of practice offered by the UCC. This small group provided an opportunity for interim ministers to share their experiences. I decided to attend the monthly meetings. When it was my turn to present, I submitted the following to the other six members:

> This congregation was gathered in 1642 in the heart of the new settlement of Woburn. Seven men from Charlestown sought to establish a new congregation to "the glory of God." Over the years the church, like the churches in other communities, played a leadership role.

The present meetinghouse, their sixth, was built in 1860 and boasts one of the largest sanctuaries and the tallest steeple in the state. Their three-manual Hook tracker organ is in good condition and one of three remaining in the country. That's the good news.

Their pastor resigned in June 2013 serving only a year and a half. Sadly the congregation has been shrinking for over thirty years. I was asked to fill their pulpit in September, a member found my name on the Internet. I was invited back on October 6th and after the coffee hour was invited to be their interim. I returned on Sunday the 20th and negotiated a job description and contract. Their budget afforded $20,000.00 for their part-time pastor, so I agreed to that amount in exchange for twenty hours, plus or minus, per week.

After preaching that first Sunday, my first thought was the obvious question, "How much longer can this congregation go on?" Their finances are very precarious, a Brazilian congregation rents on Sunday evening, and two cell towers provide some resources, but they were forced to sell their parsonage and ancient communion silver to repair the steeple that was damaged by Hurricane Sandy. They are presently spending both interest and principal from their trust funds.

I began on November 3, attendance was forty-five, but it varies greatly. I believe that God provided this opportunity for me, my wife agrees and journeys with me each week. She believes I can help lead this small group to some sort of decision about their future.

This is my first experience as an interim and
remain open to your experience and advice.
Thanks for your time,
Richard Weisenbach

The immediate advice from the ministers in the group was, "Run away!" I felt differently and believed that the gospel could bring some hope and direction.

In the fall of the year, Pat returned to the fair for the fifteenth time and our son Dave traveled to Ukraine on a mission trip. He helped build a building for the local seminary.

And for the record, I conducted five weddings, fourteen funerals, and nineteen baptisms, sixteen by immersion.

Things moved slowly at the Woburn church. Once in a while, we might have a visitor but no one ever returned. I never blamed them. The sanctuary was almost empty, and there was no Sunday school, child care, or youth group. If I were looking for a church, I would look elsewhere.

The people were just happy to be together and seemed to enjoy each other. They responded positively to Pat and me, and I know they were grateful. But the leaders were not too confident about their future, especially the moderator and the treasurer.

At the annual meeting in March 2014, the trustees reported, "We have to face the fact that our money is running out and we will be unable to continue our church as it is. As you will see by the budget statements, we have income to last about a year and a half. There have been inquiries from real estate agents interested in our property. This is something we will have to think about, perhaps some other church or organization who has the money can keep the building standing."

Repair the Steeple

There was one bright spot, an open house in April. The congregation invited the community to visit, tour the building, and celebrate the restoration of the steeple. There was a brief service with

Mayor Scott Galvin speaking, and I shared a word as well. Light refreshments were served in the vestry. Sadly, community participation was small and yielded nothing in terms of growth.

Later that month, the family gathered for the wedding of my brother Dave's son Peter to Christine Dimalanta in Pennsylvania. After the service and reception, we took a week and stayed with my brother Bill and Cynthia and toured a few of the many highlights of NYC including St. Patrick's Cathedral, Ground Zero, the Hi Line, Central Park, and an aircraft carrier.

In May, we launched an inflatable boat at our Magnolia beach. Kim and the children came up, and I pulled the boat along the shoreline allowing it to catch a wave sideways tossing the kids around. They had a ball.

We attended another wedding in August, this time in the O'Brien family. Tom and Jackie's son Michael married Danielle. We journeyed to Cincinnati and had an enjoyable time with some of the family and attended the reception to welcome Danielle into "the Outlaw Band."

We took our time coming home, visiting New York's wine country and the home of Robert Todd Lincoln, son of President Lincoln. He became an executive in the Pullman railroad car company, and his home, Hildine, is in Manchester Center, Vermont. He is buried at Arlington National Cemetery.

Later that month, we celebrated our fiftieth wedding anniversary at Moosehead (where else?). We visited my brothers in Bayside on the way up, staying in a bed and breakfast in Belfast. Bill took us to a very fancy restaurant to celebrate the occasion, and Paul and Christy gave us gifts. We went to town and were able to buy the food for our anniversary blast.

Everyone was able to join us at the lake and at the party in the basement of the People's United Methodist Church in Greenville. It was a very special time of food, videos, and sharing. All three children and their spouses took part. Pat and I are so grateful for the love of our family and the joy they bring to our hearts. They gave us

$150.00 to go to Blair Hill for a very special dinner, and Pam added to the joy by producing one of her slideshows of the event.

Sadly I had spent hours selecting portions of my videotapes to play during the meal and even rented a big-screen TV, but that big screen was cracked by the time we arrived in Greenville. Dave Goodwin provided a small substitute that was better than nothing and I had to buy the damaged screen.

Each of the children had prepared a prayer for the occasion.

Dear God,

Thanks you for Moosehead Lake and Beaver Cove Camps who had the cheapest rates in Greenville in the summer of 1964. Because of their careful allotment of funds, it brought this happy couple here fifty years and three days ago. You knew that they would be coming back here all these years, so you wanted to make it good. Thanks. It is.

So thank you for fifty years of the sight of the lake from the top of Indian Hill, for the sound of it lapping against the dock, the rustle of the leaves in the wind, the smell of the fire day and night, a stack of books, and a one-thousand-piece puzzle, the humming bird feeder and fixin's for s'mores. Thank you for a fence covered with towels and bathing suits and life preservers, a red-and-white checkered tablecloth strewn with pocketknives, potato chips, and bug spray.

Thank you for the memories of Indian dolls, Jiffy Pop, skipping stones, long canoe rides, and drift wood collecting.

I see my mother knee-deep in the lake, jeans pulled up, bandanna on her head, searching for just the right piece.

I see my dad, Nikon camera in hand, waiting for that moose on the side of the road to cross over.

Together they paddled us in canoes, split wood for the fire, and bought us coveted junk food reserved for this one time of the year.

Together they made us memories we strain to recall, memories we long to remember, memories we will never forget

Thank you, Lord, for Moosehead Lake, for each other, for my mom and dad.

With love and gratitude
Kimberly

Heavenly Father,

I am truly overwhelmed by Your faithfulness to our family. How can I possibly mention all the ways we have seen and experienced Your love, Your provision and guidance?

You have placed each of us in this wonderful family. We don't have to look very far to know how blessed we truly are. We live in something rare and precious, a family that knows You.

You have consistently met all our needs. Trusting You has never backfired. You always come thru for us when we wait for your solution. We have more than enough and we know it.

You lead us to one door at a time encouraging us to hold on to Your joy and peace in the space between. True to Your Word, Your will and plans for us are perfect and You are with us all the way.

We are grateful for Your presence and strength. What an amazing resource we have in You! We are never alone, never helpless.

We are awed by Your constant grace and forgiveness. We don't deserve it. We can never pay You back and yet Your love is never ending, never faltering. It is new and full and available every moment. Thank You.

So many in this world live without You. I can't imagine how they do it. Thank You for drawing us to Yourself, for all Your gifts and lessons, Your promises and blessings.

And most of all, thank You for the hope and joy we have in You. Continue Your faithfulness to us Lord. We don't want to live without it. Amen.

With love and gratitude
Pamela

Heavenly Father, Lord Jesus our Savior, Holy Spirit our Comforter and Guide,

We enter into your Holy presence to thank You, to praise You and to honor You.

We again want to express our gratitude for Your faithfulness and the blessing of our parents. The truth is we as their children have felt Your compassion, bathed in Your grace, experienced Your forgiveness, and have received Your unconditional love as a result of the relationship we have with Your humble servants we call Mom and Dad.

Lord Jesus, in serving You as parents, there is no greater task than to be a reflection of You to our children, and in doing so, no greater way to honor You. Father, these people have done and continue to do that in each of our lives daily. By their example, use us in our children's lives as You have used them in ours. May our children receive the same wonderful blessing of faithful parents as we have. Holy God, strengthen our faith, and enable us to do Your will, and receive our gratitude, that You alone may be glorified. I pray these things in the mighty name of Jesus our

Savior, through the power of the Holy Spirit and
for the glory of God the Father. Amen.

With love and gratitude

David

How can any father on earth be more grateful than I am to have loving, prayerful children such as these three?

Then it was off to Quebec with the Four Seasons. Dave let us use his van, which was just the right size to meet our needs. We stayed in Le'vis across the St. Lawrence River from the city of Quebec and rode a ferry each day, since our hostess gave us passes. I have two fond memories, both involve food: the amazing breakfasts we enjoyed at our Bed and Breakfast, Le Plumard and tea at the Chateau Frontenac. Both occasions were very special and delicious.

In September, we drove to Peddler's Village, Pennsylvania, for my fifty-fifth high school reunion, a dinner at the Cock 'n Bull. I remember a funny thing my friend Bob Severn said, "I love reunions. I get to hug all the girls I wasn't allowed to touch while in school!"

October was fair time again for Pat. She really enjoyed those years, especially when all the family could join us for fried dough, vegetable tempura, horse pulls, and the Musical Ride, performed by the Royal Canadian Mounted Police, forty-eight men and women riding matched horses all riding to the music. There is always a sand sculpture, farm animals, a midway with expensive rides, and the Coolidge Building where Pat had her table.

Coolidge was packed with artwork, cabinetry, needlecraft, braided rugs, quilts, handcrafted cards, canned food, and musical entertainment. We always had a great time at the fair.

In October, God blessed us with a portion of Poppy's inheritance! We decided to tithe this gift, give some to the children, and pay off the Rav4 that we bought earlier in the year and our mortgage on the condo. It was truly a blessing from our hardworking and generous father/father-in-law.

Because I was no longer in the parish, I didn't have weddings or baptisms, but I was called upon the conduct seventeen funerals that year.

The year 2015 held some exciting news; Pam and Gadar were approved to buy 70 Kirby Avenue, Warwick Neck, Rhode Island. The place was awesome—eight bedrooms, four and a half baths, an in-law apartment, swimming pool and cabana sitting on one and a half acres in a very posh neighborhood. Pam named the place the Red Door.

The previous owners could afford professional landscapers, and the grounds and gardens were large and had been well maintained. In the dead of winter, it was exciting to think of what plants and flowers the warm spring weather would reveal. As we learned, the plants, trees, and shrubs were abundant and required weekly care.

Our many trips over the four plus years were spent enjoying and laboring in those gardens. Pat's special favorite was to cut the grass using their riding mower. It was a great source of pleasure for the two of us, but our aging bodies demanded a sit-down every once in a while, often by the pool or around the firepit.

I was especially happy to use our turntable to play many of our favorite records and cassette tapes that I hadn't heard in years. Pam and Gadar were always happy to see us and catered to our every need every time we came down for a visit.

The main reason Pam and Gadar stretched to purchase their new home was to share it with the larger family, and on Easter of that year, they did. They spent hours and dollars to get ready for us. Pam had decorated all three floors, naming the bedrooms and filling them with appropriate furniture. The place was a delight to visit, especially the screened-in porch off the living room. Seeing the grandchildren playing in the pool was a particular joy.

Back to First Congregational in Woburn, I met Rev. Ken Bongiorno and Rev. Frank Passamonte, both interested in the possibility of renting space in the Woburn meetinghouse. Ken wanted to meet on Sunday morning, so the leadership voted to accommodate him by moving our worship hour to nine thirty allowing Ken and company to meet at eleven o'clock. I remember that he was hoping to make the Woburn church a satellite of his congregation located in New Bedford. His plan never worked out, and after about a month or two, he quietly left us without any explanation.

Another offer came to purchase our building from a Roman Catholic congregation meeting in a store front in another part of town, and they offered $400,000.00. The leadership rejected the offer.

St. Mark's rents our Meetinghouse

Reverend Frank, we later learned, was copastor with Rev. Sam Bombara, and together they pastored an Assembly of God congregation in Lexington. Sadly the congregation experienced great difficulties that brought about a split with Sam and Frank, leaving and taking about fifty-sixty members who were forced to find new worship space. Our meetinghouse met their needs. By September, the members of St. Paul's AG Church of Lexington, Massachusetts, moved to Woburn, changed their name to St. Mark's, and began worshiping in our building and occasionally meeting jointly with us. This decision would in time prove to be a match made in heaven.

The family again gathered at the Red Door for Memorial Day. We had hoped to attend the annual air show at Quonset Point, but the traffic was so great that we turned around and went back to 70 Kirby Avenue, much to the sadness of Pam.

Gadar, frustrated with the requirement to pay a steep percentage of his local store's profit back to 7/11's corporate offices every month, began to think of ways to manage a convenience store on his own without forking over much of the profit to someone else. Sadly this goal never came to fruition though he made several attempts to make his dream come true. These efforts were frustrating at times, but I could not find fault in his earnest search for a way to provide for his family's future.

In June, First Parish made a very important decision one I have already mentioned. The leadership believed that during the interim period between my departure and the installation of new leadership was the right time to "help the church membership take ownership of the church's direction with the help of God through Jesus Christ."

In November 2013, the congregation selected twelve persons to serve as a transition team. In the spring of 2014, under the leadership of interim pastor Ron Cousineau, the church engaged in a self-study called the Journey. Fourteen study groups sought to discover their spiritual identity. As a result they developed core values for the church—biblical principles, Christian education, fellowship, tradition, worship, and preaching biblical truth. They also committed themselves to growing in evangelism, outreach, and prayer.

The team realized that their time of transition was "the perfect time to review their connections, which included their denominational affiliation." The team took a methodical approach of evaluating each belief statement from both of their affiliations (the UCC and the CCCC) in the light of their core values, mission, and vision.

As a result of their prayer and discussions, the team concluded that First Parish was about 46 percent in alignment with the UCC and about 98 percent in alignment with the CCCC.

In April, the team's conclusions were written in a booklet and distributed to the church family. On Sunday, June 14, a special congregational meeting was called to gather after morning worship. At that meeting, First Parish Congregational Church of Wakefield voted, with a show of hands, to disassociate from the UCC, a relationship voted upon in 1960 and maintained for fifty-five years.

During my interim ministry in Woburn, it was often convenient to stop at Kim and Brian's on our way back to Magnolia. We were with Kim and Brian and family on that June Sunday and while there received several calls from church members informing us of the day's important vote. "This vote is your legacy," was the message I heard.

I had believed that the question of affiliation was best decided after a new pastor was installed not during the interim period, but I learned that the impetus for the vote came from the leadership not the interim pastor. The church leadership had heard from several in the congregation, "Get the affiliation question settled now." They did.

As I read through the booklet the team produced and observed the time and care they exercised, I became so grateful that the years of ministry Pat and I had exercised bore such fruit. To God be the glory!

We enjoyed our annual anniversary visit to Moosehead in August. Most of the family joined us for swimming, talking, shopping, fishing, eating, and of course the auction. We got back to Magnolia in time to unpack, repack, and catch a flight to Minneapolis, Minnesota, and then on to Portland, Oregon, to attend brother Dave's daughter Ona's wedding to Curt Schmidt.

On the way to the wedding site, we drove our rented Chevy sports car to Multnomah Falls, the Bonneville Dam, a fish hatchery, and several orchards, a truly delightful mountain trip.

The wedding was intimate being conducted in a small, remote hut on the slopes of Mount Hood. Bill performed the wedding service, which was then followed by a delicious reception.

The morning following the wedding, we were up at five thirty to drive back to Portland, return the car, and board Alaska Airlines to Vancouver, British Columbia, Canada, and then a bus to our cruise ship to take us along the coast of our forty-ninth state.

The next day was Sunday. Ed Whitman suggested that I might be prepared to help lead a worship service for the Protestants aboard ship, and he was right. Fr. Jim Kelleher, retired archbishop of Kansas City, Missouri, led a service for the Catholic folks and I led a service for the Protestants. We had a joyous service with singing, sentence prayers, and testimonies from many of the fifty or so in attendance. I shared some thoughts from Luke 15. I remember Father Jim's comment, "I wish I could get our people to sing the way you Protestants do!"

We spent a few rainy hours in Juneau, the capital, and then two very windy days in Skagway. (Skagway means windy place in the native language.) My Boston Red Sox hat blew off my head while watching the seals enjoy a salmon breakfast. We also were glad to see the salmon who escaped the seals' jaws swimming upstream.

When we realized that out tour did not include the meals we would need while on land, we went shopping in the local grocery store. On top of this, we were expected to tip our tour guide $10.00 per day and that totaled $100.00 for the ten days. Don't get me started on that fact!

We did enjoy visits to several museums, where we learned a great deal about the men who went searching for gold. We boarded the narrow gauge railroad train through White Pass covering the trail that most of those hopeful miners took. We enjoyed the paddle wheel ride on the Yukon River out of Dawson.

Denali was a disappointment. We endured a bumpy ride in a school bus for almost ten hours on a rainy day. We did manage to see a moose. (Honestly, we saw more wildlife at Moosehead Lake.)

The highlight of the trip was a dogsled demonstration. The enthusiastic barking of the dogs eager to run was a special treat and brought a smile to our faces.

We boarded a bubble top train to Anchorage and a city tour. Then it was up at 2:30 a.m. to catch our flight home, and we landed in bed at 11:30 p.m.

In September, Pam and Gadar decided to rent their in-law apartment. A recently divorced woman was welcomed, especially since she paid her rent for the entire year. This was a happy start, but her stay did become a bit problematic after that first year.

We drove down in October to check out the Jack-O-Lantern Spectacular held annually in the Roger Williams Zoo. It was amazing what some pumpkin carvers can create out of a vegetable.

We gathered at Brian and Kim's for our Octoberfest, celebrating two wedding anniversaries and four birthdays. The children gave me a remote starter for the car for my birthday.

I preached on Christmas Eve in the joint service with St. Mark's and then headed to Pam and Gadar's where the whole family joined together. Gadar's family came the next day to join us at the next Star War's movie. After a few days, we drove to Pennsylvania for the O'Brien Christmas party and then a visit to Jenna and Howie's new house. Jenna is Pat's niece.

For the record, I conducted one wedding, three baptisms, and seventeen funerals.

Become a Legacy Church?

From the first Sunday I visited First Congregational Church in Woburn, I believed that the possibility of becoming a legacy church should be the congregation's future. In my opinion, there was little chance of the congregation growing. When I arrived, I found a congregation of twenty to twenty-five members who were not prepared to invite others, there was no provision for children, the building needed serious repairs inside and out, and their finances were dwindling fast. There were a few members, those closest to the inner workings of the church, who saw a very dim future but were slow to accept the reality they were facing. These folks had been in the church all their lives and could not think of closing or selling.

A legacy church celebrates her past and seeks to pass on something of great significance to another congregation. However, sharing one's legacy is a hard sell but I couldn't see another alternative. I introduced the idea but never pushed it very aggressively. This was their decision and I knew it was very hard for them to even consider it.

In June, Pat wanted to attend the CTMH convention in Orlando, Florida, so we decided to drive and take time to see a bit of the South. We began in Pennsylvania at Erin Markloff's wedding to Ben Whitley. This was followed by a birthday party at Dave and Ellen's for Pam's fiftieth. Pat had worked very hard to provide a broad selection of goodies. Sadly she tripped and bent her glasses and bruised the left side of her face; fortunately she recovered by the time we got to North Carolina. We stopped in Georgia and then drove through to Merritt Island where we joined John and Barbara Wallace for lunch. Then it was on to Orlando to deliver Pat to her convention.

I returned to Ormond Beach to spend a few days with my brother Dave and his friend Emily (Molie is his name for her). Em and I took a four-mile walk each morning and then after breakfast hit a few estate sales. They do this as often as they can, finding treasures and reselling them. One afternoon, I visited the Casements, the retirement home of J. D. Rockefeller. I left with a few special gifts from Dave and Emily including an antique clock that once hung on the wall in the country store in our hometown of Southampton, Pennsylvania.

On Sunday, I picked up Pat and then headed to see Kham Vern and his family. First Parish had sponsored this family from Cambodia. They spent about a week with us at the parsonage before finding a place in Lynn.

Then it was off to St. Augustine, an old and beautiful city. We were able to tour Flagler College and the Lightner Museum and had lunch in what was once an indoor swimming pool. A talented musician provided guitar music while we ate, so we bought one of his CDs. Glad we did, we play it often and are reminded of our trip.

We continued north to Savannah, Georgia, and then Charleston, South Carolina, and a stop at the Boone Hall Plantation. We then stopped at their farm stand and bought a case of Georgia peaches, the really good kind!

We had another stop in New Bern, North Carolina, to see Tim and Darcy Hildreth, a family from First Parish, and then on to the Outer Banks of North Carolina and an interesting opportunity to explore the amazing accomplishments of the Wright brothers' first flight.

We spent a night in Delaware and then drove north to the Red Door on the Fourth of July. The family gathered along with Dom and Bonnie Mercurio, Heather Hulse, and Nick and Kerry Osgood. We distributed the peaches and presented three flamingos to Dave.

August found us at our favorite vacation spot and were joined by most of the family. We were shocked to hear Dave and Marilyn Goodwin say that they were closing the camp. With their children off to school, their dock severely damaged by a frozen lake, and Dave's physical limitations, they were left little choice. After this announcement, they quickly added, "The Weisenbachs are welcome to visit any time." We were very grateful, since Beaver Cove means so much to us all.

Our oldest daughter, Pam wrote the following:

Moosehead

Our favorite time
Our favorite place
We like to call it Moosehead

And every year
New memories made
When we go up to Moosehead

The trees are green
The air is clear
We cuddle up at Moosehead

To hear the loons
And sit and talk
That's why we go to Moosehead

Canoe the lake
And play a game
Are things we do in Moosehead

The auction's fun
Let's eat some more
It's what we do in Moosehead

Wait for the kids
If they don't come
We'll still have fun at Moosehead

And when we're home
We know the loons
Will call back to Moosehead

Thanks, Pam!

Later that month, it was off to Buffalo, New York, for the wedding of Molly to Mark Vanderkooi. Molly arranged for the church and reception, and Dave was the perfect father of the bride providing an after-wedding breakfast at the hotel. It was special to see Dave and Diana O'Brien, Kurt and Ona Schmidt, Pete and Christine Weisenbach, and most of the Reynolds family.

We lingered after the festivities for a visit to Niagara Falls and the Buffalo Zoo and a ride through the locks of the Erie Canal. Mark and Molly drove off to Kennebunkport, ME for their honeymoon.

We traveled back to Pennsylvania in September to celebrate with the members of the WTHS class of 1958. While there, we visited with several O'Brien families and then off to Oyster Bay, Long Island, in search of Sagamore Hill, the summer home of our twenty-sixth president, Theodore Roosevelt. The house itself was closed but we did get to walk the grounds, sit in the rocking chairs on the porch, and listen to prerecorded information at various stops on the grounds that I could access from my phone. We ended the trip at Pam and Gadar's.

Global Evangelical Church (Ugandan) rents our Meetinghouse

A second congregation came to the Woburn church asking if we might provide them with worship space. The leadership was eager to consider this possibility, and by September, the 250 members of the Global Evangelical Church (Ugandan) began to worship at four o'clock every Sunday afternoon. Their presence provided a great financial boost. They also showed interest in repairing and purchasing the meetinghouse. This offer pleased some and offended others.

In October, on the recommendation of my primary care doctor, Dr. Sahel Midha, I had a PSA test. This is a blood test used to screen for prostate cancer. The test measures the amount of prostate-specific antigen (PSA) in the blood. In November, I had a biopsy of my prostate and learned in December 12 that I had cancer. Dr. Bill Faust ordered a bone scan and body scan to see if the disease had spread. I learned in January 3 that the scans revealed good news, no metastasis, but radiation will be required.

The family again gathered at the Red Door for Christmas. Pat and I stayed to do some gardening and then off to the O'Brien Christmas party.

Here are some brief notes. Pat and I spent a few days in Camden, Maine, in February, Jack and Maddie were baptized on Easter Sunday at Genesis, and Pat reduced her hours at the Topsfield Fair.

And for the record, I conducted two weddings and twenty-four funerals.

375th Anniversary

Here is what I wrote for my 2017 annual report to the Woburn congregation.

> The year began with our congregation's participation in the 375th anniversary of the city of Woburn. This was indeed a wonderful Sunday afternoon celebration. A large group of church and community folk filled the sanctuary on January 8th to mark the beginnings of our city in 1642. It was certainly appropriate to begin the year's celebration where it all began with the establishment of a Christian church in "the wilderness." As Mayor Scott Galvin wrote in his introductory greetings, "It is fitting that we begin this yearlong commemoration in this special place, the First Congregational Church, a national landmark and historic link to our past."
>
> The service was planned by the mayor's office. Participants included Mayor Galvin, Sen. Edward Markey, Pastor Eric Malloy, pastor of the Charlestown Congregational Church (the seven men who were sent forth to establish a church were members of this church), and yours truly. Several groups provided music including the praise band of the Global Evangelical Church. The highlight of the afternoon was a reenactment of the ordination service of Rev. Thomas Carter, our first pastor. All agreed that this was

a very special service and a great opportunity for
First Church to serve the community. Thanks be
to God!

Two days later, Pat slipped on Kim's steps and fractured her left
tibial plateau so no weight-bearing for four to six weeks. Fortunately
Pat is a strong woman and adapts quickly to whatever is demanded
of her.

In February, I received three gold markers to guide the radiation
and then an MRI and a simulation of what I should expect in terms
of the radiation procedure. The radiation itself began in March 6
and would continue every day, except the weekend, through May 5.
Every day I drove to a cancer center in Winchester. It was an hour
round trip, and the radiation took about ten minutes. It was painless
and conducted by a team of men and women who were very professional. At the conclusion of the sessions, I was allowed to ring a bell
marking the occasion. The staff clapped and offered congratulations,
and I distributed twelve packs of Pat's handmade cards to everyone.
Pat had made dinner reservations at the Beauport Restaurant in
Gloucester to celebrate.

I continue to get checkups every six months to monitor my PSA
level. So far they are undetectable. Praise the Lord!

In March, Pat got her "walking papers" and was able to take
down the Christmas decorations and then travel with Kim to Pam's
to paint some of her furniture.

Then Kim and Brian gave us a two-day getaway to the Cliff
House in Ogunquit, Maine, to mark Pat's progress and the end of
my radiation. The weather was unusually warm, and I even went
swimming. We enjoyed breakfast on our lanai and were able to walk
the Marginal Way and eat our lunch at the Anchorage Restaurant.
We went shopping and then stopped at the Stonewall Kitchen and
When Pigs Fly, a bakery in Kittery, Maine.

I was ordained at Union Congregational Church in October
1967, so in June I was invited by the Massachusetts Conference of
the UCC to attend the annual meeting in Hartford, Connecticut,

to receive the conference's congratulations and appreciation for fifty years of pastoral ministry.

The meeting was in Connecticut to mark the first annual meeting of the new triconference of Southern New England. The Massachusetts Conference merged with the conferences of Connecticut and Rhode Island, a necessity due to shrinking membership and finances. The new name is the Southern New England Conference of the UCC (SNEUCC).

We left Hartford after lunch and drove through rural Connecticut to visit and celebrate Pam's fifty-first birthday. The family was there and we enjoyed the pool, food, and firepit. Dave was kept busy with repairs to outdoor lighting, basement flood control and the kitchen faucet repair.

In July, we heard the scary news that Gadar has decided to sell their 7/11 store. Added to this was the fact that the occupant in the in-law apartment refused to leave. We were very concerned about their future and their finances, and they would both need to get jobs and perhaps sell the house.

We were back at Moosehead in August; on Sunday we were enjoying a cup of coffee after church and glanced out the window to see a fire engine racing up the street. "Oh, what a shame," we said to each other. "Someone is in trouble." Minutes later, we received a call from Marilyn Goodwin telling us that there had been a fire in Beaver, *our* cabin! Fortunately their daughter was walking their dog and smelled smoke. Dave put the fire out but some damage had been done to the floor and to several items that we had placed on the space heater. We always used this heater as a convenient shelf not realizing that this heater could fire up if the temperature dropped. Well, the temperature did drop, and since the heater had been turned on by the previous campers, it fired up.

We lost a bag of games (Mille Bornes, Qwirkle, Pit, Five Crowns, Takaradi, and Kim's game board) and puzzles, several DVDs (*Seabiscuit, Amazing Grace,* and *A Night at the Museum*), birthday cards containing $25.00 each for Ben and Sam, and Pat's crocheting bag and its contents. The dipping jar was so hot I couldn't touch it. The dipping jar, a family tradition, is filled with coins. Any family member celebrating a birthday is invited to dip in the jar and scoop as much cash as possible.

We were devastated and embarrassed. Pat felt like going home. We cleaned the place and gathered everything that had been thrown out onto the lawn. We moved into Kit, the cabin next to Beaver, and slept and ate there till the smell was blown away. When the kids arrived, we had quite a story to share.

I was able to go to the craft fair held each year and purchase a new loon bag for Pat.

We did salvage our time by driving to Spencer Pond to meet Chick and Ann Howe's granddaughter and son-in-law who had purchased the place. They told us that Chick was in a nursing home in Bangor, so we decided to take the time to visit him. He was surprised to see us and very grateful that we made the effort to visit. We always felt a warm feeling for the Howes, especially Chick. He told us once, "I always feel better when you two are here."

The family arrived, and Dave drove his new camper, a fifty-eight-foot mobile home. He had packed it with chairs, his grill, and all the kitchen tools except the kitchen sink. He blessed us with several meals.

We left Greenville and headed for Bayside to see my brothers and their families and then to Standish, Maine, to conduct the wedding for Kenny Hodgson and Candice Pagliarulo. They rented a place on the shores of Lake Sebago. We had a grand time, especially teaching Ken and Pam, Kenny's parents, two of our favorite games.

When we returned home, we got a call from Mark Hatheway, moderator at First Parish. He was sad to share that their newly installed pastor was filing for divorce. The church offered him a leave of absence, but he refused to use the time to repair his marriage. He said it was all his wife's fault. After a long and difficult road, he was asked to leave forcing the church to hire another interim pastor, Rev. Rick Toroni then a third, Rev. Dr. Bob Leroe, who served till Rev. John Dale was secured as the next settled pastor.

By September, Pam realized that she could keep the house by providing accommodations for traveling nurses. She went to work rearranging the rooms, developing a Web site, and welcoming nurses who worked in local hospitals for a season and then moved on. It seemed to be an ideal arrangement for Pam and Gadar and the nurses.

This worked fine till their neighbor complained that she was running a rooming house! They were forced to halt their plans and were eventually forced to put the house on the market. After a long wait, it was sold in April 2019. They moved temporarily to Plainville, Massachusetts. In June, they moved to their new apartment in Ando-ver. We were glad to have them much closer to us, but the sale of the Red Door was sad, since the family and several friends, including the Four Seasons, had spent time there. It was a great place for family celebrations and has provided some wonderful memories over the years.

Pat was told to see a urologist in September. "We see a spot on your bladder." A biopsy was taken, and in October 16 we learned that she had bladder cancer. I was with her and will not forget the flushed expression that came over her face upon hearing the news. We were not expecting this. On the sixteenth, we spoke to Dr. Andrea Sorchini at Lahey Clinic in Burlington. He is a very empathetic surgeon and explained every detail of the upcoming surgery, which was conducted in December15.

We were up at 4:30 a.m. and were met by Kim when we arrived at the hospital. Pat received excellent care and came home in December 20. This was followed by a few visits from a visiting nurse who helped Pat become accustomed to her new reality. I told her that I was proud and thankful for her strength and quick adjustment to these new circumstances. She took her time to regain her energy and appetite, and she made steady progress. Help from our church family and children reminded us of God's presence and support.

In the midst of this major challenge, we attended the fiftieth reunion of Gordon Divinity School graduates. Dean Pedersen, Ed Whitman, Dr. Lloyd Carr, and I had been meeting and planning with Rhonda Gibson of the Alumni Office for about eighteen months. It was a gathering of those students who studied in Frost Hall from 1965 to 1969 before Gordon's merger with Conwell School of Theology and the big move to the hilltop location of the former Carmel-ite School in Hamilton.

We enjoyed a dinner on Friday night and a Saturday tour of a few historic places in Puritan New England narrated by Dr. Garth

Roswell and Dr. David Horn. Dr. Scott Gibson led a panel discussion and Dr. Ramsey Michaels, the only one of our professors still living, led us in worship. Rev. Ryan Ackerman, pastor of Cornerstone Church in Manchester, Massachusetts, conducted our service of communion. We had a great time and even toured the much altered Frost Hall. It took me a while but I was able to discover the room Takeo Miyamura and I shared during my first year (1963–1964).

Another major event occurred in October 22—Casey O'Brien married Matthew Sames. Almost all the hundred plus members of the family gathered in a refurbished barn in Quakertown, Pennsylvania, on a beautiful Saturday afternoon. Rev. Ron Markloff conducted the ceremony and a green tractor stood in the field overlooking the event.

All of us immediately thought of Poppy and were somehow moved by the sight of that John Deere tractor standing silently by. Many of the families had pictures taken as they gathered around that happy reminder.

We again gathered at the lakeside log cabin of Dave and Sharon for Thanksgiving. We had a very enjoyable time of sharing, singing, and eating.

We were saddened to hear that Randy Hongo passed away in December 16. He and Gay were headed to a concert, but he never made it. He died in the parking lot. The funeral was held at KUC in December 23, and we were able to view the service on the Internet. It was filled with hope, humor, and lots of music, including the Hallelujah Chorus. His son Andrew participated and then flew to California to marry Meghan, his sweetheart. They will live in Mobile, Alabama, where she will practice as a pediatrician and he will teach journalism in a nearby college.

For the record, I conducted one wedding, one baptism, and sixteen funerals.

2017 started with the safe arrival of Remus Cayed, born to Mark and Molly on Epiphany, January 6, our first great-grandchild. After Remus's arrival, Mark and Molly decided to move east from Mark's hometown of Buffalo, New York. They stayed with Dave and

Sharon for a month or two, and by God's grace, Dave was able to make a connection for Mark at P&E Plumbing and Heating. A job was secured and then a move to an apartment owned by Mark's boss.

Leaving FCCW

About a week later, I received a phone call from George Saraceno telling me that the council of First Congregational Church in Woburn wanted him to become their pastor. George was introduced to the congregation when his church, St. Mark's, began worshipping with us a few years back. He is eager and humble and possesses pastoral gifts, but he has little training or experience. Understanding his church background, in the Assembly of God, it is easy to see that one's training is not considered as important as one's desire to serve God. After the initial shock of George's call, it took me about fifteen seconds to realize that his call was a signal that I should resign.

We began on November 3, 2013, and decided to announce our departure at the next annual meeting on March 11, 2018. During those four plus years, the congregation had become stabilized, provided worship space for two other congregations, celebrated the 375th anniversary of the city of Woburn, and discovered a new pastor from within St. Mark's.

I must confess that I felt relieved to be leaving; driving from Magnolia every Sunday morning, preparing a sermon, and providing the necessary pastoral care was a chore. It was a gift from God to be able to share my gifts and experience, but seeing so little spiritual or numerical growth was disappointing.

I conducted an informal service of installation for George in March 11 and wrote the following in the church's annual report:

> I am grateful to God for the four plus years that
> Pat and I have been able to minister among you
> till new leadership was provided. Over the years
> I have conducted ten funerals for First Congre-
> gational members, four baptisms, two weddings,

fifty plus home/hospital visits, attended several
committee meetings, and preached 182 sermons.

Pat and I have also been grateful for the
opportunity to sing in the choir, supporting the
music ministry of Marguerite and Renelle.

We are truly grateful to God and the people
of First Congregational Church for the years we
have been privileged to be with you. May God
bless and lead Pastor George and the people of
this congregation.

After I left, I wrote in my journal, "I do not see this change [the
hiring of George Saraceno as pastor] as a realistic step. I cannot think
of a more difficult situation for a young inexperienced man who is
already fully employed as the city engineer of a neighboring community, becoming the part-time unpaid pastor of a congregation that
has been deteriorating for the last thirty-forty years."

On Sunday, September 29, 2019, Pat and I left our church's
retreat in Maine to bid farewell to Marguerite Upton who was retiring as soloist from the Woburn church after forty-one years. We were
pleased to see some progress within the church body. The two congregations had formally merged including their budgets, there were a
few new faces, the leadership decided to drop the term congregational
from their name, and they had refurbished the ladies' bathroom and
added significant improvements to the Annie Murray Room.

I believe the First Congregational Church in Woburn had left
a legacy to a new church in the center of the city. We were greatly
encouraged after the visit.

Then, in November 19, a call came from Dr. Lee Maynard, the
church's moderator, who shared with me that after twenty months,
George Saraceno has resigned from his position as pastor and he and
his family (his wife Grace was the church's secretary) left the church.
The church did not want him to leave, but expected a greater sense
of cooperation and communication between him and the leadership;
sadly this could not be worked out.

Lee made it clear that I was welcome to fill the pulpit on any Sunday, and this will be a decision of Pastor Frank Passamonte. If he invites me, I will consider his invitation. At the moment, things look pretty sad for this congregation. Pat and I are praying for God's help and direction. Pastor Frank did invite me to attend and preach on the first Sunday of Advent and again in February to help mark the gift from Anne Eastman of two paintings in memory of her husband Gary who was a faithful member of the congregation

In April of 2018, we traveled to Maine to welcome our second great-grandchild, Conor Thomas Weisenbach, born to Dave and Britany on the tenth of April. We greeted this child with very mixed feelings. Our grandson Dave has had a relationship with Britany since 2016. We met her on Thanksgiving of that year. Their behavior was a bit disconcerting to say the least. Over the two plus years, their relationship has been tumultuous. They have had a second child, born on March 19, 2019—Daniel Albert—and this situation continues as a great challenge. Cutting them off from the family will not help, but accepting the present circumstances would not be the right decision either. I must add that they have weathered many a storm and continue to be together. Pat and I pray and share some cash once in a while as does Dave and Sharon, but this has added great stress to all of us. May God's Holy Spirit speak, correct, and lead this young couple to a healthy future!

On Sunday, June 23, I was invited to say a few words at the retirement service for Peter Brown. We were peers and prayer partners for many years. He and JoAnne moved back to their native Rhode Island.

Pastor Emeritus of First Parish

In September 16, I was honored by First Parish as their Pastor Emeritus. This basically means that I retain my position as pastor but without the responsibilities. My name is included on the order of worship each Sunday and I get to park in the clergy spot. Not bad!

I preached from 2 Peter 1:12–22 at that special service and told the children's story. Our family was there along with the Whitmans and Pedersens. It was a grand day.

Pat and I traveled to Pennsylvania in September 21–23 for the sixtieth high school reunion of WTHS class of 1958. The highlight for me was the opportunity to see Coach Dick Acker. He was our track coach and the main reason I went to Muhlenberg College, his alma mater.

Katsuko Sato came to Magnolia in October 1. She had asked me if we might spread her husband Yuki's ashes into the ocean. Two of her three sons attended with her. After a brief service, we all moved toward the sea. Katsuko had prepared several biodegradable bags filled with a small portion of Yuki's ashes, and we all tossed our bags into the sea. After the service, we offered to take her to the Topsfield Fair. We have been friends since they came to GDS in 1963.

Pastor Peter Brown retired in June, and then in October 23, the huge meeting house of First Baptist was struck by lighting and burned to the ground. The congregation has been meeting in the Chapel of First Parish. They have decided to rebuild but it will be a few years before they occupy their new space. In the meantime, a good relationship has developed between the two congregations.

I got a call from my brother Bill checking to make sure that I was planning to attend my brother Paul's retirement party on December 7–8. Paul had been with Rewold Construction Company for thirty-one years. He had become the backbone of the company's sales force. I flew out to Detroit for the celebration and enjoyed the time together with my brothers and the Rewold family.

The family gathered at the Red Door for our last Christmas celebration, and then we drove to Pennsylvania for the O'Brien party.

For the record, I conducted one wedding and twelve funerals and preached nineteen times in Magnolia, Wakefield, and Pigeon Cove.

This year, 2019, was Ty's senior year at Clark, and one of the school's requirements was for each graduate to secure a three-month internship followed by a written summary of their experience. We were all wondering what Ty could find to fulfill this responsibility. Kim wondered if I might use my connections with the town of Wakefield and investigate any opportunities that might be available.

I was able to see Steve Maio, town manager, and ask if he might have any ideas. He said that he had been thinking of instituting an annual internship program and suggested that Ty might be the town's first student! Ty worked with the town's building department for three months and wrote a description of his experience for his class. He was then hired by the town as a summer worker and got paid! At the end of the summer, he was told that he was welcome to return next year if he wanted to do so. He began studies at Bunker Hill Community College in the fall.

At the end of the month, we journeyed to Connecticut for the wedding of Pat's brother Dan's son Jonathan to Emelisa. Our family along with Tom and Jackie and Dave and Diana got rooms at the Ethan Allen Hotel in Danbury. We drove to a church in New York for the ceremony conducted by Dan. The reception followed in a local fire hall. All eight O'Brien siblings were in attendance. I welcomed Em to the Outlaw Band, and Pam and Dave O'Brien Jr. did a fabulous rendition of "A Love like This."

A week later, I discovered sharp pain in my left hip, and it turned out to be arthritis. I was unable to tie my left shoe or put on my sock. I thought I might need a hip replacement but the doctor suggested physical therapy first. I was amazed and thankful for the difference four to six sessions could make. I was given seven exercises that I should do at home, and these have helped me maintain a close to normal lifestyle.

In February, Barbara Wallace called to say that her husband John had died suddenly, and she was hoping that I could conduct his funeral. I flew to Orlando, Florida, in March 4. The service was scheduled for the sixth at their church. I stayed with Mark and Andrea, neighbors up the street. They were good friends of Barbara and provided everything I needed. Both David and Katie, John's children, were able to join us. It was a privilege to share God's promises and hope for the grieving.

Pat and I met the Wallaces when I served as chaplain in Kwajalein. We were able to keep in contact with them when they returned to their home in Hopkinton, Massachusetts. They were faithful friends and very generous toward us.

John was a spiritual searcher so I was heartened to hear his pastor tell me that he grew in his faith in Christ during his years at the church. Barbara said, "You were the one minister that got through to John." What a privilege.

Abram asked if I might conduct the Easter sunrise service this year. We gathered on the rocks by the ocean, the same place we had gathered back in the late 1960s. I tripped as I climbed back to the street, though I only sustained a severe blow to my ego. The breakfast and worship service were wonderful as was the time with the family at Brian and Kim's home later in the day.

A CT scan revealed a shadow on Pat's kidney in April, and a biopsy was taken that indicated no cancer. We were very grateful, but the doctor had his doubts. He ordered a second biopsy that revealed his suspicions. A second surgery was scheduled for September 8 to remove Pat's left kidney. This news was cause for us and the family to call upon God's Holy Spirit for His calm and comfort. Pat is trusting in God's will and so am I.

During last year's Kiwanis auction in Greenville, we bid on two tickets for the Thursday night prime rib dinner a West Branch Camps in celebration of our fifty-fifth wedding anniversary; it was delicious and we encountered a moose along the road. We also bid on two tickets for a cruise on the Kate.

Thinking that we might need to make reservations, I stopped at the Moosehead Museum and Office. I didn't need a reservation but got to chatting with the woman at the desk. She and her husband were recently retired and living in Rockwood for the summer. I mentioned that we had been raised in Pennsylvania and been coming to Beaver Cove ever since 1964 and was now a minister in Massachusetts. After a few minutes, we discovered that her father had been the pastor of DVBC in Pennsylvania. I told her, "My family attended that church in the fifties. Pastor Morrison led me to Christ." At this news, the woman was close to tears, so happy to discover some of the spiritual fruit her dad had initiated. It was quite a surprise for both of us. I went out to the car and urged Pat to come meet Florence for herself. Flo remembered the O'Brien family and remarked at how wonderful and amazing was the grace of God. We plan to make a connection next year, Lord willing. The whole family was able to join us at the lake for another grand time together.

We put everyone's name in a hat to determine who might get to ride on the Kate, and Pam and Dave were selected.

Kim and I accompanied Pat to Lahey Hospital in September 5. She entered the operating room at 10:00 a.m. and left at 4:00 p.m. Kim and I saw her at 6:00 p.m. She was groggy but grateful. Dr. Soricini told us that all went well and was able to perform the operation laparoscopically. This avoided another scar but disturbed Pat's intestines a fact that required several weeks for her to regain normalcy. I asked the doctor about the possibility of metastasis, and he said, "About 4 percent. That sounded pretty good to us but we are in the Lord's hands and happy to be so.

Cancer struck again, and this time it was Gadar. He had been experiencing stomach pains for months and finally saw Dr. Goodman who performed surgery at Tufts Medical Center on Tuesday, September 17. He reported that the operation went well, but he was sad to say that the cancer on his pancreas was inoperable. He will have to undergo chemotherapy for three months. He has been able to return to work at Atlantic Fisheries, a factory in Gloucester purchased by his longtime friend, Nick Osgood. We have since learned that Gadar's chemotherapy has removed all signs of cancer! "You are cancer free...for now," The Dr. said.

Gadar decided to continue his therapy to keep a strong defense against any recurrence, We all praise God for this news.

I traveled to Pennsylvania to celebrate the sixtieth high school of the class of 1959. I drove alone and enjoyed seeing about thirty-five classmates and their spouses. I was asked to say grace, which I was happy to do. I'm always impressed to experience these gatherings, especially how the maturity of each of us facilitates a level of mutual respect that was absent while in high school.

In November, we were invited to attend and participate in the 375th anniversary of First Parish Congregational Church. What a privilege! The service was well planned—honoring veterans, welcoming five new members, reading our ancient covenant, viewing a video, and hearing a brief message from Pastor John Dale.

He is growing into the position and is warmly welcomed by the congregation. This is wonderful to see and we rejoice in the blessing of God. After the two services, traditional and contemporary, we enjoyed a luncheon and then visits to both Kim and Brian and Gadar and Pam. We are so blessed.

A week later, I received a note from Pastor John, "Thanks so much for coming to the 375th! We had a great time and are so grateful for your impact on FPCC. In Christ, John."

We again gathered at 10 Highpoint Circle for our Thanksgiving celebration. I spoke briefly about the challenges of the past year but ever grateful for God's word and wisdom. We spent the night and enjoyed breakfast with our three children, while everyone else had to leave. It felt like old times.

Pastor John Dale and his wife Kathy invited us to their first annual Christmas open house. We were able to attend and enjoyed the fellowship and an opportunity to see the parsonage, first time in six years. We stopped by John Sofia's open house and then a brief visit to see Dick and Mary Jennings, our former neighbors; they were very surprised and happy to see us.

Many ministers will take off the Sunday after Christmas. Pastor John Dale asked if I might preach that Sunday, giving him opportunity to return to his house in upper state New York. Being the first Sunday after Christmas, I spoke from Matthew 2:1–2, emphasizing the deep desire of God to offer salvation to all the earth, even "outsiders" like the Magi.

For the record, I preached nine times and conducted seven funerals.

Final Reflections

They say that a minister never retires. I guess that is true. After retiring from First Parish in Wakefield in 2013 and from First Congregational Church in Woburn in 2018, I continued to be given opportunities to preach God's Word and conduct funerals for grieving families.

I am very fortunate that my calling as a pastor doesn't require me to have a strong and vigorous body or a toolbox filled with heavy tools. What I need is faith and trust in God grace to take up the next opportunity that He brings my way. I believe that as long as God brings such opportunities to my doorstep, He believes that I can serve His glory adequately. When the opportunities stop coming, I will assume that I have finished the course.

I would agree with Julian Freeman, pastor of Grace Fellowship Church in Toronto, Canada, who observes that being a Christian pastor is a paradoxical calling. He writes:

> We are called to proclaim a message with the power of God to change people, but we can't even change ourselves. We say that numbers don't matter but long for many more to be saved and realize that an increase only multiplies our accountability. We try to express the infinite and eternal in twenty minutes—give or take; obviously, we fail, so we try again next week. We spend our lives studying Holy Scripture that we will never fully grasp and labor to explain it to

the people who can't understand it apart from the work of a third party—the Holy Spirit. And the more we study, the more certain we become of the wisdom of God and our own foolishness, and yet we must preach on. We are told that not many should be teachers and that there will be stricter judgment for those who are, and yet we cannot fight off the compulsion to preach.

We are called to toil in the Word of God and in prayer, yet there is nothing our enemy opposes more actively. We preach a gospel of joy but are often hard pressed by a temptation toward depression.

We must preach with passion and pastor with patience. We must be gentle with the sheep and fierce with the wolves, and we better know the difference! We must labor with all our strength but never ever rely on it.

I came across this bit of poetry by W. Alexander McEachern entitled, *I Am the very Model of the Busy Modern Minister* (with apologies to Gilbert and Sullivan).

> I have to meet the problems of the man who gets too mystical
> And says that God has told him all his friends are atheistical.
> I have to show the sexton how to spread a box of Vigero
> And tell the first soprano that she isn't singing Figaro.
> I have to shake a hundred hands and never be mechanical,
> And exercise my leadership, but never be tyrannical.
> I have to be a statue of stability personified

When dealing with young ladies who are not yet
  matrimonified.
I have to listen quietly to the loudest of polemicals
Against the type of music in the latest of our
  hymnicals.
And despite the lovely spirit when I meet with
  brother's clerical
I really ought to have on hand new miracles
  numerical—
And though I strive to keep my preaching sound
  and clear and clarion,
Some listener is sure to ask, "Are you a Unitarian?"
In short, in matters sociable or socialist or sinister,
I am the very model of the busy modern minister.

Over the years, I have admired the ministry of Rev. Chuck
Swindoll. He served First Evangelical Free Church of Fullerton,
California, for twenty-three years. When he left to take up the pres-
idency of his alma mater, Dallas Theological Seminary, he listed
"Stuff I've Learned" in his newsletter. Because I liked how he wrote,
I subscribed to that letter and was able to read and agree with most
all of his observations about pastoral ministry. Here are a few truths
that touched me.

- I've learned that I should tell people how I feel about them
  now, not later. Later seldom comes. I've walked away from
  too many funerals asking myself, Why didn't I tell him or
  her those things when they were alive?
- I've learned that things I'm not even aware of are being
  noticed and remembered. You wouldn't believe the things
  folks have mentioned that encouraged them—a smile, a
  pat on the back, a glance, an arm around the shoulder. It
  is really true; small things mean a lot, which can be a little
  scary.

- I've learned that days of maintenance are far more in number than days of magnificence. Over half the job is just showing up. Staying faithful pays great dividends.
- I've learned that some people aren't going to change no matter what! It was a great moment in my life when I realized that "You can't win them all Rich."
- I've learned that it is often the case that perception overcomes reality. How people perceive things is to them more convincing than a truckload of evidence. I hate that, but it's a fact.
- I've learned that time spent with my family is a good investment. I am so grateful that I realized that Mondays off with Pat or an overnight together, the friendship, love and counsel of our now grown children, the acceptance, and hugs and kisses of the grandchildren. Family is one of God's greatest ideas!
- I've learned to trust and rest in the sovereignty of God. God has a plan that is unfolding whether I like it or not, whether I understand it or not.
- I've learned that some things are worth all the energy and faith I can muster, not the big programs and bold plans but the intangible things, like telling the truth, admitting inadequacy, emphasizing quality, expressing gratitude, saying "I'm sorry," being generous, studying hard and demonstrating affection, and most importantly loving and trusting my heavenly Father.

Pastoring a church has to be the highest of all callings. It includes the greatest privileges: walking with a grieving family, celebrating a wedding and dancing at the reception, being remembered for a service rendered, receiving a loving note of appreciation, or praying before an operation. Folks want their pastor to be with them during these times—what a priceless privilege!

All these years have been extended to me by the grace of God.

The Grace of God

To succeed without ability and create without
     talent;
To be confident in doubt and secure in turmoil;
To have joy in sorrow and peace in battle;
To believe when doubtful and trust when suspi-
     cious;
To love when hated and care when rejected;
To walk straight on a crooked path and firmly on
     shifting sand;
To make judgments sounder than my understand-
     ing and decisions wiser than my knowledge.
The grace of God is God acting in me despite me.
Wallace Alcon

I would guess that many of us remember Dr. Bill Bright of Campus Crusade. He was the Christian leader who wrote the little booklet he called, *The Four Spiritual Laws*. Rule number one: "God loves you and has a wonderful plan for your life." Every believer would agree with rule one.

But I came across this very poignant variation written by Mark Galli in an article he wrote in *Christianity Today* (September 2005): "God loves you and has a difficult plan for your life."

God the Father announces that He is well pleased with His beloved Son (Mark 1:11), then the Spirit promptly drives him into the wilderness to face severe temptation.

This has been my experience in pastoral ministry, and I wouldn't trade it for the world!

CPSIA information can be obtained
at www.ICGtesting.com
Printed in the USA
BVHW081006150421
605029BV00002B/99

9 781098 069940